2ND EDITION

Classic
WOODEN
TOYS

STEP-BY-STEP INSTRUCTIONS FOR
22 BUILT-TO-LAST PROJECTS

EDITED BY
Jim Harrold

CEDAR LANE PRESS

CONTENTS

Imaginative Play

Trucks & More

Pull-Toy Pals

Toy Storage

PLAYTIME EASEL

Biscuits and knock-down hardware make for an easy build

BY ANDY RAE

What's more fun than to build a child's easel and watch your kids get creative? This stand-up play station offers two artists' areas: a blackboard with a chalk tray for spur-of-the-moment designs and a more studious side equipped with an almost limitless roll of drawing paper and a supply box, ready for lasting creations that can be separated from the roll via a clever tearing mechanism. Fun, colorful shapes face-glued to the frame entice youngsters to play. Two of these decorative blocks are outfitted with magnets that mate with magnets in the drawing panel to hold down the corners of the paper. I used cherry for the solid-wood parts of this project, but any clear and relatively straight-grained hardwood will do. This easel is fun to build and makes for an enjoyable weekend project. Consider enlisting a young'un to help.

Make the frame and panels

1 Mill the stiles (A), rails (B, C), and panels (D, E) to the sizes in the Cut List (page 11).

2 Ease all the edges on the stiles, rails, and panels with a ⅛" round-over bit.

3 Sand the stiles and rails through 220 grit, as well as the panel faces—but not the panel edges.

4 Lay out the holes for the magnets in the drawing panel (D) and in the top rail (B) above it, as shown in Figure 1 on page 7. Bore the holes to a depth of $\frac{9}{64}$", using a ½"-Forstner bit in the drill press.

5 Lay out and cut slots for #20 biscuits in the stiles, rails, and panels, approximately where shown in Figure 1. Adjust the cutter to center the slots across the panels' thickness, with the exterior faces oriented upward, and referencing the joiner's fence, as shown in Photo A (page 6).

6 Spray one coat of blackboard paint on the exterior face of the blackboard panel (E). After this dries, scuff-sand with 320 grit. Then spray on another coat, and let it dry for 24 hours before handling. To "charge" the unsanded surface before assembly, rub a piece of chalk lengthwise over it, and then wipe off the excess with a chalk eraser.

Assemble the frames and panels

1 Initially assemble the blackboard panel frame, as shown in Photo B, applying glue in the biscuit slots and along the mating edges of the assembly parts.

2 Unclamp the stile, and place the assembly onto bar clamps. Pull the joints home, and check for square and flat (Photo C) before leaving the frame to dry.

3 Repeat the procedure for the drawing panel frame assembly.

Make the box and tray

1 Mill the box and tray parts (F, G, H, J, K, & L), except for the corner blocks (I), to the dimensions in the Cut List, mitering the sides (G), the box bottom (H), and the aprons (J, L) to 12°, as shown in Figure 1. Don't rip the 12° bevel on the tray (K) for now.

2 Bevel the aprons (J, L) on the tablesaw by angling your tablesaw blade to 12° (Photo D). For reference, the sawn surface is the face that will contact the easel. Alternatively, this cut can be made on the bandsaw.

3 To prevent a starved joint, size the end-grain at the ends of the bottom (H) by applying a light coat of glue, waiting a few moments before adding fresh glue, and then clamping the sides (G) to the bottom. Check the assembly for square before setting it aside to dry.

4 Join the front (F) to the side/bottom assembly (G, H), this time sizing the end grain of the sides before adding a fresh coat of glue to all the mating areas, and clamping as before.

5 Make the triangular corner blocks (I) by beveling the edge of a board and then ripping the beveled section free. Crosscut pieces to length, and glue them into the corners. No clamps needed; just rub them in place.

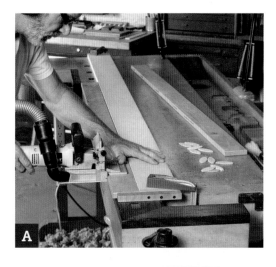

A

Clamp an L-shaped stick assembly to the bench to safely hold the stock while you slot the stiles for #20 biscuits.

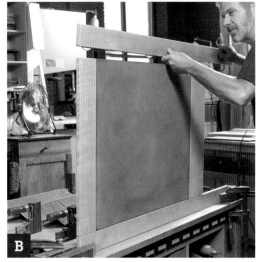

B

To assemble a frame, clamp one stile to the bench, and attach the two rails and the panel. Then cap the assembly with the remaining stile.

C

Bath towel

Clamp in both directions to ensure a good bond between the parts, making sure the assembly is square. Then use a straightedge to check for flatness.

D

Tilt the blade to 12° and adjust the fence so the cut results in a sharp edge on the thickest portion of the blank. Use a pushstick to keep fingers safe.

Figure 1: Easel Exploded View

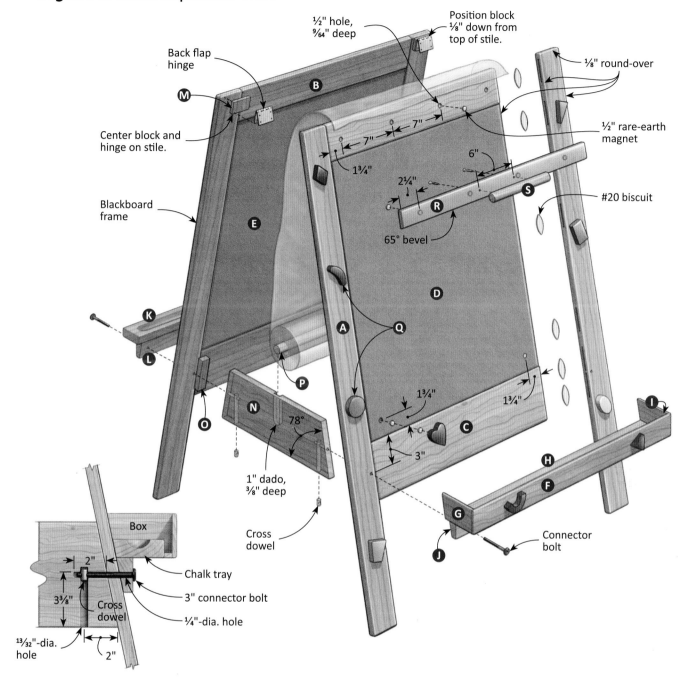

½" hole, ⁹⁄₆₄" deep

Position block ⅛" down from top of stile.

Back flap hinge

⅛" round-over

Center block and hinge on stile.

½" rare-earth magnet

7" 7"

Blackboard frame

1¾"

6"

2¼"

#20 biscuit

65° bevel

1¾" 1¾"

78°

1" dado, ⅜" deep

3"

Cross dowel

Connector bolt

Box

2"

Chalk tray

3⅜"

3" connector bolt

Cross dowel

¼"-dia. hole

¹³⁄₃₂"-dia. hole

2"

QUICK TIP

Bath towels make great protectors for blemish-free bar-clamp glue-ups. Just cover the bars with a towel to protect the work from scratches and dings.

6 Rout the ½"-deep stopped groove in the chalk tray (K) using a 1½" core box bit. Outfit your router table with stopblocks mounted on an auxiliary fence, as shown in Photo E. Make the cut in several passes, the last being a skim cut for a smooth surface.

7 With your tablesaw bevel gauge set to 12°, rip the 78° bevel on the chalk tray (K).

8 Lay out and drill ¼" through-holes in the box and tray aprons (J, L), where shown in Figure 2 (page 8). Be sure to reference the front face of the aprons on the drill press table to keep the holes aligned properly. Slightly chamfer the holes on the outermost face so the connector bolts will seat properly.

9 Glue and clamp the box apron (J) flush with the rear edges of its mating parts (G, H). Also glue and clamp the tray apron (L) flush with the rear edge of the tray (K).

10 Temporarily clamp the chalk tray to the blackboard panel and the box to the drawing panel, centering them across the width of the easel and aligning the holes in the aprons so they're 3" below the top edge of the bottom rails (C), where shown in Figure 1. Guiding a ¼" bit through your apron holes, drill through the stiles (A).

Hinge the panels together

1 Glue and pin-nail or clamp the hinge blocks (M) to the top of the stiles (A), where shown in Figure 1. Make sure to orient the grain horizontally.

2 Lay the two panels head-to-head on the bench, with their inside surfaces facing up. Check that the panels are in line with each other by laying a long straightedge against one edge of the panels. (A straight piece of plywood works fine.) Attach the hinges, as shown in Photo F.

Make the side rails

1 Refer to the Cut List to mill the side rails (N) to thickness and width, and crosscut the ends to 78°, as shown in Figure 1.

2 Lay out the 1" hole for the paper roll dowel (P) on the inside face of each side rail, centering it across the rail's length and width. Drill ⅜" deep into each rail with a 1" Forstner bit on the drill press.

3 Chuck a 1"-diameter straight bit in a plunge router and set it for a ⅜"-deep cut. Then set up a fence to rout the channel for the dowel, as shown in Photo G.

4 Temporarily clamp the side rails (N) to the frames using blocks clamped to the stiles so that the edges of each side rail

Figure 2: Box and Tray Construction

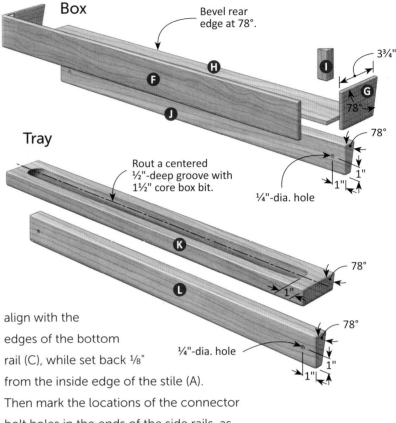

align with the edges of the bottom rail (C), while set back ⅛" from the inside edge of the stile (A). Then mark the locations of the connector bolt holes in the ends of the side rails, as shown in Photo H.

5 Clamp each side rail in the bench vise, and use a ¼" bit to drill about 2" into each rail end (Photo I on page 10).

6 Drill the intersecting holes for the cross dowels using a ¹³⁄₃₂" brad-point bit on the drill press, as shown in Photo J (page 10).

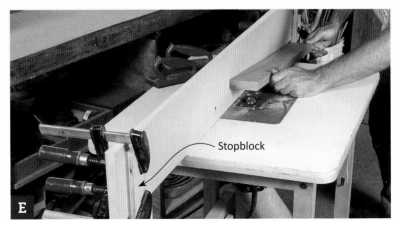

When routing the pencil tray, hold the work against the first block, lower it onto the bit, push until it reaches the second block, and then lift.

Pull the top edges of the aligned panels together by clamping the hinge blocks. Then drill pilot holes for the screws, and install the hinges.

7 Working on a low bench or the floor, fold the assembly on its side in an "A," and install the side rails, box, and tray using the connector bolts and cross dowels.

8 Make the shoulder blocks (O) to the size in the Cut List. Glue and pin each block to the inside face of the bottom rail (C), with the block centered on the inside face of the side rail (N). Avoid spreading glue onto the side rails.

Make the decorative blocks

1 Make the decorative blocks (Q) from any wood you like. Figured woods such as curly maple can really pop when colored with dye. Trace the outlines on a ⁹⁄₁₆"-thick board.

2 Use a ¼" or narrower blade on the bandsaw to cut closely to the outlines. Refine the shapes using files and power sanders, finishing up with hand-sanding through 220 grit.

3 Round over one face of each block using a ⅛" round-over bit on the router table. For safety, feed the pieces using a jig made from ¼"-thick acrylic outfitted with scrap wood handles (Photo K; page 10). Round

Rout the channel that connects the hole to the edge of the side rail by guiding the base of the router against a fence clamped to the workpiece and bench.

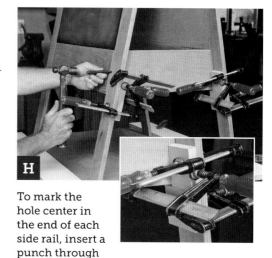

To mark the hole center in the end of each side rail, insert a punch through the hole in the stile, holding the punch level and in line with the rail.

QUICK TIP

For trial-fitting of hinges, use steel screws, as brass screws can strip or deform from repeated installation. When the fitting is done, replace the steel screws with brass.

over both faces of the two blocks you choose for the paper holders.

4 Drill a hole for a magnet in each paper holder. Center the hole on the back face of the holder, and use a ½" Forstner bit in the drill press as you did with the top rail (B), drilling ⁹⁄₆₄" deep.

5 Dye the blocks using bright-colored aniline dyes, and then apply a single sealer coat of clear finish.

6 For easy block attachment, remove the box, tray, side rails, and hinges. Lay out the blocks in a pleasing pattern on each panel (avoiding the top rail on the drawing paper side), and glue and clamp them in place. Spread glue judiciously to prevent squeeze-out, and use clamping pads.

Make the paper cutter

1 Select a dense hardwood for the cutter (R), and mill it to the dimensions shown in the Cut List. Bevel one long edge of the cutter at 65° to create a knife edge on the workpiece.

2 Lay out the holes for the magnets, as shown in Figure 1, and drill them ⁹⁄₆₄" deep, as you did with the top rail (B), using a ½"-Forstner bit in the drill press.

3 Using the excess from the 36"-long paper roll dowel, cut the handle (S) to the length shown in the Cut List, clamp it to the bench, and plane a ⅛"-wide flat along one edge.

4 Center the handle on the cutter with clamps, drill countersunk through-holes in the back of the cutter, drill pilot holes in the handle, and secure the handle with glue and 1" brass screws.

Apply the finish and magnets

1 Sand all of the parts, making particularly sure that the corners and edges are kid-friendly.

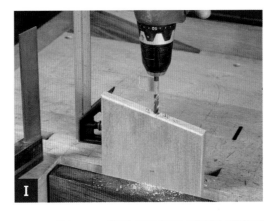

Using tape as a depth gauge, drill a hole in each end of the side rails. Two squares placed 90° to each other help you drill straight and square.

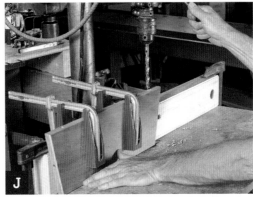

Drill the 3⅜"-deep hole for each cross dowel on the drill press by clamping the inverted rail against a tall fence.

Use double-faced tape to hold three or more decorative blocks to the jig for stability when rounding their edges.

2 Disassemble everything, mask off the blackboard, and apply at least three coats of wiping varnish to protect against grimy li'l hands.

3 Orient each magnet to its mate so they attract each other, and mark them for assembly.

4 Brush epoxy into the magnet holes in the top rail (A), drawing panel (D), paper cutter (R, S), and the two paper holder decorative blocks (Q). Press and twist the magnets into the holes until they're level or just slightly

Cut List: Playtime Easel

	Part	Thickness	Width	Length	Qty.	Mat'l
A	Stiles	11/16"	3"	53"	4	C
B	Top rails	11/16"	4"	24½"	2	C
C	Bottom rails	11/16"	6"	24½"	2	C
D	Drawing panel	½"	24½"	30"	1	MDF
E	Blackboard panel	½"	24½"	30"	1	MDF
F	Box front	¼"	2½"	28½"	1	C
G*	Box sides	¼"	2½"	3¾"	2	C
H	Box bottom	¼"	3¼"	28"	1	C
I*	Corner blocks	11/16"	1 1/16"	2"	2	C
J*	Box apron	1"	2"	27½"	1	C
K	Chalk tray	1"	3"	28½"	1	C
L	Chalk tray apron	1"	2"	27½"	1	C
M	Hinge block	⅜"	1½"	2¼"	4	C
N**	Side rails	11/16"	6"	17¾"	2	C
O	Shoulder blocks	11/16"	1"	4"	4	C
P	Paper holder	1" dia.		25½"	1	C
Q	Decorative Blocks	9/16"	2½"	2½"	24	M
R	Paper cutter bar	½"	2"	26½"	1	M
S	Paper cutter handle	1" dia.		8"	1	C

* Indicates parts are initially cut oversized. See instructions.
** Measure from long points of miters
Materials: C=Cherry, MDF=Medium Density Fiberboard, M=Maple or other suitable dense hardwood

below the surface. Wipe away any excess epoxy with denatured alcohol. Wait a day for the epoxy to cure before putting the cutter into use on the frame.

Put it all together

1 Remount the hinges using brass screws, and reassemble the easel with the connector bolts and cross dowels as before.
2 Cut the dowel (P) to fit between the pockets in the side rails (N). (Note: Don't apply finish to the dowel, as the paper roll spins better on bare wood.)
3 Stand the easel upright, and slip the dowel through the roll of paper and into the side rail pockets. Pull the paper up and over the drawing surface frame, and snap it in place with the paper cutter and paper holders. Stock the box with drawing supplies—and watch someone get creative!

Patterns: Decorative Blocks

Enlarge 200%.

Overall dimensions:
37½"w × 13½"d × 27"h

KID-PLEASING ROCKING PONY

While not every child wants a horse, they all want a pony.

BY CHUCK HEDLUND WITH KEN BRADY

WRITTEN BY ROBERT J. SETTICH

We used three criteria to design this galloping steed. First, we wanted a pony that could withstand decades of hard riding. Here, the tough cherry rocker base, maple body, and walnut saddle provide durability where needed. We wanted it easy to build. By providing patterns for the parts, success lies only a weekend or two away. And, finally, our pony had to pass the cute test and serve as a charming home accent. We'll let you be the judge.

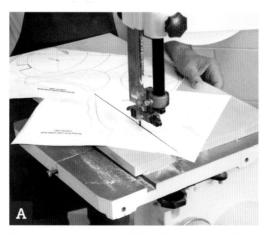

Using the pattern's solid cutlines as a guide, saw the center body layer (A) at the head and tail.

Laminate the body

1 From ¾" maple, cut three blanks to 13 × 24" for the center body layer (A) and the two outer body layers (B). (You may need to edge-glue narrower stock to obtain the needed width.) Stack the blanks, aligning their edges and ends. Measure to the center of the width and length, and use a pencil and square to draw centerlines on each edge and end. Unstack the blanks, and extend the centerlines 1" onto the faces of the three blanks.

2 Print and assemble the patterns. Adhere the composite pattern for the center body layer (A) to one blank and the composite pattern for the outer body layers (B) to another blank. In both cases, align the centerlines printed on the pattern with the centerlines you marked on the blanks.

3 Using a bandsaw, cut the center body layer (A) along the solid green lines (Photo A) and then remove the pattern. We used a ¼"-wide blade with four teeth per inch for all bandsaw cuts.

4 Using double-faced tape, sandwich the center body layer (A) between the two outer body layers (B), carefully aligning the edges, ends, and centerlines.

5 Chuck a ¼" bit into your drill press and drill two holes through the stacked blanks where shown on the pattern. You'll use these holes to align the body layers (A, B) during glue-up and also to position the legs. Unstack the blanks and remove the tape.

6 Spread glue to laminate the center and outer body layers (A, B), insert ¼" drill bits into the holes to keep the pieces aligned (Photo B), and then clamp them together. Unclamp and remove the drill bits after the glue has cured overnight.

Drill and shape the body

1 Chuck a ¾" Forstner bit into your drill press and drill the handle hole through the lamination (A, B) where marked on the pattern. Use a scrap backing board to prevent tear-out.

2 Drill a ⅛" hole through the lamination (A, B) at the center of the eye. (A ⅛" bit 6" long is a common hardware store item.) Using these holes on each side of the lamination as guides, drill ⅞" counterbores ⅛" deep as eye sockets. Finally, drill ⅜" holes 1¼" deep.

3 Bandsaw the perimeter of the body lamination (A, B), staying on the waste side of the solid cutline.

4 Sand to the line, using a drum or spindle sander. Tight curves and corners may require some hand-sanding.

5 On the pattern, you'll see that one centerline of each ¼" hole extends to the edge of the body lamination (A, B). Use a pencil and square to transfer the lines onto the edge. Refer to Photo E on page 16 to see how these lines guide leg placement.

6 Strip off the pattern and sand both faces of the body lamination (A, B).

7 Chuck a ¼" round-over bit into your router and round over the perimeter of both faces of the body lamination (A, B) where shown in Figure 1.

B Drill bit alignment pins and a boatload of clamps help ensure a stress- and gap-free glue up. (In this photo, the paper pattern is facing down.)

C Cut just to the waste side of the taper line on each leg. A slow feed rate promotes a straight cut.

Figure 1: Pony Exploded View

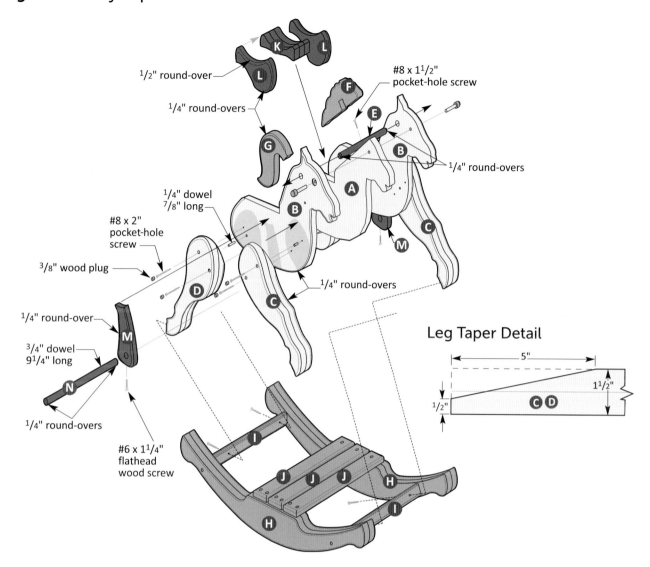

$1/2$" round-over

$1/4$" round-overs

#8 x $1^1/2$"
pocket-hole screw

$1/4$" round-overs

$1/4$" dowel
$7/8$" long

#8 x 2"
pocket-hole
screw

$3/8$" wood plug

$1/4$" round-overs

$1/4$" round-over

$3/4$" dowel
$9^1/4$" long

$1/4$" round-overs

#6 x $1^1/4$"
flathead
wood screw

Leg Taper Detail

5"

$1^1/2$"

$1/2$"

C D

Cut and shape the legs

1 Laminate pairs of $3/4$" maple boards to make four oversized blanks for the front legs (C) and rear legs (D). Rip and crosscut the blanks to 6" wide by 18" long, ensuring that the end cuts are square. Mark centerlines along the full length of both faces and on both ends.

2 All legs have an identical taper on the top inner face. Referring to the Leg Taper Detail, above, mark cutlines on each blank. Bandsaw the taper (Photo C), and save the scrap wedges.

3 Flatten the taper with a block plane or a random-orbit sander. To check the taper's flatness, hold a straightedge across it in several directions.

4 Adhere a leg pattern on the untapered side of the blank. Align the pattern's centerline with the line drawn on the blank and position the top of the pattern (or leg) flush with the tapered end.

5 Chuck a $3/8$" brad-point bit in your drill press and drill the $1/2$"-deep counterbores in each blank where shown on the pattern. Switch to a $1/8$" bit and drill holes through the blanks centered in the counterbores.

6 On the tapered face, mark the location of the ¼" hole used to help position the legs. To do this, mark a centerline on the taper and then draw a line connecting the centers of the ⅛" holes. The intersection of these two lines is the centerpoint of the ¼" hole.

7 Chuck a ¼" brad-point bit in your drill press. Shim the workpiece to make the beveled face of the leg blank perpendicular to the drill bit, as shown in Photo D, and then drill a ½"-deep hole. Repeat for the remaining legs.

8 Bandsaw the legs to shape and sand the edges.

9 Referring to the End View Detail on the pattern, you'll see that the bottoms of the back legs have a 4° back bevel. You can shape this quickly and accurately by tilting the table of your disc sander to 4°. Make

the bevels so that they tilt toward the inner face of the leg

10 Transfer marks from the pattern to the inner face of the leg indicating where to stop the round-overs. Using a router and a ¼" round-over bit, shape the stopped round-overs on the inner faces of the legs. Strip off the pattern, and rout the full perimeter of each leg's outer face. Don't get rid of the centerlines penciled on the blanks.

Attach the legs

1 Cut four ¼" dowels toi ⅞" long. Place the body assembly (A, B) on its side, and insert the dowels into the holes in the tapered faces of the legs.

2 Choose an appropriate leg and engage the dowel in the corresponding hole in the body. Referring to the inset in Photo E, align the centerline on the inner face of the leg with the index mark on the lower edge

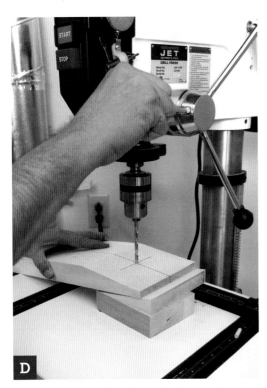

D Use the wedge offcut from the leg and a spacer to position the tapered face perpendicular to the bit.

Body

Leg   Leg

E Matching the centerlines on the inner face of the leg with the body (Inset) guarantees that the legs are attached symmetrically. Screwing the leg in place eliminates the need for a tricky clamping setup.

A slightly crushed corrugated carton can serve as a temporary horse support, enabling you to screw the supports to the legs.

of the body assembly (A, B). Push an awl through each hole in the leg to transfer the locations to the body.

3 Remove the leg and drill pilot holes into the body assembly (A, B). After you've positioned all the legs, use an eraser and sandpaper to remove the pencil marks.

4 Attach the legs (C, D) with glue and screws as shown in Photo E.

Make the handle, mane, and tail

1 Cut the handle (E) 7¼" long from a ¾" walnut dowel. Sand an even ¼" round-over at the ends of the handle. Drill a ⅛" hole through the midpoint of the handle.

2 Insert the handle (E) into the body assembly (A, B), centering the handle's hole in the thickness of the body. Using that handle hole as a guide, drill a pilot hole into the body. Reposition the handle, and drive the 1½"-long screw, as shown in Figure 1 (page 15), to secure it in place.

4 Adhere patterns for the mane (F) and tail (G) to ¾" cherry. Bandsaw along the waste side of the line, and sand up to the edges.

5 Mark the end points of the round-overs onto the edges of the tail (G). Strip the patterns from both the mane (F) and tail (G). Rout the edges where shown with a router and ¼" round-over bit.

6 Check the fit of the mane (F) and tail (G) into their recesses. If necessary, sand the surface or edges of these parts until they slide into place. Brush glue into the body cavities and press the parts into place. Wipe away squeeze-out with a damp rag.

Make the rocker base parts

1 Laminate pairs of ¾" cherry boards to make two oversized blanks for the rockers (H). Cut the blanks 8" wide by 38" long. Stack the blanks, joining them with double-faced tape.

2 Assemble the two parts of the rocker pattern and then adhere it to a piece of ¼" hardwood or plywood. Bandsaw the shape and sand the edges to create a full-sized half pattern. Drill the ⅛" holes where shown.

3 To use the half pattern, first draw a centerline across the width of the stacked blanks. With the paper pattern facing up, align the pattern's centerline with the one on the wood, then trace the outline and mark the location of the ⅛" hole used to secure the rear leg support (I). Now flip the pattern onto the other side, align its edge on the blank's centerline, and trace the opposite end. Finally, mark the location of the ⅛" hole to secure the front leg support (I).

4 Drill the ⅛" holes through both blanks, and then drill the ⅜" counterbores on the outside faces.

5 Bandsaw the perimeter of the rockers (H) and sand the edges smooth. Separate the blanks.

Figure 2: Base Detail

$3/8"$ tapered wood plug

#8 x $1^{1}/2"$ pocket-hole screw

$13^{1}/8"$

J

$2^{5}/8"$

$3/8"$ counterbore $3/8"$ deep with a $1/8"$ hole centered inside

$1/4"$ round-overs edge and ends

$3/8"$ gap

$1/4"$ round-overs

#8 x $2^{1}/2"$ flathead wood screw

$1^{1}/2"$

I

$10^{1}/2"$

$3/4"$

J J H

$3/4"$

5° bevel

5° bevel

I

H

$3/8"$ tapered wood plug

$3/8"$ counterbore $3/8"$ deep with a $1/8"$ hole centered inside

H

$1/4"$ round-overs

6 Rout a ¼" round-over along the perimeter of both faces of each rocker (H) where shown on Figure 2.

7 Referring to the Cut List, make the supports (I). Note that the top edges have 5° bevel. After cutting these parts to length, drill the counterbores and holes at the locations marked.

8 Cut the three rocker platform slats (J). Rout a ¼" round-over along the top edges and top ends. Referring to Figure 2, drill the counterbores and holes into the slats to attach the slats to the rockers.

Assemble the base and add the pony

1 Screw the supports (I) between the rockers (H) without glue. Leave the screws loose to allow the supports to rotate as needed to align with the bottoms of the legs (C and D).

2 Using the rocker half pattern as a guide, position the center slat (J) on the rocker assembly (H, I). Center the slat atop the rockers (front to back and side to side) and clamp it in place. Hold a square against a rocker and each support to ensure a square assembly. Using the holes in the slat as guides, drill pilot holes into the rockers. Attach the slat to the rockers using screws but no glue.

3 Attach the remaining two slats (J) to the rockers (H), using ⅜" scrapwood spacers to position the slats.

4 Use the holes in the supports (I) to drill pilot holes into the legs (C, D). Referring to Photo F (page 17), drive the screws through the supports (I) into the legs (C, D). Finally, tighten the screws used to attach the rockers (H) to the supports (I).

Rocking Pony Cutting Diagram

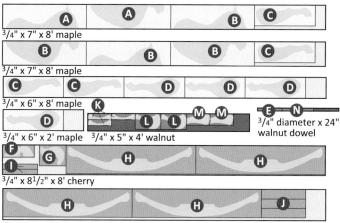

3/4" x 7" x 8' maple

3/4" x 7" x 8' maple

3/4" x 6" x 8' maple

3/4" x 6" x 2' maple   3/4" x 5" x 4' walnut   3/4" diameter x 24" walnut dowel

3/4" x 8 1/2" x 8' cherry

3/4" x 9" x 8' cherry

Cut List: Rocking Pony

	Part	Thickness	Width	Length	Qty.	Mat'l
*A	Center body layer	3/4"	12 1/4"	21 7/8"	1	M
*B	Outer body layer	3/4"	12 1/4"	21 7/8"	2	M
*C	Front legs	1 1/2"	5"	16 5/8"	2	LM
*D	Rear legs	1 1/2"	6"	16 1/2"	2	LM
E	Handle	3/4" dia.		7 1/4"	1	W
*F	Mane	3/4"	3 1/4"	9 1/4"	1	C
*G	Tail	3/4"	5 1/2"	7 3/4"	1	C
*H	Rockers	1 1/2"	4 3/8"	37"	2	LC
I	Supports	3/4"	1 1/2"	10 1/2"	2	C
J	Slats	3/4"	2 3/4"	13 1/8"	3	C
*K	Saddle seat	2 1/4"	1 5/8"	6 15/16"	1	LW
*L	Saddle sides	3/4"	4 1/2"	7 5/8"	2	W
*M	Stirrup straps	1/2"	3 1/4"	7"	2	W
N	Footrest	3/4" dia.		9 1/4"	1	W

*Parts initially cut oversized.
M=Maple LM=Laminated Maple C=Cherry
LC=Laminated Cherry LW=Laminated Walnut
Supplies: 3/4"-diameter whitewood dowel, piece of 1/4"
plywood for rocker half-pattern

Shape and mount the saddle

1 Laminate three pieces of 3/4 × 1 3/4 × 7" walnut to make a blank for the saddle seat (K). Adhere the seat pattern to the blank's edge. Bandsaw and sand.

2 Stack two pieces of 3/4" walnut, join them with double-faced tape, and adhere the pattern for the saddle sides (L). Bandsaw just outside the line, strip off the pattern, and separate the parts.

3 Glue and clamp the saddle sides (L) to the saddle seat (K). After the glue has dried, sand the edges flush.

4 Rout a 1/4" round-over along the edges of the saddle assembly (K, L) where shown in Figure 1 (page 15) and the pattern. Next, rout the 1/2" round-overs along the top edges of the saddle.

5 Glue and clamp the saddle assembly (K, L) in place.

6 From 1/2" walnut, stack-cut and edge-sand the stirrup straps (M). Drill the 3/4" hole through each strap with a Forstner bit and the 1/8" shank hole in the bottom ends with a twist bit.

7 Strip the pattern from the stacked stirrup straps (M). Rout a 1/4" round-over along their perimeter except for the top ends, and then separate the parts.

8 Cut a 3/4" walnut dowel 9 1/4" long for the footrest (N). Sand a 1/4" round-over on the ends to prevent chipping.

9 Insert the footrest (N) through the stirrup straps (M), and then glue and clamp the stirrup straps to the sides of the horse.

10 Center the footrest (N), and use the holes in the ends of the stirrup straps (M) to drill pilot holes into the footrest. You will need to remove the center slat (J) to drive these screws.

Make the eyes

1 Cut a ¾"-diameter dowel to 4" long. Use a handscrew clamp to hold the dowel vertically on your drill press table and drill a ⅜ × ¼" deep hole in the center of each dowel end with a brad point bit. Cut two ⅜" dowels 1⅛" long and glue them into the holes.

2 Cut ½" from each end of the ¾" dowel. Referring to Photo G, sand a ¼" round-over on the end to form the eye domes.

3 Sand the rim of each eye socket to a slight round-over (about ¹⁄₁₆"). Finally, glue the eyes in place.

Finishing touches

1 Plug the counterbores with tapered side-grain plugs. Try to pick plugs that match the figure and color of the legs for a virtually invisible installation. Level the plugs with a random-orbit sander or block plane.

2 Finish-sand the entire project with 220 grit and remove all dust. We applied three coats of finish: two coats of polyacrylic gloss followed by a final coat of polyacrylic satin. Lightly sand between coats with 220-grit sandpaper.

3 To make the bridle and reins, cut leather strips ⅜" wide, using a metal straightedge and a new blade in an X-acto knife. (We purchased the materials at a local crafts store.) Punch holes in the leather with an awl, and use rivets to make looped ends as shown in Photo H. Join the looped strips with split key rings. Make sure you thread the leather through the mane during the bridle-assembly process.

G

Use 100-grit sandpaper and a sanding block to shape the eye.

H

You can make a convincing bridle and reins using a few craft store items. Wrap the pliers' jaws with tape to prevent scratching the rivet.

Patterns: Center
Body Section

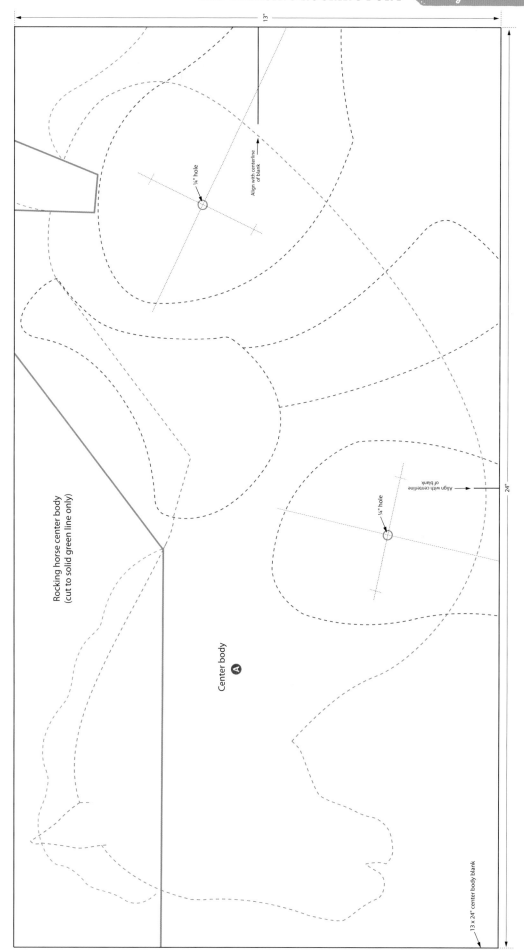

Enlarge 250%.

Patterns:
Outside Body
Section
(2 required)

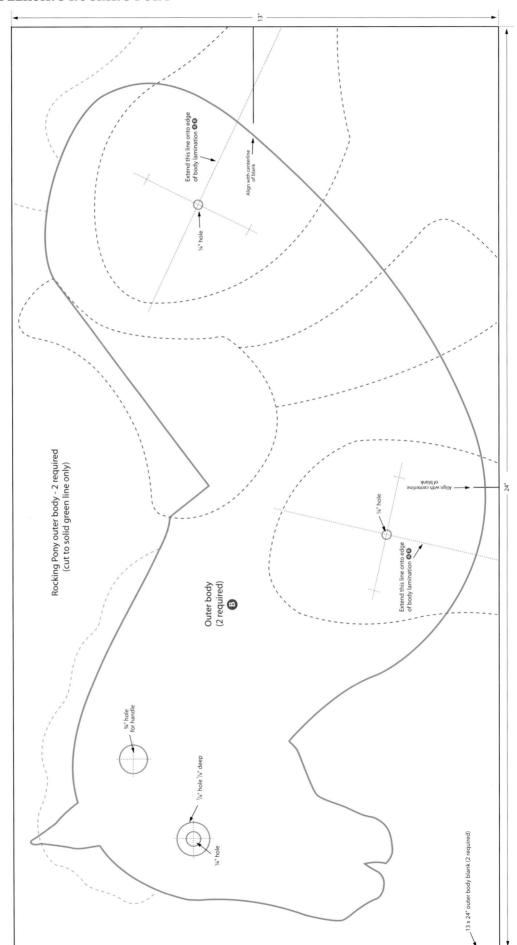

Rocking Pony outer body - 2 required
(cut to solid green line only)

Outer body
(2 required) **B**

¾" hole
for handle

⁷⁄₁₆" hole ¹⁄₈" deep

¼" hole

¼" hole

Extend this line onto edge
of body lamination ❹❺

Align with centerline
of blank

13"

24"

¼" hole

Align with centerline
of blank

Extend this line onto edge
of body lamination ❹❺

13 x 24" outer body blank (2 required)

Enlarge 250%.

Patterns: Left Legs

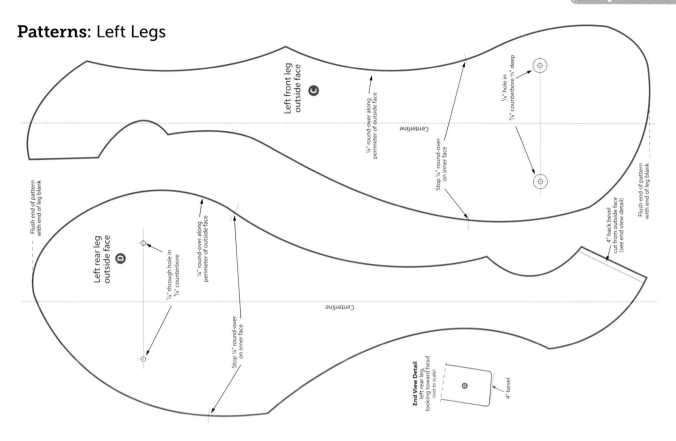

Patterns: Right Legs

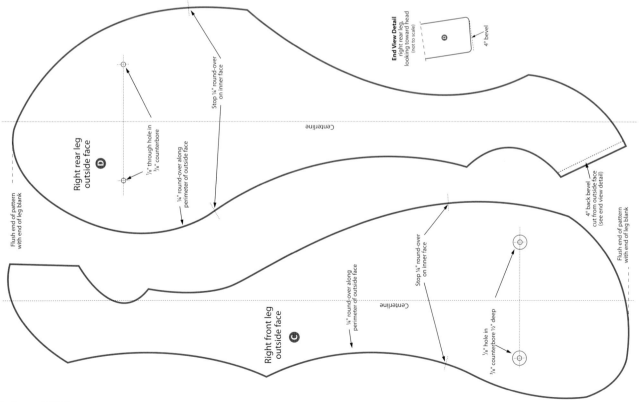

Enlarge 250%.

Patterns

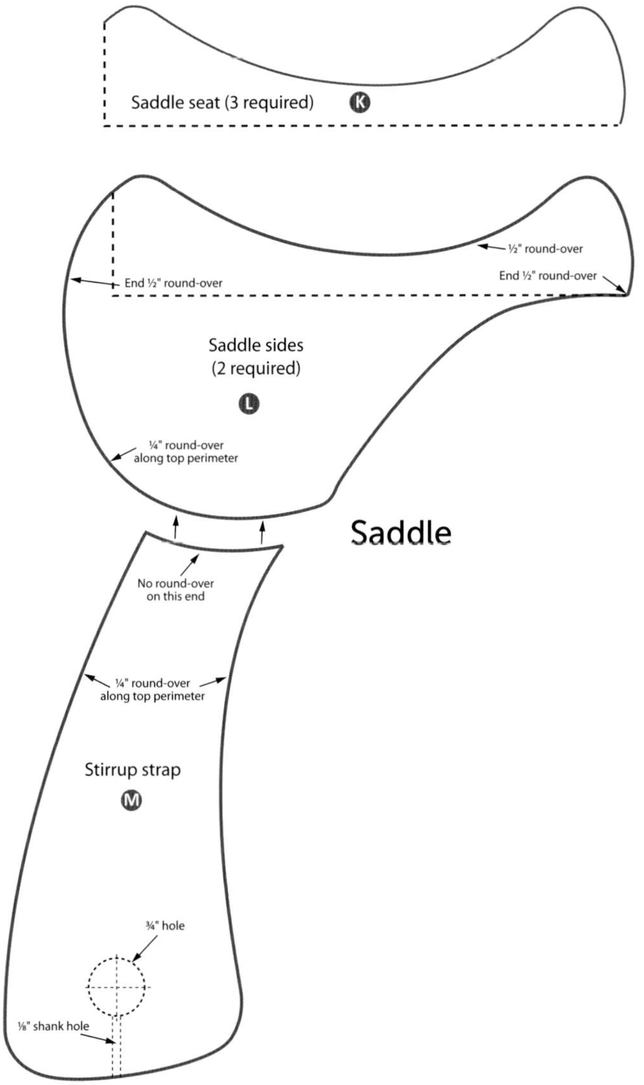

Saddle seat (3 required) K
½" round-over
End ½" round-over
End ½" round-over
Saddle sides
(2 required)
L
¼" round-over
along top perimeter
Saddle
No round-over
on this end
¼" round-over
along top perimeter
Stirrup strap
M
¾" hole
⅛" shank hole

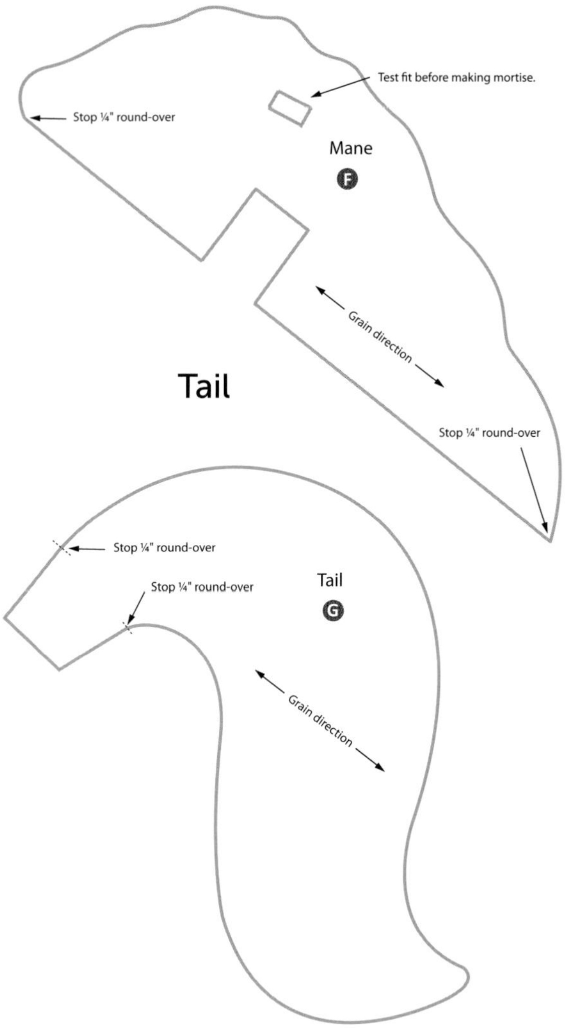

Test fit before making mortise.
Stop ¼" round-over
Mane
F
Grain direction
Tail
Stop ¼" round-over
Stop ¼" round-over
Stop ¼" round-over
Tail
G
Grain direction

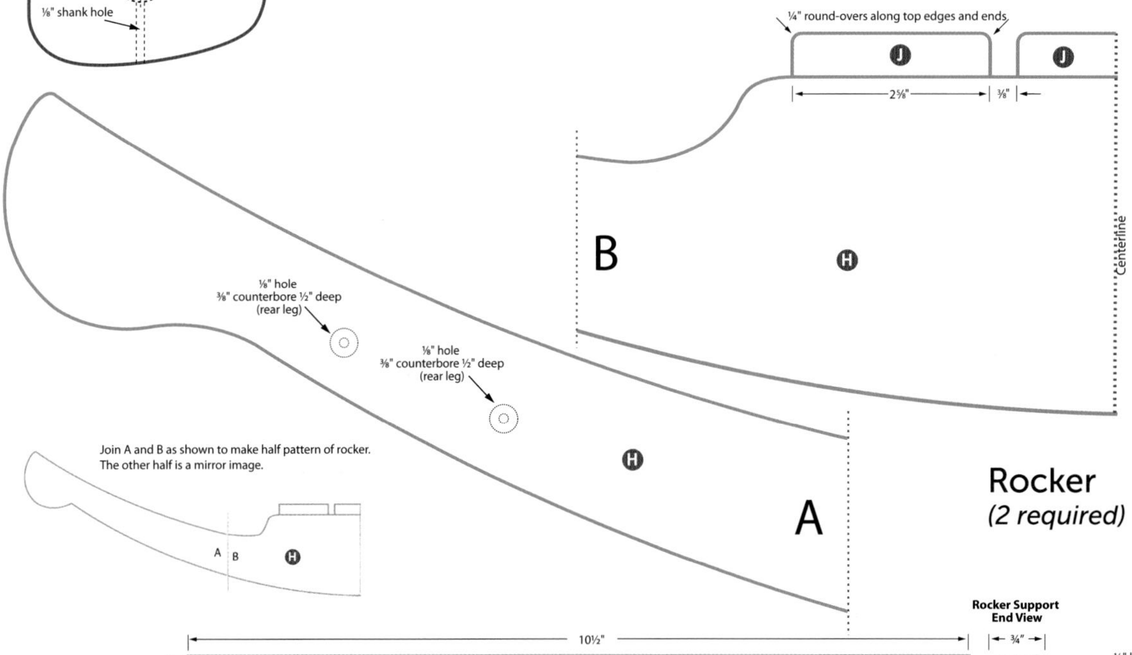

¼" round-overs along top edges and ends
J
J
2⅝"
⅜"
B
H
Centerline
⅛" hole
⅜" counterbore ½" deep
(rear leg)
⅛" hole
⅜" counterbore ½" deep
(rear leg)
H
A
Join A and B as shown to make half pattern of rocker.
The other half is a mirror image.
A B H
Rocker
(2 required)

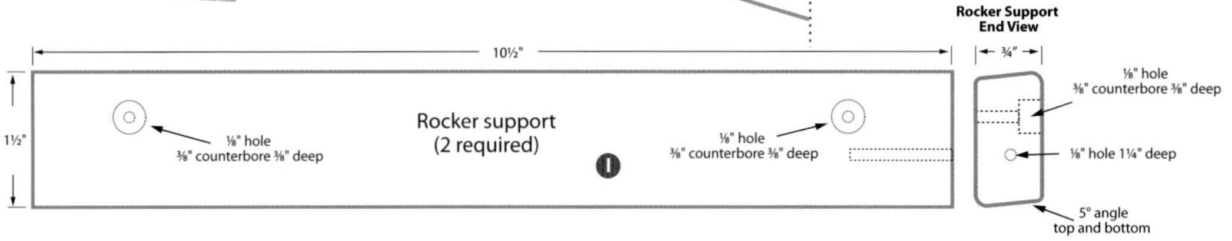

10½"
1½"
⅛" hole
⅜" counterbore ⅜" deep
Rocker support
(2 required)
I
⅛" hole
⅜" counterbore ⅜" deep
Rocker Support
End View
¾"
⅛" hole
⅜" counterbore ⅜" deep
⅛" hole 1¼" deep
5° angle
top and bottom

Enlarge 250%.

MARBLE RACE

Building blocks with a built-in race track

BY SCOTT EMCH

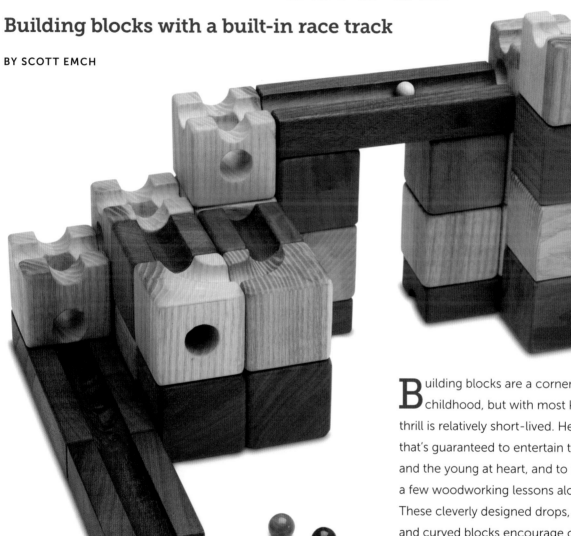

Building blocks are a cornerstone of childhood, but with most kids, the thrill is relatively short-lived. Here's a set that's guaranteed to entertain the young and the young at heart, and to teach you a few woodworking lessons along the way. These cleverly designed drops, chutes, and curved blocks encourage creative minds to assemble tall towers that double as marble raceways.

This simple scrapwood project also offers lessons in accurate production work. The parts must be milled precisely in order for the marbles to roll without a hitch.

With the following step-by-step instructions and jigs, you can make a starter set in a weekend. Keep the jigs handy—you'll likely get requests for more parts or another set, before the holiday season ends.

SAFETY ALERT

The blocks are suitable for all ages, but ⅝"-diameter marbles are a choking hazard for small children.

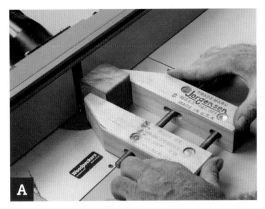

Secure the small blocks in a wooden handscrew to keep fingers clear of the router bit.

Mill the stock

1 From ⁵⁄₄ (1¼") stock, mill chute stock to 1" thick. From ¹⁰⁄₄ (2½") stock, mill block stock to 2" thick. Consider milling extra chute and block stock now. If you're short on time, you can forgo the routing and make plain-faced blocks for stackers.

2 Rip the block and chute stock to 2". Crosscut the chute stock to about 12¼" long. Now using a stop, carefully cut all of your block stock to 2" cubes.

3 Set up your router table with a ⅛"-radius round-over bit. Using a pushblock for the chute stock and a handscrew to safely hold the blocks, round over all edges (Photo A).

Make the jigs and mill the parts

1 From ¾"-thick plywood and block scrap, make both slotting jigs, as shown in Figure 1.

2 Using a plunge router equipped with a bearing-guided cove bit, adjust the bit height (and set the depth stop) to rout a ⅜"-deep groove. Using your bench vise, clamp a piece of chute stock (A) in the straight slot jig and rout a groove (Photo B). If needed, insert a shim against the stop so that the groove is centered on your stock.

3 Continue routing straight grooves on your chute stock (A), curve (B) and drop

Figure 1: Slotting Jigs

Straight Slot

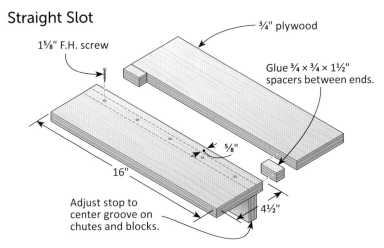

Curved Slot

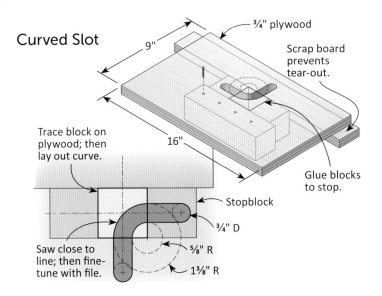

Figure 2: Chute

Use a vise to secure chute stock and blocks to the straight slot jig, and rout the groove.

Scrap stock

Clamp a block in the curved slot jig and feed the router counterclockwise The scrap stock controls tear-out and protects the vise.

blocks (C and D), using the figures on page 38 as reference. To make the castle-topped drop blocks (C and D), rotate the block 90°, and rout a second groove perpendicular to the first.

4 Clamp a block into the curved slot jig, and rout a groove to make the curved slot block (B), as shown in Photo C.

5 Using a mitersaw and stop, trim the chute stock to make short, medium, and long chutes, where shown in Figure 2.

Drill the drops

1 Using a center gauge, mark out the centers on the unrouted faces of curve blocks (B). Make sure your drill press table is perpendicular to the chuck, and then drill ¾"-diameter through-holes where shown in Figure 3 (page 28).

2 Clamp a starter drop block (C) into an adjustable angle vise. Using the grooves as a guide, center the bit on the top of the block, and drill a stopped hole as shown in Figure 3 (page 28) and Photo D.

3 Adjust the vise angle to 26° (or the tilt of your table), and drill a second stopped hole through the front, as shown in Photo E.

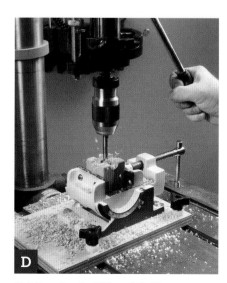

Set the vise to 90° and drill a stopped hole into the top of each of the drop blocks.

Set the angle, reposition the vise and then drill the angled hole in the front face of the drop block.

Use the router bit to shave away any tear-out and round the inside corner.

4 To round the intersection between the holes, chuck the bearing guided cove bit (used to rout grooves) into your drill press. Drilling at the slowest speed, lightly clean out the hole as needed to allow clearance for the marble (Photo F; page 27).

5 Repeat the drilling sequence for the standard drop blocks (D), making sure to adjust the hole depth and vise angle, where shown in Figure 3.

Build the box and finish the blocks

1 From hardwood and/or Baltic birch plywood, cut the box ends, sides, and bottom to the sizes listed in Figure 4.

2 Using a tablesaw equipped with a dado set, dado and rabbet the box ends where shown.

3 Glue and clamp the bottom and sides to the ends.

4 Sand the parts to 220 grit, and then apply a kid-friendly finish to the blocks and box. (I wiped on a coat of walnut oil, let it soak in for about 10 minutes, and then wiped off the excess.)

5 Give the blocks a test run. You may need to sand or plane a corner or face to make a fast rolling track.

Figure 3: 2 x 2" Blocks

Curve

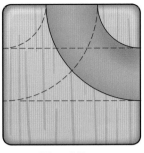

Top View

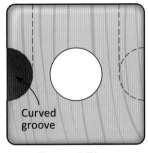

Front View

Starter Drop

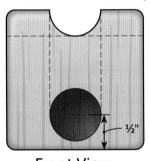

Front View

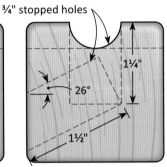

Side View

Standard Drop

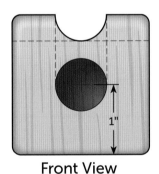

Front View

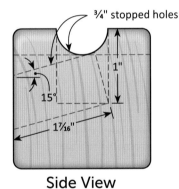

Side View

	Part	Thickness	Width	Length	Qty.	Mat'l
A*	Chutes	1"	2"	2" (short) 4" (med.) 6" (long)	4+ 4+ 4+	W
B	Curve blocks	2"	2"	2"	10+	A, W
C	Starter drops	2"	2"	2"	6+	A, W
D	Standard drops	2"	2"	2"	10+	A, W

Cut List: Marble Race

*Indicates parts that are initially cut oversized. See instructions.
+More blocks are better, but the above quantity will fit inside the block box.
Materials: W=Walnut, A=Ash

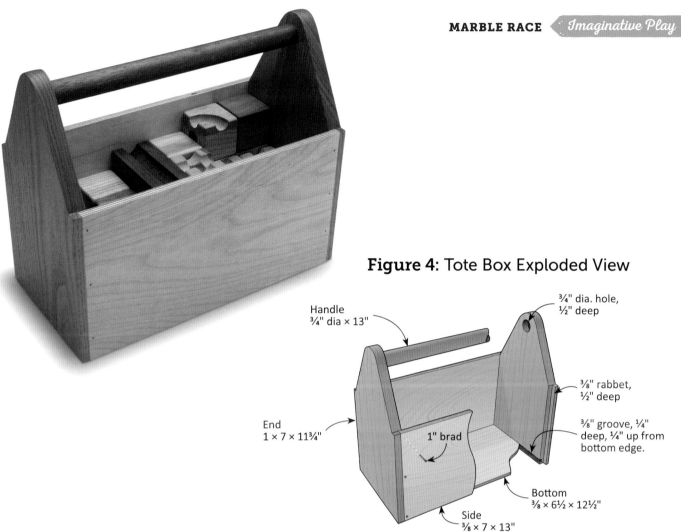

Figure 4: Tote Box Exploded View

¾" dia. hole,
½" deep

Handle
¾" dia × 13"

End
1 × 7 × 11¾"

1" brad

⅜" rabbet,
½" deep

⅜" groove, ¼"
deep, ¼" up from
bottom edge.

Bottom
⅜ × 6½ × 12½"

Side
⅜ × 7 × 13"

Pattern: Tote Box End

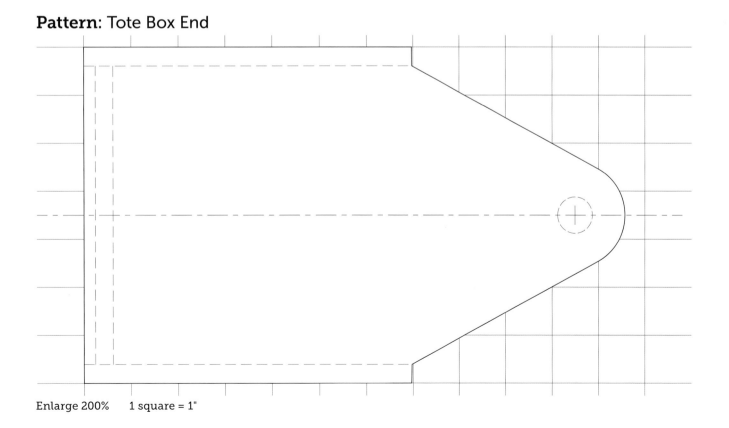

Enlarge 200%   1 square = 1"

MAGIC COIN BANK

Mystery and illusion via a tricky mirror

BY KEN BURTON

This fun and mysterious bank is sure to delight children of all ages. Coins dropped in the slot seem to disappear, leaving the box empty except for a small wooden cube which appears to float in the center. The secret to the illusion is an internal mirror set at a 45° angle, creating the impression that the bank is hollow, while the money drops into the section behind the mirror.

There's no magic to building this project, but you'll certainly learn some woodworking tricks. They include a great lesson in spline joinery, with hidden splines used to attach the case parts, and keyed splines used to join the mitered front and rear frames. The only specialty supplies involved are a "front-surface" mirror—easily found online—and a and a checkerboard-patterned paper liner for the interior which you can copy from page 35.

I made this box from sassafras, which is relatively soft and easy to work with both hand and power tools. As an added bonus, freshly cut sassafras exudes a delightful, spicy aroma

Miter the ends of the box sides so the waste is located under the leaning blade, not above it.

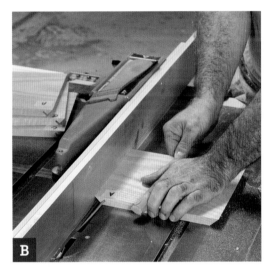

Adjust the fence and blade height to cut the 3/8"-deep spline slots 1/8" in from the inside edge of the miter.

that will leave your shop smelling exotic for several days. However, you can use any wood of your choosing to build the bank. Although you could use glass for the front of the box, I chose to use acrylic to provide for child safety.

Make the case

1 Mill a 36" length of stock for the box sides to the thickness and width shown in the Cut List (page 34). Then cut each side (A) about 1/8" oversized in length for now. Mark the mating ends for reassembly later in their

original sequence to ensure grain continuity around the box. Orient the mismatched corner to be on the underside; then mark the top piece to identify it as such.

2 Tilt the blade on your tablesaw to 45°, and miter one end of each side (A). Use a stop on your miter gauge fence to help keep the pieces from slipping as you cut. Reset the stop to cut the pieces to final length while mitering the other ends, as shown in Photo A.

3 With the saw blade still tilted at 45°, position your rip fence to cut the 3/8"-deep spline slots in the mitered ends, where shown in Figure 1 on page 32. Guide the mitered ends along the fence to make the cuts as shown in Photo B.

4 Cut a piece of 3/4"-thick stock to 2 1/4" wide × 18" long to use as spline stock. Then use scrap to set up the saw for a 1/8"-thick rip that creates a snug fit in your spline slots. With that saw setting, resaw two lengths of 2 1/4"-wide stock from your 18"-long piece; then crosscut 12 pieces 1 1/16" long from that to use as case splines. Save the rest of the material for the frame splines to be made later.

5 Chuck a 1/4" straight bit in your table-mounted router, and cut the coin slot, centering it in the top piece as shown in Photo C (page 33).

6 Lay out the grooves for the mirror on the two opposing box sides (A), as shown in Figure 2 (page 32). Make the cuts on the tablesaw, as shown in Photos D and E on page 33. You can use the same stop setting for both pieces, but you'll need to load the pieces onto the miter gauge in two different orientations. On one piece, the mitered end rests against the fence, and on the other, the side goes against the fence. Use a plywood backer to minimize exit tear-out.

Figure 1: Magic Coin Bank Exploded View

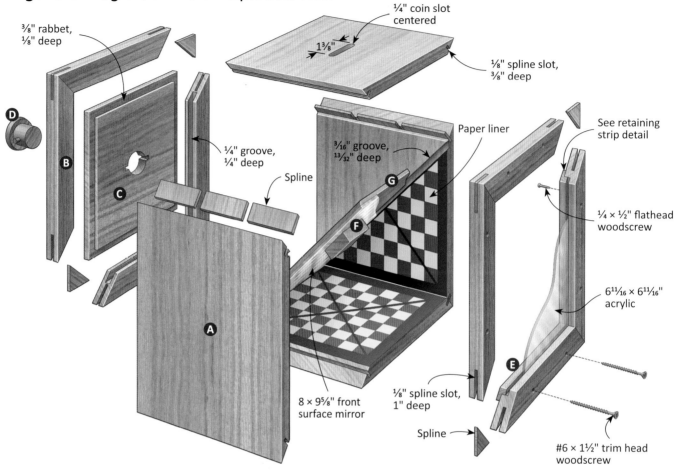

⅜" rabbet, ⅛" deep

¼" coin slot centered

1⅜"

⅛" spline slot, ⅜" deep

¼" groove, ¼" deep

³⁄₁₆" groove, ¹³⁄₃₂" deep

Paper liner

Spline

See retaining strip detail

¼ × ½" flathead woodscrew

6¹¹⁄₁₆ × 6¹¹⁄₁₆" acrylic

8 × 9⅝" front surface mirror

⅛" spline slot, 1" deep

Spline

#6 × 1½" trim head woodscrew

D B C A G F E

Back Hole and Plug Detail

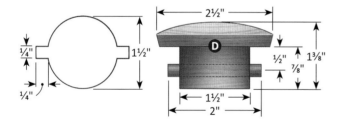

2½"
1½"
¼"
¼"
½"
7⁄8"
1⅜"
1½"
2"
D

Retaining Strip Detail

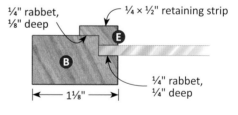

¼" rabbet, ⅛" deep

¼ × ½" retaining strip

E

B

¼" rabbet, ¼" deep

1⅛"

After making both initial cuts, reposition the stop and make a second pass on each piece to widen the cuts to ³⁄₁₆".

7 Make up four 7 × 8" clamping cauls from scraps of ¼"-thick plywood with 45° strips glued and screwed at either end. Clamp the cauls to the sides; then dry-fit the four sides together, as shown in Photo F (page 34). When you are happy with the fit, glue the box together.

Make the frames

1 Cut the front and back frame pieces (B) about ¹⁄₁₆" longer than the sizes shown in the Cut List. This will create slightly oversized frames that you'll trim flush to the case after assembly.

2 Using a miter gauge and stop, miter the ends of the pieces to 45°. Glue four of the pieces together to make up the front frame, as shown in Photo G (page 34).

QUICK TIP

Instruction on cutting mirror is available on the Internet, including a lesson at *wikihow.com/Cut-Glass*. Or, your local glass supplier will usually do the job for you at minimal cost.

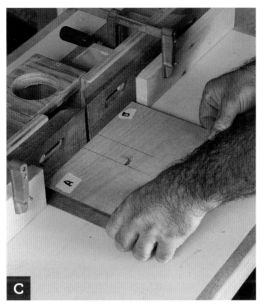

Cut the coin slot on the router table in two passes, using stopblocks to limit the slot's length.

Sawing the Grooves

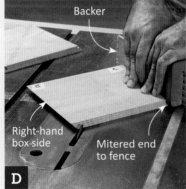

Backer

Right-hand box-side

Mitered end to fence

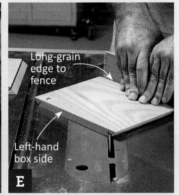

Long-grain edge to fence

Left-hand box side

Saw the ¹³/₃₂"-deep grooves for the mirror. Set the miter gauge at 45° to the blade, and use the same stop position for both opposing cuts. Cut the right-hand piece with its end against the fence and the left-hand piece with its side against the fence.

Figure 2: Groove Detail

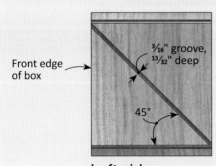

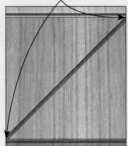

Grooves should run from corner to corner.

Front edge of box

³/₁₆" groove, ¹³/₃₂" deep

45°

Left side   Right side

3 Cut centered ¼"-wide × ¼"-deep grooves in the remaining four frame pieces, where shown in Figure 1, to accept the back panel (C).

4 Cut a piece of stock for the back panel to the size shown in the Cut List. Saw or rout ⅜"-wide rabbets in the edges to create tongues that fit in the rear frame grooves.

5 Drill a 1½"-diameter hole through the center of the back panel. Then use a coping saw to cut opposing notches at the perimeter, as shown in the Back Hole and Plug Detail in Figure 1.

6 Glue the back frame together as you did with the front frame. Be sure to slip the back panel (C) in its grooves before clamping the pieces (B) together.

7 Turn a 1½"-diameter plug (D) with a ⅞" long spigot, as shown in the Back Hole and Plug Detail in Figure 1. (If you don't have a thick enough piece of sassafras, either glue up thinner pieces or use another species such as oak.) Test the fit of the spigot in its hole. Drill a ¼"-diameter hole through the spigot, and glue a 2" length of ¼"-diameter dowel in place to serve as a lock.

8 With the blade raised 1", saw centered spline slots in the corners of both frames by carrying each across the blade at a 45° angle, using a jig like the one shown in Photo H (page 34).

9 Cut the previously unused spline material into slightly oversized triangular splines to fit in the slots. Swab the pieces with glue, and tap them home, as shown in Photo I (page 35). When dry, trim the splines flush with a chisel and block plane.

10 Rout a ¼"-wide × ¼"-deep rabbet around the inside of the front frame, and then square the corners with a chisel.

11 Make the retaining strips (E) that hold in the acrylic panel, as shown in the Retaining

Strip Detail in Figure 1 (page 32). The best approach here is to saw or rout the ⅛" × ¼" rabbet in the edge of a ½"-thick board; then rip the ¼"-wide retaining strip from the rabbeted edge. Crosscut the strips to the length; then miter the pieces to fit the rabbet in the front frame.

Assemble and finish the box

1 Glue the back frame to the back of the box.

2 Print out the liners on cover stock or other heavy paper, and trim them to fit inside the box. If you need to make the pieces smaller, trim an equal amount off each side to keep the borders an even width. Brush rubber cement on the back side of the liner pieces and on the inside surfaces of the box and allow it to dry. Then carefully adhere the liners to the inside of the box.

3 Cut the mirror to 8 × 9⅝". Note: This mirror is very thin. To avoid cracking it, handle it carefully when removing the protective plastic covering and when cutting it.

4 Saw the acrylic to 6¹¹⁄₁₆ × 6¹¹⁄₁₆". A standard carbide combination blade on the tablesaw will do the job fine.

5 Cut the floating block (F) to the size shown in the Cut List, using quartersawn material so the grain pattern doesn't spoil the illusion in the mirror (Figure 1). Finish the block with shellac; then affix it to the mirror at its center, using cyanoacrylate (CA) glue.

6 Cut a piece of ⅛"-thick plywood to 8 × 9⅝" to serve as a backer (G) for the mirror. Then carefully slip the backer and mirror into their grooves at the same time, as hown in Photo J.

Glue triangular strips to scrap plywood; then clamp across the box corners to close the miter joints.

Glue up the front frame with a band clamp or self-squaring frame clamp, like the one shown here.

Make a simple V-shaped carrier to hold the frames for sawing the spline slots in the corners.

Cut List: Magic Coin Bank

	Part	Thickness	Width	Length	Qty.	Mat'l
A*	Sides	⅝"	7¼"	8½"	4	S
B*	Frame pieces	⅝"	1⅛"	8½"	8	S
C	Back panel	⅜"	6¹¹⁄₁₆"	6¹¹⁄₁₆"	1	S
D*	Plug	1⅜"	2½" diameter		1	S
E*	Retaining strips	¼"	½"	7¼"	4	S
F	Floating block	⅝"	1¼"	1¼"	1	QO
G	Mirror backer	⅛"	8"	9⅝"	1	P

*Indicates parts that are initially cut oversized. See instructions.
Materials: S=Sassafras, QO=Quartersawn Oak, P=Plywood
Hardware: (8) #4 × ½" wood screws; (8) #6 × 1½" trim head screws

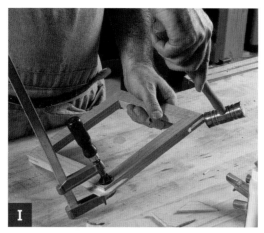

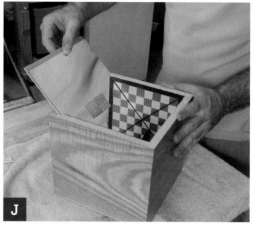

Glue the splines into their slots, and then tap them home to fully seat them before clamping at the frame corners.

7 Place the acrylic in its rabbets in the front frame, and then attach the retaining strips (E) to the frame using #4 × ½" wood screws. Clean the inside surface of the acrylic thoroughly.

8 Screw the front frame to the box with eight #6 × 1½" trim head screws. Plane,

To avoid breaking the mirror, carefully slide both it and the backer into the box grooves at the same time.

scrape, and sand the edges of both frames to flush them to the box sides. Then sand the whole box through 220 grit.

9 Temporarily apply masking tape to the acrylic to protect it, and then apply several coats of your favorite wood finish. I used spray shellac.

Patterns: Magic Coin Bank

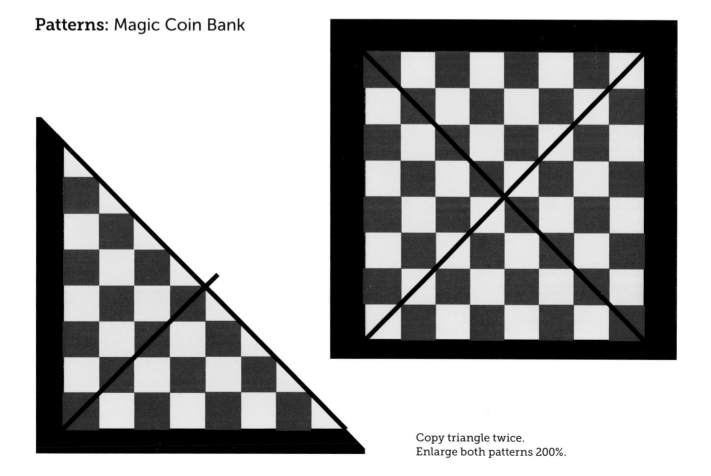

Copy triangle twice.
Enlarge both patterns 200%.

RAINBOW THROWER

A fascinating but simple toy for kids and adults that uses an item from an unexpected source: military surplus

BY WILLIAM MCDOWELL

It was probably close to 50 years ago that I bought my first surplus tank prism taken from a periscope housing. I remember being amazed at the colorful spectrum it projected across a room when placed in direct sunlight. A few years ago I rediscovered some of these precisely ground pieces of glass and decided to build

a functional cradle that allows for a more controlled aiming of the rainbow.

It is possible to use a prism by just standing it on end on a sunny windowsill, but you will get much better results by

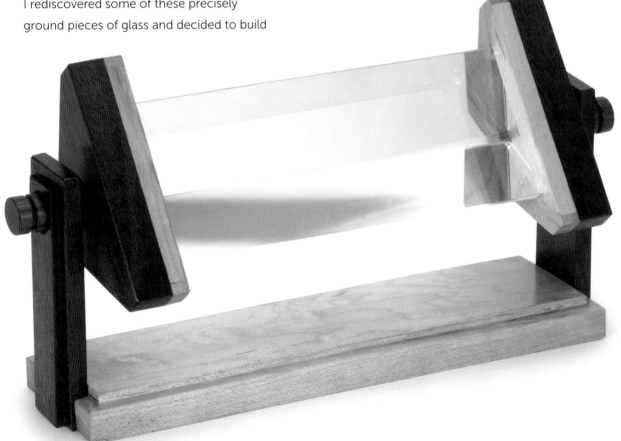

constructing a stand that will allow for horizontal mounting and making fine adjustments to compensate for the daily changes in the sun's position in the sky.

Before we begin, there are a few things you should know about these surplus prisms. They are available in three configurations: mounted in the original metal housing, one side silvered (a mirror coating), and plain unsilvered. You want the plain ones. You can usually save a few bucks by purchasing one in the original housing, but remember these were built under contract from Uncle Sam for use in military combat vehicles. To say they are ruggedly mounted is an understatement. Trying to extract one may result in the invention of new swearwords and a broken prism.

You should also remember that these are takeouts from surplus military gear and may have some minor flaws such as little chips or fogging of the glass. If there are areas of the glass with a gray coating that glass cleaner won't remove, a solvent such as acetone or paint thinner with fine steel wool will usually do the trick.

These prisms are ground, not cast, glass, and are very fragile. If one is standing on end on your workbench and falls over, it can easily break in half. This will definitely have an effect on the performance of your rainbow thrower—unlike small chips, which will usually not cause any noticeable problems.

Tools: Bandsaw, disc or edge sander, square

Time: A few hours

Materials: Prism, wood stock, ½" dowels, chipboard or heavy paper, CA glue, sandpaper, wood filler, mirror adhesive or silicone

Choose your wood

Your first decision is what kind of wood to use. Unlike most woodworking projects, this one will intentionally be placed in direct sunlight—something we usually try to avoid). A more stable wood will work better. Mahogany and teak are good choices, and if you prefer domestics, I've had good luck with walnut. Poplar would be a good choice for those of you who prefer working with softer woods; and, of course, the closer you can get to a true quartersawn board the better, regardless of your choice. I always like to mix different species, and this has presented no problems when the gluing process is done correctly.

These prisms sit in direct sunlight and can get quite warm, so woods with dramatically different expansion/contraction rates should be avoided. Don't worry about your project becoming a fire hazard; unlike magnifying glasses, rainbow throwers do not concentrate sunlight.

Make the end pieces

Making the two end pieces that will hold the prism is the first step. Trace the outline of the prism end near the center of a piece of heavy paper or thin cardboard at least 3" x 3" square (Photo A; page 38). The location is not critical. I use single-ply chipboard for all my patterns. It is cheap, available at art stores, easy to cut with a sharp knife and durable, even for repeated use.

Cut some ¼" x ¼" stock, which you will use to make the triangular frames that secure the prism to the endpiece backing parts. The dimension of this stock isn't critical either, but the thicker it is, the larger the area of the prism faces it will cover, decreasing the size of the projected rainbow. You can make it wider, but keep

A

Much of the process for making the ends involves simple "eyeballing" rather than taking exact measurements.

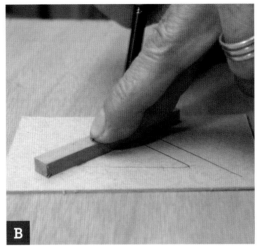

B

Learn to be accurate in tracing or outlining by using a sharp pencil held at a consistent angle.

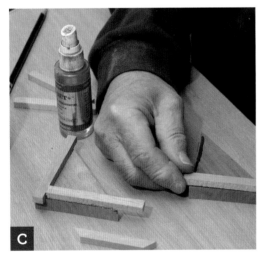

C

The more you use CA glue for small parts, the more you will appreciate what it can do.

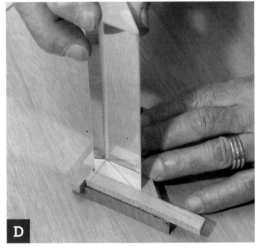

D

"Sanding to fit" makes it possible to remove much smaller amounts than with cutting tools.

the thickness to about the recommended ¼". The smaller the finished cradle, the better, as it will fit on more windowsills, and some of the newer sills are pretty skinny.

Place the prism back on the cardboard pattern where you previously marked its outline, and using a piece of the framing stock, mark another outline the width of the stock (Photo B). This will be the size of your backing parts. Cut out your new pattern.

Trace the shape onto your choice of stock, which should be at least ½" thick. You will need two for each rainbow thrower

you are making. Cut out these pieces "fat" (outside the line). I just use the bandsaw, as the parts will be sanded to the line after the framing strips are added.

Cut six framing strips to length for each cradle. Four should be a bit longer than the sides of the backing parts and two can be a bit shorter, as they will fit inside the other two. Cut a few extra of these, as we are going to use the trial-and-error method for fitting them. Glue the two longer ones to the backing plates right inside the line you previously traced (Photo C). I use thick cyanoacrylate, or CA glue, more commonly known as superglue.

The next step is the only tricky part of this project, fitting the third framing piece between the two you have previously glued onto the backing parts. It's time to get into angle cuts, or as I prefer, *freehand angle sanding*. You can calculate the length and angle of the cuts you will make on this piece, but for me, sanding gives me the needed control.

You will need either a disc or edge sander to make this part fit perfectly. Place the prism upright between the two previously glued framing strips. Be careful here, this is where they can fall over and break. Sand the ends and the angles of the third piece until you have a pretty good fit (Photo D).

This fit should be a little sloppy, a bit oversize to allow for seasonal wood movement. Let the prism move about 1/64" in all directions. Glue this last strip in place, using wood filler (if necessary) to neaten it all up, and use your sander (Photo E) to finish the job. I have made a number of these, and on some I have squared off both

ends of the long side of the triangle. See the finished sample shown on the first page of this article, and the exploded drawing on the next page.

The final step in completing these parts is drilling the ½" holes for the pivot dowels. These should be centered in the triangle defined by your framing parts. I suppose their exact locations could be calculated, but I'm satisfied to just eyeball it.

Design your base

Take a deep breath and relax; all the hard stuff has been done. Having framed the prism, the only step left is making the base, the design of which is pretty much up to you. Fitting and placement of the pivot dowels is important, but once again not critical. Let's make the base and be done with this one.

The base unit consists of five parts: two uprights to support the prism assembly, two ½" dowels about 1½" long, and the baseplate itself.

The uprights are the first parts to make. They must be long enough to attach

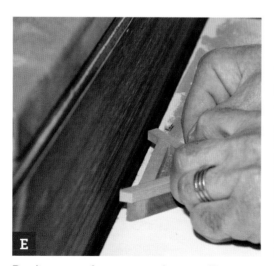

Don't use much pressure when sanding small parts to fit. Save your workpiece and your knuckles.

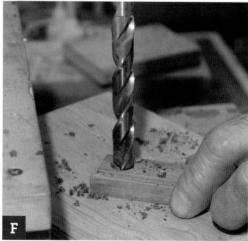

If you're drilling a number of identical parts, set up a jig for support and positioning.

Figure 1: Rainbow Thrower Exploded View

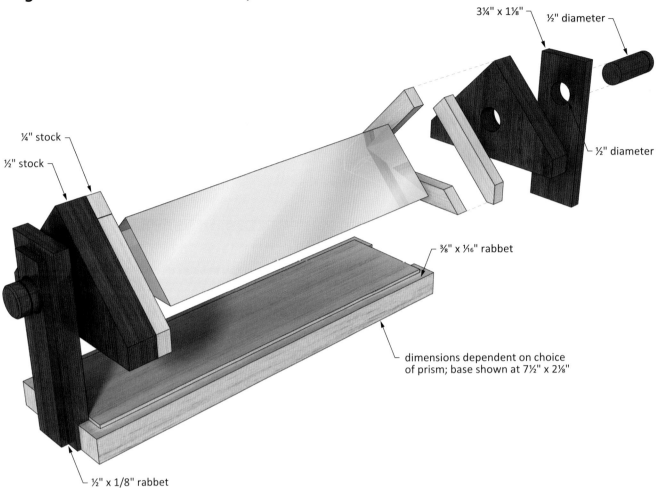

3¼" x 1⅛"

½" diameter

½" diameter

¼" stock

½" stock

⅜" x ¹⁄₁₆" rabbet

dimensions dependent on choice
of prism; base shown at 7½" x 2⅛"

½" x 1/8" rabbet

securely to the baseplate while allowing
the prism assembly to rotate above it. Their
exact length will depend on how large you
made the backing plates and the thickness
of your base. Keep them as short as possible
to add stability. They must be wide enough
to drill a ½" hole through. Fabricate these
parts and drill the holes (Photo F; page 39).

Select your dowels for a snug fit in the
holes in both the uprights and backing
plates. The rotating parts will wear over time,
so I use thin CA glue to strengthen them.
This also can be used to build up the dowel
size and pivot hole in the backing plate if
the fit is a bit sloppy. Just apply the CA to
one end of the dowel up to about as far as
it will fit in the backing plate and around

the entire circumference of the hole. If you
need multiple coats, use a CA accelerator
to speed up the process. You don't need to
treat the other end of the dowel or the hole
in the upright, as these will be permanently
glued together after finishing.

The base can be as simple or complex as
you like. The joint for attaching the uprights
is your choice; it would be a perfect
application for a dovetail, but to keep things
simple, I just used a captured dado. Make
the base long enough so when the uprights
are fitted you have about ¼" clearance from
the prism assembly on each end. Cut your
joint, test everything with a dry fit (Photo G).
If it all works together, glue the uprights to
the base.

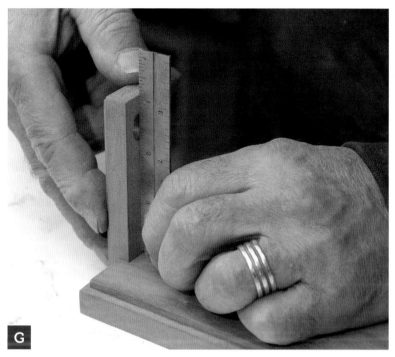

G

Accuracy at this stage will make everything easier during the final steps of construction.

H

Use a tabletop to help line up the dowels in the prism. The prism turns around the dowels, and the dowels are solid in the uprights.

Finish up

Apply a finish of your choice to all the parts before final assembly. When dry, the next step is fastening the end plates to the prism. Clean the prism thoroughly and use a small dab of mirror adhesive or silicone in each corner. Flexibility is necessary here to allow for seasonal wood changes.

Lay the base down on its side and push the dowels into the holes on the uprights. Move the prism assembly into position and push the dowels the rest of the way through until they seat against the prism itself (Photo H). Adjust their depths to get the prism centered between the two uprights. As the prism will pivot on the inside ends of the dowels, it's time to glue the outer ends to the uprights. This is another great application for thin CA. Use a piece of wire or other pointed implement to touch a drop of CA to the joint between the dowel and the upright. It will wick right in through capillary action. Three or four drops is plenty.

Well, that's it; you're done. Except for one more step...finding a sunny window!

Overall dimensions:
12¾"w × 15 ⅜"d × 33¾"h

DOLL HIGH CHAIR

Make this a memorable gift for a deserving daughter or granddaughter

BY CHUCK HEDLUND

Bring a smile to the face of a future mom with this child-pleasing project. Biscuits, dowels, and screws bond the maple parts together, while store-bought turned spindles speed construction. I sized the overall design to suit dolls 15" to 18" long, like the Grace Farmgirl Butterflies doll shown. Just like full-sized high chairs, the food tray rotates up, making it easy to sit dolly or remove her after her feeding. And remember: the high chair is for dolls only.

Build the base side frames

Note: Purchase (or make yourself) the spindles and other essential materials and confirm sizes before you begin building.
1 From ¾"-thick stock, cut the high chair base parts (A-H) to width plus 1" longer than listed in the Cut List. (page 51). As you cut the pieces, mark the part letter on the face of each with chalk, referring to Figure 1 (page 44). Set aside all but the base side frame parts (A-D).
2 Using a quality crosscut blade, cut the top ends of the legs (A) at a 5° angle and bevel (Photo A). To do this, mark the outside or best faces for the left front, left

back, right front, and right back legs. Now, adjust the saw blade and miter gauge for the compound cuts. With a left-tilt blade and the miter gauge and extension fence in the left-hand slot, cut two leg top ends with their outside faces up. Without changing the settings, move the miter gauge and extension fence to the other side of the blade, place the remaining two legs outside face down, and cut their top ends. This will result in two sets of front and back legs, or one set for each side.
3 With the blade at 90°, cut the 5° angles on the ends of side rails (B), (C), and (D),

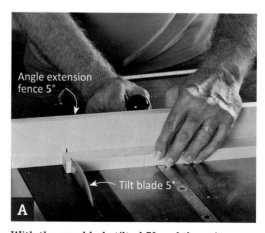

With the saw blade tilted 5° and the miter gauge extension fence angled at 5°, cut the leg top ends.

as shown in Figure 2. Use a stop on the extension fence to ensure that part pairs are cut to identical lengths.

4 Adjust the fence, tilt the blade 5° away from the fence, and bevel-rip the top edge of parts (B) to match the top ends of legs (A).

5 Then, on a flat surface, position rails (B), (C), and (D) between the sets of front and back legs. Fit the top side rails (B) flush with the top ends of the legs. Fit the other rails below, making sure the joints are snug. They should match the dimensions in the Base Side View in Figure 2. Mark centered biscuit slot locations on the ends of the rails and corresponding locations on the legs. Mark the centers for the biscuit locations on the front edges of the front legs and back edges of the back legs. Note that the side assemblies (A, B, C, D) require slots for #20 biscuits and that the front and back rails (E, F, G) require slots for #0 biscuits.

6 Now make the Leg-Slotting Jig and Rail-Slotting Jig shown in Figure 3 (page 47).

7 Using the leg-slotting jig, cut biscuit slots in the legs' inside edges and faces. When slotting the faces, gang the two legs together to provide bearing for the biscuit joiner's fence, as shown in Photo B. Note that edge slots are centered across the legs' thickness while face slots are ³⁄₈" in from outside edges.

8 Clamp the rail-slotting jig to the bench and position and clamp a rail in place, flush with the edge of the jig. Use a stop to center the joiner's cutter on the rail's end and aligned with the cut line. Now make the cut. Keeping the same face up, rotate the rail and move it to the other side of the jig. Repeat the process to cut a slot in the rail's opposite end (Photo C). Cut slots in the remaining rails.

9 Working off a centerline, lay out the locations for the turned spindles in the side rails, spacing them 1½" apart, as shown in Figure 2. Check the hole diameter for the tenons by making a test hole. Now drill the centered ¼" holes ⁹⁄₁₆" deep (Photo D; page 46).

Figure 1: Doll High Chair Exploded View

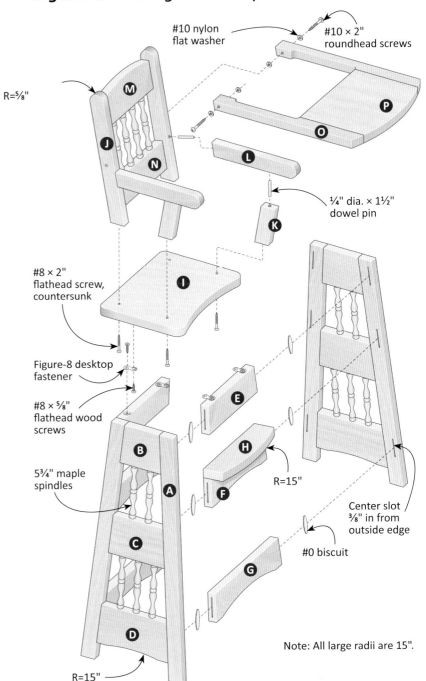

#10 nylon flat washer

#10 × 2" roundhead screws

R=⅝"

¼" dia. × 1½" dowel pin

#8 × 2" flathead screw, countersunk

Figure-8 desktop fastener

#8 × ⅝" flathead wood screws

5¾" maple spindles

R=15"

R=15"

Center slot ³⁄₈" in from outside edge

#0 biscuit

Note: All large radii are 15".

QUICK TIP

For consistent results, set the miter gauge only once, test it, and leave it at that setting for all cuts requiring the same angle.

B

Clamp the legs in the leg-slotting jig, and biscuit-cut the slots at the marked locations for the side, front, and back rails.

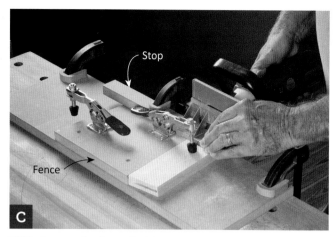

Stop

Fence

C

With the toggle clamp holding the rail snug to the jig's fence, place the joiner against the stop and biscuit-cut a centered slot.

Figure 2: Base Side and Front Views

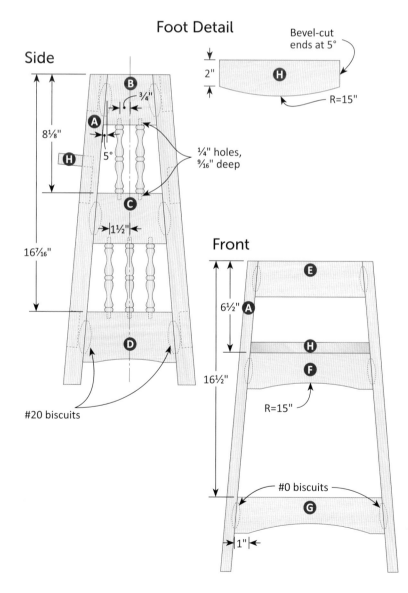

Side

Foot Detail

Bevel-cut ends at 5°

2"

H

R=15"

8⅛"

B

¾"

A

5°

H

¼" holes, 9⁄16" deep

C

16⁷⁄16"

1½"

Front

D

E

6½" **A**

16½"

H

F

R=15"

#20 biscuits

#0 biscuits

G

1"

10 Lay out an arc with a 15" radius on a piece of plywood or MDF. Use it to lay out the arcs on the bottom edges of the bottom side rails (D), where shown in Figure 2, as well as later arcs. Bandsaw the bottom side rails to final shape; sand smooth.

11 Make four Tapered Clamping Cauls like the ones in Figure 3 (page 47). I started with two ¾ × 3¾ × 22" pieces of MDF and taper-cut each piece at 5° on the bandsaw, where shown, to make four tapered wedges. Then I cleaned the sawn edges on the jointer. To prevent the cauls from slipping in use, screw and glue on small ¼ × ¾ × 2" hardwood cleats on the 1" ends, or stick strips of self-adhesive sandpaper on the cauls' tapered edges.

12 On a flat surface, position and dry-fit the parts, including the spindles, for one side to assure a proper fit. Now, use biscuits to bond the rails to the legs, using glue having a longer open time (Photo E; page 46). Remove glue squeeze-out with a clean, moistened rag. Glue up the second side assembly. Set both aside to dry.

13 With the miter gauge extension fence set at 5° and the saw blade at 5°, bevel the ends of the side assemblies (Photo F; page 46).

Cut more rails and assemble the base

1 Gather up the top, middle, and bottom front and rear rails (E, F, G, respectively) and footrest (H). On the top rails (E), rip a 5° bevel on the upper edge, where shown in Figure 2. Now trim all of the front and rear rails to final length by angle-cutting the ends at 5°.

2 Mark centerlines on the ends of the rails and biscuit-cut slots for #0 biscuits, using the Rail Slotting Jig.

3 Lay out the arcs on the center rails (F) and bottom rails (G), and cut to shape; sand smooth.

4 Working on a raised surface, place a side assembly (A/B/C/D) face down on top of the Tapered Clamping Cauls. Apply glue to the biscuit slots in the side and to the slots in the mating ends of the top, middle, and bottom front and back rails (E, F, G). Add the biscuits and join the rails to the side. Dry-fit the remaining side to the glue-up, add two more tapered clamping cauls, and clamp, as shown in Photo G (page 48).

5 After the glue has dried in one rail and side assembly (A/B/C/D/E/F/G), undo the clamps and remove the dry-fit side. Now, add glue, and biscuit-join the remaining side to the rails, again, using the tapered clamping cauls and clamps for even clamping pressure. Remove any squeeze-out, and check for square.

6 Hold the oversized part for footrest (H) to the legs at its intended location and mark the ends. Bevel-cut the ends at 5°. Now, mark the radius, bandsaw, and sand. Glue and clamp the footrest to the middle front rail (F).

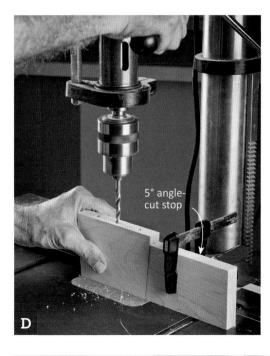

Using a fence and a scrap stop with a 5° end, drill the holes in the side rails for the spindle tenons.

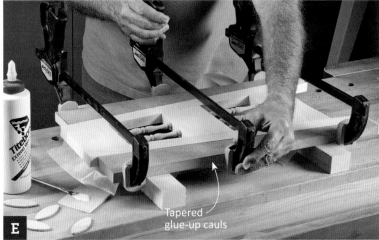

Apply glue in the biscuit slots, and assemble the side parts on blocks, using tapered cauls to evenly distribute clamping pressure.

With the side assemblies outside face down and the stop clamped to the extension fence, cut the legs to final length.

Figure 3: Doll High Chair Jigs

Tapered Clamping Cauls

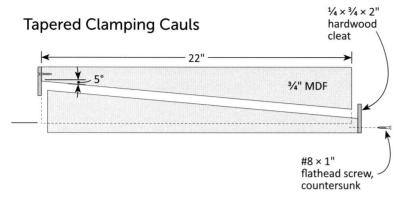

22"

5°

¾" MDF

¼ × ¾ × 2" hardwood cleat

#8 × 1" flathead screw, countersunk

Leg Slotting Jig

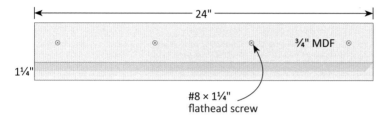

24"

¾" MDF

1¼"

#8 × 1¼" flathead screw

Rail Slotting Jig

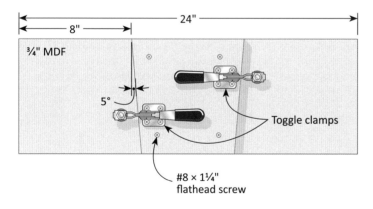

24"

8"

¾" MDF

5°

Toggle clamps

#8 × 1¼" flathead screw

Make the seat

1 To make the seat (I), edge-glue ¾"-thick pieces to make the overall size. Sand the surface smooth.

2 Lay out and saw the seat (I) to the shape in Figure 4. Sand the edges smooth.

3 Drill and countersink holes on the bottom face of the seat (I), where shown in Figure 4, for #8 × 2" flathead wood screws. These are for attaching the arm and chair back assemblies.

QUICK TIP

Countersink the holes on both faces of the workpiece to capture any wood filings or crumbs that exit the screw hole.

Add the arms

1 Next cut the back supports (J), arm supports (K), and the arms (L) to length with a 10° angle at one end.

2 Lay out, cut, and sand the rounded ends of the back supports (J) and arms (L). See Figure 4.

3 To attach the upper and lower back rails (M, N) to the back supports (J), lay out the biscuit slot locations. Employ the slotting jigs to cut the slots for #0 biscuits.

4 Lay out and then drill the ¼" dowel holes, ¹³/₁₆" deep in the back supports (J),

Figure 4: Chair Seat Front and Side Views

#0 Biscuits

Ⓜ

¼" hole, ⁹/₁₆" deep

Ⓙ

1½" 1½"

Ⓝ

1"

Ⓘ

Ⓞ

R=⅝"

Ⓛ

10°

¾"

Ⓙ

Ⓘ

Seat View

1"

R=15"

⁵/₃₂" shank hole, countersunk

Ⓘ

5⅞"

1⅛"

1⅜"

G

With the marks of the rails and one side aligned and glue applied, biscuit-join the parts, using the dry-fit opposite side as a spacer.

H

Clamp the workpiece to the bench, align and tighten the doweling jig on the piece, and bore the hole.

I

Working on a flat surface, apply glue and insert the dowels in the mating arm assembly parts, snugging the joints with clamps.

arm supports (K), and arms (L) using a doweling jig (Photo H).

5 Now glue and clamp up the arm assembly parts (J, K, L), as shown in Photo I. After the glue dries, remove clamps and sand smooth.

Now for the back

1 Crosscut the upper back rail (M) and lower back rail (N) to length.

2 Cut the slots in the ends of the rails (M, N).

3 Lay out and drill the holes for the turned spindles.

4 Lay out the arc on the upper back rail (M). Bandsaw and sand the arc.

5 Dry-fit the back rails (M, N) and spindles to the arm assemblies (J/K/L). Then, apply glue to the slots, assemble the parts with biscuits, and clamp. (I used a little glue in the spindle holes on one rail to prevent rattling.)

Assemble the doll high chair

1 Position the seat back/arm assembly (J/K/L/M/N) upside down on the workbench, centering it from side to side (or ¾" in from the side and back edges of the seat [I]). Clamp it in place. With the holes as guides, drill pilot holes and drive the screws (Photo J).

2 Using a ¾" Forstner bit, slowly drill recesses in the top inside edges of side top rails (B) for four figure-8 tabletop fasteners. I located them 2" in from the outside edge and ½" in from the outside faces. Test the fit. You want them a hair deeper than the thickness of the fasteners. Drill a pilot hole, and then screw them in place with #8 × ⅝" flathead wood screws. Now, attach the seat/arm/back assembly to the chair base, as shown in Photo K.

Clamp the seat to the back/arm assembly, drill pilot holes, and drive #8 × 2" flathead wood screws to secure it.

With the high chair upside down on the bench, use a cordless drill and bit extensions to screw the seat to the base where shown.

Drive screws through tray supports and into the back assembly to complete the project.

Build and add the tray

1 Cut the tray supports (O) and the tray (P) to size plus 1" long. To get the exact width of the tray, measure the width of the back of the chair plus the thickness of two flat washers. Now edge-glue the tray supports to the tray. After the glue dries, scrape and sand the joints.

2 Use the dimensional information in the Figure 5 Tray View to lay out the tray assembly (O/P) on the glue-up. Set the miter gauge extension fence to 0° and angle the blade at 10°. Next, bevel-cut the back ends of the tray supports (O) to match the angled back supports (J).

Figure 5: Tray View

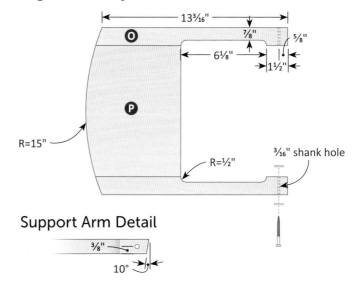

13³⁄₁₆"
⅞"
⁵⁄₈"
6⅛"
1½"
O
P
R=15"
R=½"
³⁄₁₆" shank hole

Support Arm Detail

³⁄₈"
10°

Cut List: Doll High Chair

	Part	Thickness	Width	Length	Qty.	Mat'l
A	Legs	3/4"	1 1/4"	21 3/4"	4	M
B	Side top rails	3/4"	3 1/2"	3 7/8"	2	M
C	Middle side rails	3/4"	3 1/2"	5 5/16"	2	M
D	Bottom side rails	3/4"	3 1/2"	6 3/4"	2	M
E	Front and rear top rails	3/4"	2 1/2"	7 15/16"	2	M
F	Middle front and rear rails	3/4"	2 1/2"	9 1/16"	2	M
G	Bottom front and rear rails	3/4"	2 1/2"	10 13/16"	2	M
H	Footrest	3/4"	2 1/2"	8 5/8"	1	M
I	Seat	3/4"	10 1/2"	7 3/4"	1	M
J	Back supports	3/4"	1 1/4"	11 3/4"	2	M
K	Arm supports	3/4"	1 1/4"	3 13/16"	2	M
L	Arms	3/4"	1 1/4"	8"	2	M
M	Upper back rail	3/4"	3"	7 1/2"	2	M
N	Lower back rail	3/4"	2 1/2"	7 1/2"	2	M
O*	Tray supports	3/4"	1 1/4"	16"	2	M
P*	Tray	3/4"	9 1/16"	6 3/4"	1	M

*Indicates parts that are initially cut oversized. See instructions.
Materials: M=Maple
Hardware/Supplies: (4) #8 × 2" flathead wood screws; (8) #8 × 5/8" flathead wood screws; (2) #10 × 2" roundhead wood screws; (4) #10 flat nylon washers

3 Lay out the shank holes for #10 × 2" roundhead screws, 5/8" in from the back ends of (O) and centered. Drill the holes at the drill press.

4 Bandsaw the notched areas and the arc along the front edge of the tray assembly (O/P). Sand the edges smooth.

5 To attach the tray assembly (O/P), clamp it to the arms (L), and align it with the back supports (J). Using the shank holes and a small brad-point bit, locate and mark the hole locations on the back supports. Remove the tray assembly, and drill pilot holes for #10 × 2" roundhead screws. Now position the four flat washers, where shown in Figure 1; page 44, and drive the screws (Photo L).

Note: If you are concerned about the tray pinching small fingers, consider screwing the tray to the arms from underneath.

6 To finish, remove the tray assembly (O/P), and sand all surfaces to 220 grit, easing all edges. **Then apply three coats of water-based polyurethane, sanding between coats. Reassemble.**

BACKYARD WAGON

Easy-to-Build Wagon Hauls Plenty of Giggles

WRITTEN BY JIM HARROLD, PROJECTS DESIGNED AND BUILT BY TIM BIRKELAND AND BOB POLING

When you consider the fun of hauling your giggling kids around the yard in a wooden wagon, it is no wonder this classic has a place on every woodworker's "to make" list. This project takes a four-wheel chassis and adds a sturdy flatbed base with a classic stake top. You can buy new lumber or use workshop scrap to complete the wagon. You can find an affordable chassis at Northern Tool, Millside, or online. If necessary, adjust the drilling pattern to fit the chassis you purchase.

Figure 1: Stake Wagon Exploded View

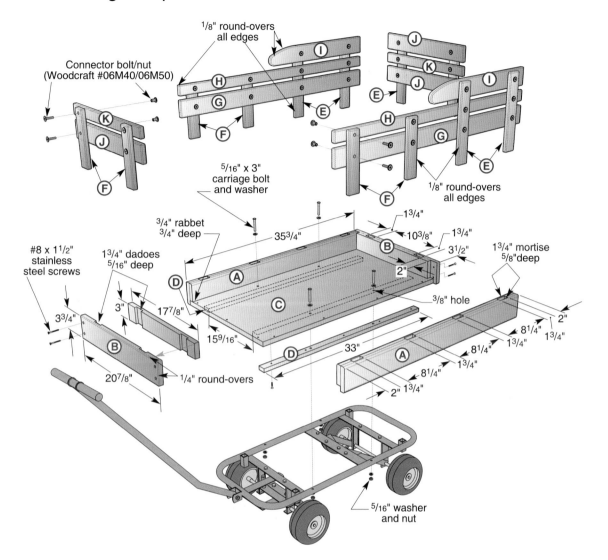

Connector bolt/nut
(Woodcraft #06M40/06M50)

1/8" round-overs all edges

5/16" x 3" carriage bolt and washer

1/8" round-overs all edges

3/4" rabbet 3/4" deep

35 3/4"

1 3/4"

10 3/8"   1 3/4"

3 1/2"

1 3/4" mortise 5/8" deep

2"

#8 x 1 1/2" stainless steel screws

1 3/4" dadoes 5/16" deep

3"

3/8" hole

2"

8 1/4"

8 1/4"   1 3/4"   1 3/4"

3 3/4"

17 7/8"

15 9/16"

33"

8 1/4"   1 3/4"

20 7/8"

1/4" round-overs

2" 1 3/4"

5/16" washer and nut

Backyard wagon

Who hasn't enjoyed a little red wagon somewhere in their past? This versatile model—complete with removable stake sides—offers the same familiar looks with a lot more capacity. We used cypress for the stake sides and base frame, along with exterior grade plywood for the base bottom.

Start with the base

1 From ¾" stock, cut parts for the base sides (A), and front and back (B) to the widths and lengths shown in the Cut List (page 56) and Figure 1. Note that it takes two pieces—one 3" wide and the other 3¾" wide—to make up each side, the front, and the back. Note also that the inside parts for the front and back are cut 3" shorter.

2 Referring to Figure 1, mark the locations for the dadoes and cut them on your table saw using a dado blade, miter gauge extension fence, and stopblock as shown in Photo A (page 54). Now align and glue the mating pieces as shown in Photo B to make the base sides (A) and the base front and back (B). Ensure the top edges for each mating pair are flush.

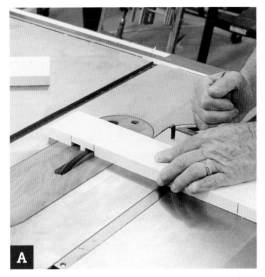

Using a dado blade in your table saw, cut 1³/₄" dadoes just over ⁵/₁₆" deep in the base parts (left), and then glue-join mating parts, flushing the top edges and aligning the dadoes to form through mortises.

3 Join and square the base sides (A) to the base front and back (B) using screws where shown in Figure 1 (page 53) to create the base frame. With a ¼" round-over bit, round over all the exterior edges and corners, as well as the inside top edges.

4 Measure and cut a ¾" piece of exterior grade plywood for the base bottom (C) to fit in the rabbet along the bottom inside edges of the base frame. Turn the base upside down to screw the bottom in place (we used pocket-hole screws.)

5 Cut the cleats (D) to the sizes in the Cut List. Ease the outside edges of the cleats and glue and screw them to the base bottom. Paint and finish the wagon base. (We used brick red milk paint and two coats of gloss polyacrylic.) Rub out the painted finish with deluxing compound.

Cut and assemble the stake sides, front, and back

1 Plane enough ¾" stock (two 1"×6"×8') to ⁵/₈" thick for the stakes and rails listed in the Cut List. Now rip and crosscut the long stakes (E), short stakes (F), the bottom side rails (G), middle side rails (H), top side rails

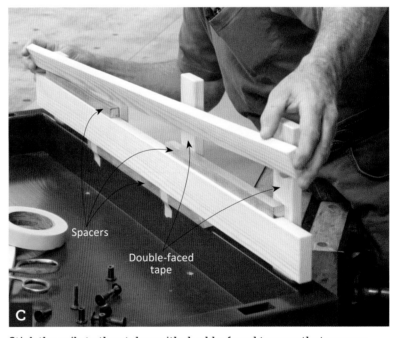

Spacers

Double-faced tape

Stick the rails to the stakes with double-faced tape so that you can drill bolt holes through both pieces at the same time.

(I), bottom and top front and back rails (J), and middle and top rails (K) to size. See also the Cut List and the parts view (Figure 2) for reference.

2 Stick the two top rails (I) together with double-faced tape, and transfer the tapered radius from Figure 2 onto one end. Now bandsaw both side rails to shape at the same time and sand.

QUICK TIP

When drilling through-holes, use a wood backer to prevent splintering the back of the workpiece where the bit exits.

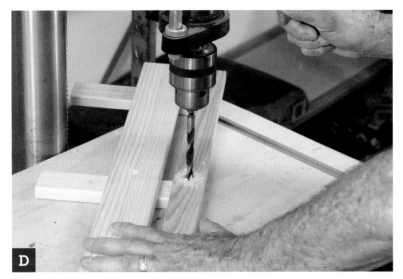

D

Mark the location of the centered ³/₈" holes in the taped stake and rail assemblies and drill them for the connector bolt/nut combo.

3 Install a ¹/₈" round-over bit in your table-mounted router and round over all of the edges and ends of the stakes and rails. Sand these parts through 220 grit. Apply an outdoor oil finish and let dry.

4 Cut three ⁵/₈×⁵/₈" spacers anywhere from 12" to 18" long. Fit the stakes for one side in the mortises in the wagon base. Next,

place the spacer between the top edge of the base (you may need to tape it in place) and a bottom side rail (G). Adhere 1"-square pieces of double-faced tape just above the spacer onto the inside faces of the stakes. Now center the bottom side rail (G) between the ends of the base and press it temporarily in place. Add a second spacer and similarly press the middle side rail (H) in place as shown in Photo C. Add a top side rail (I). In the same manner, create the opposing side stake and rail assembly and the front and rear stake and rail assemblies.

5 With the assemblies lying flat on your workbench, strike vertical centerlines down the stakes and mark hole locations centered on the rails where shown in Figure 1 (page 53). Carefully take the assemblies to your drill press and drill ³/₈" holes at the marked locations as shown in Photo D. Now, leaving the thin double-faced tape in place ont he stock, secure the assemblies

Figure 2: Parts View

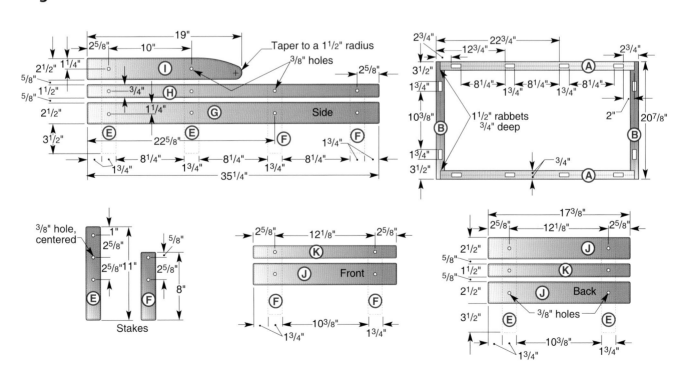

with connector bolts and nuts (30 needed), snugging the two together.

6 With the stake and rail assemblies complete, place them into the mortises to test the fit. The stakes should rest somewhat loosely in the mortises. Sand the stakes if needed.

7 To install the wagon base, center it on the chassis, and use an awl to mark the 5/16" carriage bolt holes on the plywood bottom, poking up through the four holes in the metal frame. Drill the holes, replace the base on the chassis, and secure it with carriage bolts, washers, and nuts.

Cut List: Backyard Wagon

		Thickness	Width	Length	Qty.	Mat'l
A	Base sides, outside	3/4"	3 3/4"	35 3/4"	2	C
A	Base sides, inside	3/4"	3"	35 3/4"	2	C
B	Base front and back, outside	3/4"	3 3/4"	20 7/8"	2	C
B	Base front and back, inside	3/4"	3"	17 7/8"	2	C
C	Base bottom	3/4"	19 3/8"	35 3/4"	1	EP
D	Cleats	5/8"	1 1/4"	33"	2	C
E	Long stakes	5/8"	1 3/4"	11"	6	C
F	Short stakes	5/8"	1 3/4"	8"	6	C
G	Bottom side rails	5/8"	2 1/2"	35 1/4"	2	C
H	Middle side rails	5/8"	1 1/2"	35 1/4"	2	C
I	Top side rails	5/8"	2 1/2"	19"	2	C
J	Bottom and top front and back rails	5/8"	2 1/2"	17 3/8"	3	C
K	Middle rails, back and front	5/8"	1 1/2"	17 3/8"	2	C

Backyard Wagon Cutting Diagram

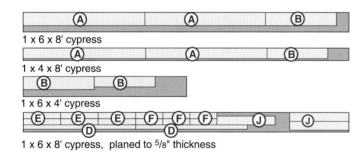

1 x 6 x 8' cypress

1 x 4 x 8' cypress

1 x 6 x 4' cypress

1 x 6 x 8' cypress, planed to 5/8" thickness

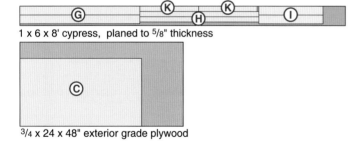

1 x 6 x 8' cypress, planed to 5/8" thickness

3/4 x 24 x 48" exterior grade plywood

DOUBLE-DUTY DOLLHOUSE

A not-so-big home for dolls or books, with a secret storage spot

BY TOM WHALLEY AND
MARLEN KEMMET

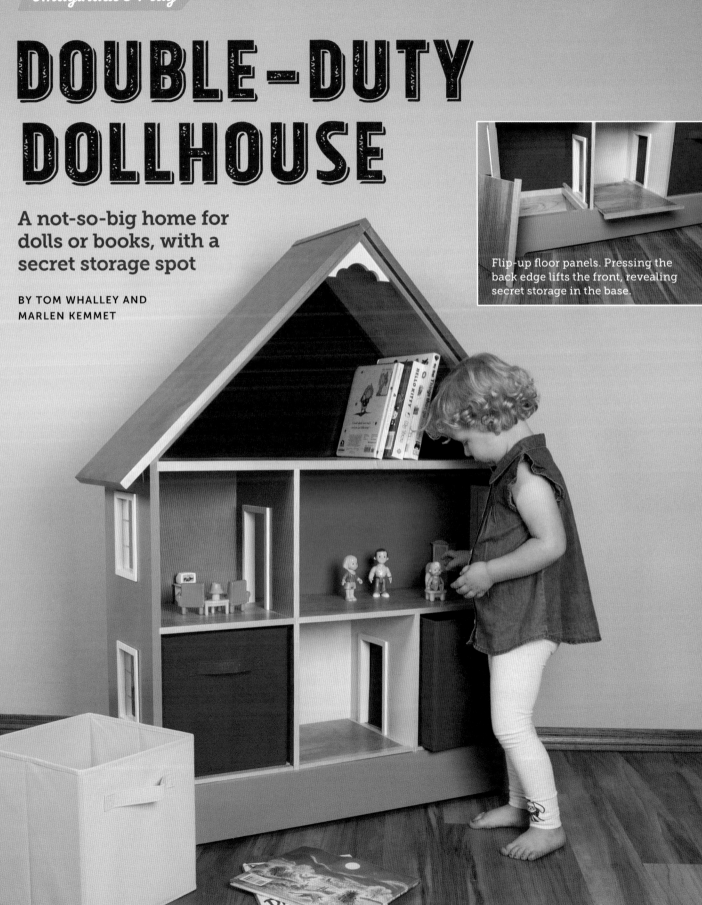

Flip-up floor panels. Pressing the back edge lifts the front, revealing secret storage in the base.

The problem with kids isn't just that they grow up so quickly, it's also that they quickly outgrow the gifts you build for them. Here's a dual-purpose project designed to pass the test of time. In "play" mode, you have a fully functional dollhouse with rooms sized to hold commonly available lightweight boxes. But this multi-colored mansion can easily serve as a bookcase when its dollhouse days are over.

Like any good dollhouse, this one has enough architectural detail to inspire fun play time: brightly colored rooms, windows, doors, and multiple levels. Construction materials are pretty basic: plywood, iron-on edging, solid wood trim and a few pieces of clear acrylic.

Figure 1: Dollhouse Exploded View

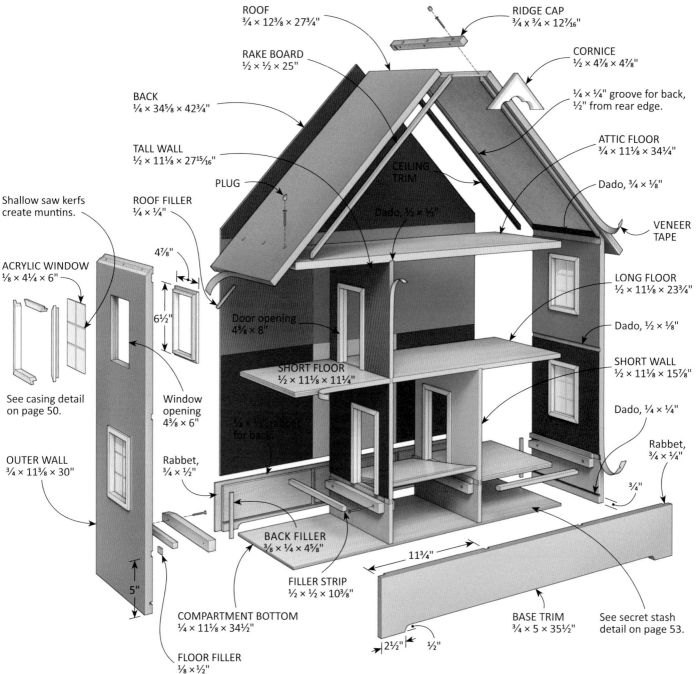

ROOF
¾ × 12⅜ × 27¾"

RIDGE CAP
¾ × ¾ × 12⁷⁄₁₆"

RAKE BOARD
½ × ½ × 25"

CORNICE
½ × 4⅞ × 4⅞"

BACK
¼ × 34⅝ × 42¾"

¼ × ¼" groove for back, ½" from rear edge.

ATTIC FLOOR
¾ × 11⅛ × 34¼"

TALL WALL
½ × 11⅛ × 27¹⁵⁄₁₆"

CEILING TRIM

Dado, ¾ × ⅛"

PLUG

Dado, ½ × ½"

VENEER TAPE

Shallow saw kerfs create muntins.

ROOF FILLER
¼ × ¼"

4⅞"

LONG FLOOR
½ × 11⅛ × 23¾"

ACRYLIC WINDOW
⅛ × 4¼ × 6"

6½"

Door opening
4⅜ × 8"

Dado, ½ × ⅛"

SHORT WALL
½ × 11⅛ × 15⅞"

SHORT FLOOR
½ × 11⅛ × 11¼"

Dado, ¼ × ¼"

See casing detail on page 50.

Window opening
4⅜ × 6"

⅛ × ½" rabbet for back.

Rabbet,
¾ × ¼"

OUTER WALL
¾ × 11⅜ × 30"

Rabbet,
¾ × ½"

¾"

5"

BACK FILLER
⅜ × ¼ × 4⅝"

11¾"

COMPARTMENT BOTTOM
¼ × 11⅛ × 34½"

FILLER STRIP
½ × ½ × 10⅜"

BASE TRIM
¾ × 5 × 35½"

See secret stash detail on page 53.

2½" ½"

FLOOR FILLER
⅛ × ½"

Figure 2: Dollhouse Drawing

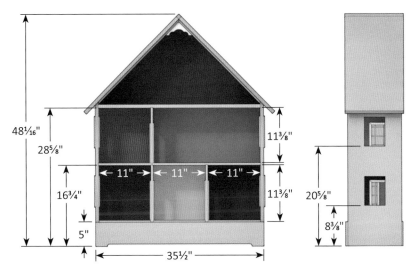

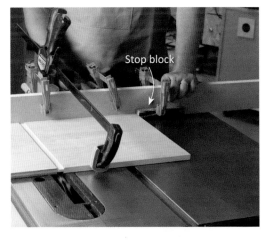

Eliminate alignment errors. After applying veneer tape to the front edges of the walls and attic floor, cut the dadoes using a miter gauge outfitted with an auxiliary fence and a stop.

House raising: walls, floors, windows & doors, plus paint & trim

Though the joinery and materials in this project mark it as a bookcase, architectural details make the construction process a little unusual. Follow these construction steps:

1 Cut the base, walls, floors, and compartment bottom to finished sizes. Leave the tilt-up bottom floor panels (see pages 63 and 64) for the very end.

2 Apply the iron-on veneer to the front edges of the walls and floors, as shown in the drawing.

3 Cut the dadoes where the walls and floors join. Test-fit the wall and floor joints for snug, square assembly.

4 Cut the window and door openings. Sand the bottom edges of all door openings flush with the floor dadoes.

5 Cut and assemble the mitered casings for all the windows and doors. Rabbet the casings to fit the sawn openings.

6 Prefinish the walls and casings with spray enamel, masking the edges of the openings as shown at left. Top off the pieces with a coat of clear lacquer.

Smooth the sill. Trim covers the rough-sawn edges around the windows and doors, but the bottom edge of each doorway remains exposed. To sand the bottoms flush with the dadoes, set a pair of scrapwood guides into the floor dadoes as shown.

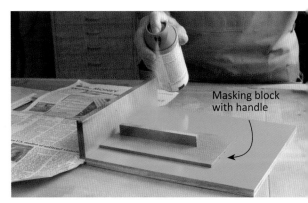

Mask, then spray. Finishing the rooms is easier now than after assembly, but you'll need to mask off the rabbets, grooves, and dadoes to ensure a solid glue bond. Custom-made masking blocks keep paint off a 3/16" strip around windows and doors.

7 Install the door and window casings on interior wall openings using glue.

8 Assemble the case (see photo, below).

9 Paint and install the back of the case.

10 Assemble and then raise the roof (see page 62). Paint, then install the trim.

11 Cut, score, and install the acrylic windows. Then, attach the exterior window casings.

12 Install the tapered cleats for tilt-up floor panels. Carefully measure and fit the tilting floor panels on the first floor.

Prefab window & door casings

To start, mill about 40' of ½ × ½" trim stock. As you tape and glue the mitered window trim pieces together, make certain that the joints are tight and the assembly flat. After the glue has cured, sand each door and window frame smooth, and then paint the three outer faces. Rabbet the inside (bare) edges of the window and door frames. Adjust the depth of the window casing rabbets so that the acrylic fits between the inner and outer frames. To make a pair of door casings, saw a double-length door casing assembly in half, using a miter box and model saw.

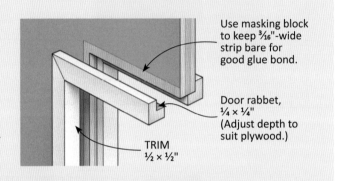

Use masking block to keep ³⁄₁₆"-wide strip bare for good glue bond.

Door rabbet, ¼ × ¼" (Adjust depth to suit plywood.)

TRIM ½ × ½"

Rabbetting

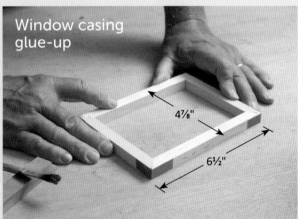

Window casing glue-up

4⅞"

6½"

Cutting 2 doors

17" min.

8¼"

4⅞"

Make sure walls and floors are square before attaching back.

Use clamp pads.

Extend clamp through window and door openings.

Install interior casing, but leave exterior casing off.

Final framing: adding the back & roof

Made from ¼" plywood, the back stiffens the case assembly when glued and nailed to walls and floors. After installing it, cut the roof panels to finished size and groove their rear edges to fit over the back's top edges. Join the roof panels together by screwing and gluing them to the ridge cap. Then install the back, screwing into outer walls, as shown below. When adding the decorative cornice and rake board trim, feel free to develop your own design and color scheme.

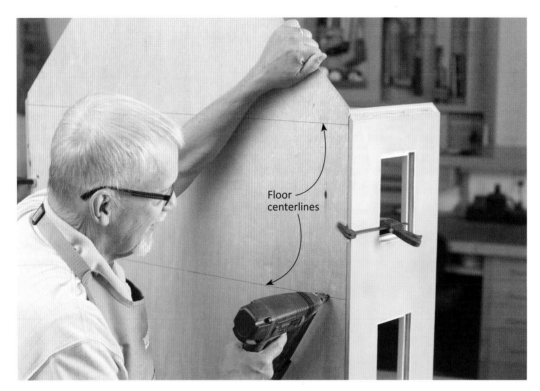

Floor centerlines

Tack the back. After cutting the back to fit, and painting the front to match your rooms, attach it to the case using glue and pin nails. Mark the locations of the floors so that your pins don't miss their target.

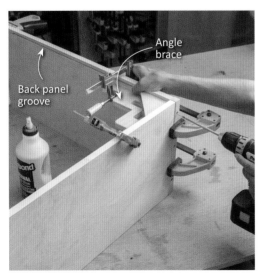

Angle brace

Back panel groove

Square peak. I temporarily set a piece of ¼" plywood in the roof panel grooves and used a shop-made right-angle brace to make sure the roof panels were aligned and perfectly square before joining them to the ridge cap.

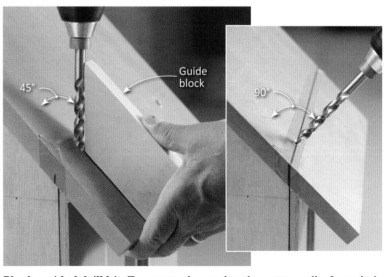

45°

Guide block

90°

Block-guided drill bit. To secure the roof to the outer walls, I needed to drill angled pilot holes through the roof and into the outer walls. Using a ⅜" pocket-hole drill bit I started the holes perpendicular to the surface, then used an angled guide block to finish the hole. After installing the screws, plug the holes, trim them flush, and sand smooth.

Muntin maker. Using a pushblock for support, cut 1/64"-deep kerfs (just enough to score the surface) in the acrylic panels to simulate muntins.

Press-fit windows. Insert the acrylic windows with the grooves facing inward, and glue the outer window trim assemblies in place on the outside walls.

Window glazing

The last few steps qualify as "punch-list items" in carpentry parlance—small details that make a difference—so take your time.

To create kid-safe windows I used 1/8"-thick acrylic. After cutting the acrylic to fit, I cut shallow grooves to simulate muntins, using a blade that cuts a flat-bottom kerf. Fit the acrylic in the window opening, and then install the exterior window casing as shown.

QUICK TIP

To prevent scratching the acrylic, leave the protective wrap in place until you have finished cutting the muntin lines.

Secret stash: fitting the flip-up floors

In order for the compartments to be a secret, the floor panels must fit perfectly. Measure the floor openings and then subtract just 1/16" from the dimensions to size each floor panel's depth and width. Allow for solid wood trim on front edges, with 1/4 × 1/8" rabbets to fit over the top edge of the base.

Take a moment to fill in any remaining gaps. I plugged the dadoes in the underside of the roof and on either edge of the compartments with filler strips and then dabbed on a bit of finish to match the surrounding wood.

Figure 3: Dollhouse Floor

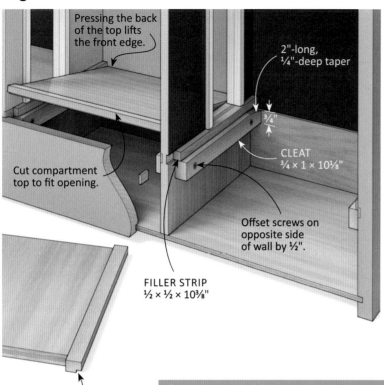

Pressing the back of the top lifts the front edge.

2"-long, ¼"-deep taper

¾"

CLEAT
¾ × 1 × 10⅛"

Cut compartment top to fit opening.

Offset screws on opposite side of wall by ½".

FILLER STRIP
½ × ½ × 10⅜"

¼ × ⅛" rabbet

Cut List: Double-Duty Dollhouse					
	Thickness	Width	Length	Qty.	Notes
Roof	¾"	12⅜"	27¾"	2	
Rake Board	½"	½"	25"	2	
Veneer Tape		½"	25"	2	
Back	¼"	34⅝"	42¾"	1	
Tall Wall	½"	11⅛"	27⁸⁄₉"	1	
Outer Wall	¾"	11⅜"	30 "	2	
Roof Filler (Strips)	¼"	¼"	3 "	TBD	As Needed
Cornice	½"	4⅞"	4⅞"	1	
Ridge Cap	¾"	¾"	12⁴⁄₉"	1	
Attic Floor	¾"	11⅛"	34¼"	1	
Short Wall	½"	11⅛"	15⅞"	1	
Long Floor	½"	11⅛"	23¾"	1	
Short Floor	½"	11⅛"	11¼"	1	
Acrylic Window	⅛"	4¼"	6 "	4	
Window Casing - Top / Sill	½"	½"	4⅞"	12	See Page 60
Window Casing - Side	½"	½"	6½"	12	See Page 60
Door Casing - Top	½"	½"	4⅞"	6	See Page 60
Door Casing - Side	½"	½"	17 "	12	See Page 60
Floor Cleat	¾"	1"	10⅛"	6	
Flip Up Secret Floor	½"	TBD	TBD	3	See Pages 63 & 64
Back Filler	⅜"	¼"	4⅝"	2	
Filler Strip	½"	½"	10⅜"	6	
Compartment Bottom	¼"	11⅛"	34½"	1	
Floor Filler	⅛"	½"	1"	12	
Base Trim	¾"	5 "	35½"	1	

TOY TRUCKS FROM 2×4S

You could build just one, but that's no fun. Turn your shop into an automotive assembly line and create a fleet of four wheelers.

BY BY DON RUSSELL

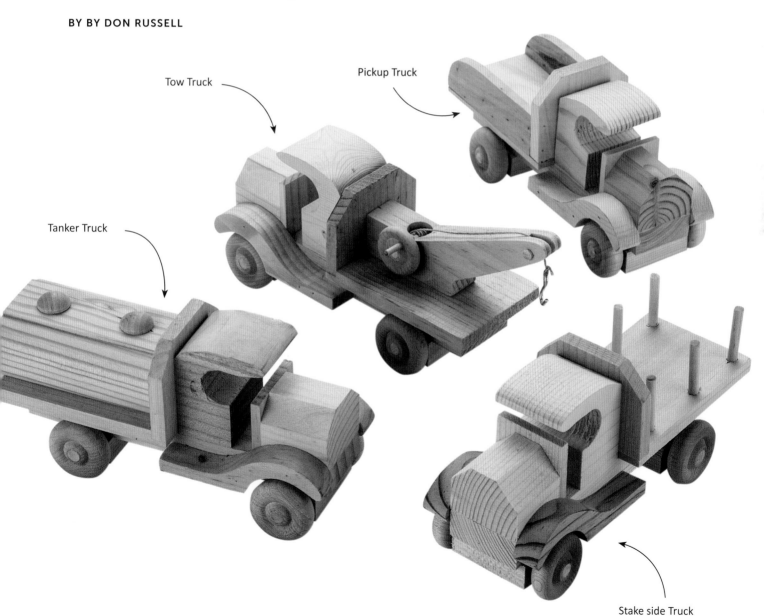

Tow Truck

Pickup Truck

Tanker Truck

Stake side Truck

Woodworkers don't have to go to the mall when someone needs a gift. We always have the opportunity to create something special right at home. That's why I've come to love building these toy trucks.

It's challenging and fun to figure out how to mass-produce all the parts and create my own assembly line process (I'll share some of my techniques on the pages ahead). It's great that the raw material for this woodworking adventure is cheap and easy to find. You can raid your scrap pile for truck parts, or head to the lumber yard for 2x stock.

What I like most about this truck project is that it's fun to do as a group. Round up your buddies, or organize a truck-making afternoon with your woodworking guild.

Finished trucks are great items to donate to toy banks or charity auctions. Kids can get involved in the construction process too. Who knows—a child who has a hand in building a few trucks might just grow up to be a great woodworker.

6 truck parts + wheels & axles

You can create many variations of this truck—from stake side pickups to oil tankers and tow trucks (See p. 71). But they all are built on the basic cab-and-chassis assembly shown below. This "core" vehicle requires a couple of ready-made components: wheels and ¼" dowel rod for axles. The remaining six parts can all be cut from 1½"-thick 2x stock. As shown on page 69, you'll have an easy time mass-producing these six parts if you set up different workstations.

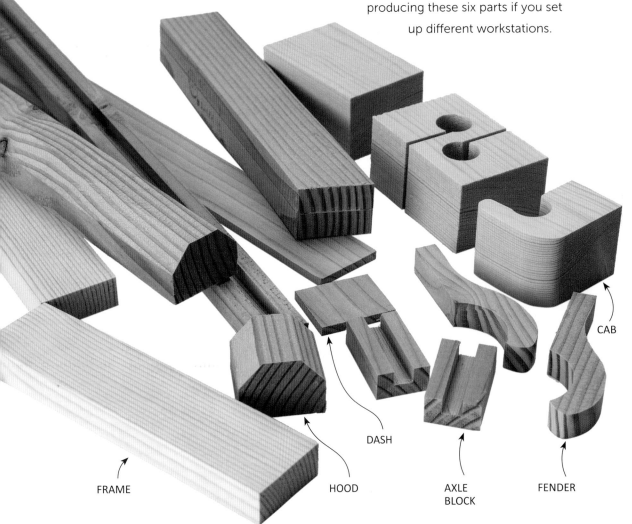

FRAME

HOOD

DASH

AXLE BLOCK

FENDER

CAB

Photos: Larry Hamel-Lambert

Cut List: Toy Trucks from 2x4s – Basic Chassis

	Thickness	Width	Length	Qty.
Frame	9/16"	1 1/2"	6 1/4"	1
Cab	1 1/2"	1 7/8"	2"	1
Dash	3/16"	1 1/2"	1 3/16"	1
Hood	1 1/8"	1 1/2"	1 1/4"	1
Axle Block	1/2"	1"	1 5/8"	1
Axle	1/4"	1/4"	2"	2
Fender	1/2"	1"	3 1/2"	2
Wheel		1 1/4"		4

Figure 1: Basic Chassis Exploded View and Patterns

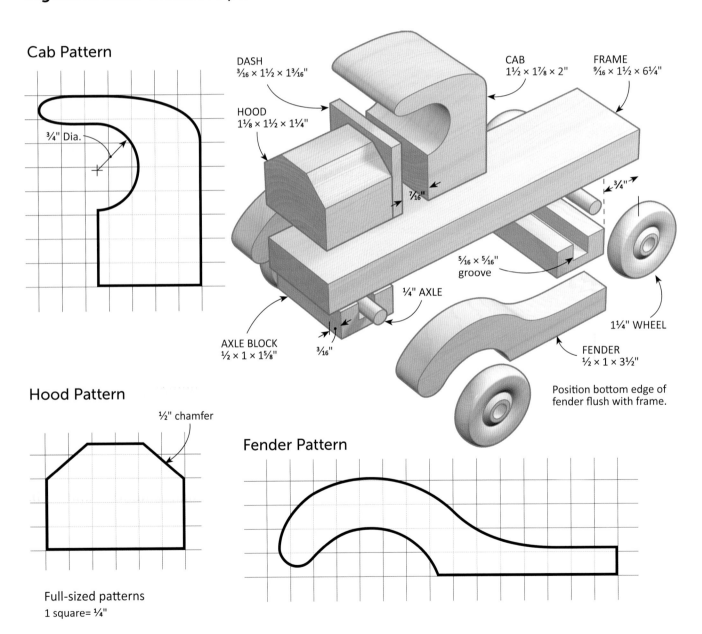

Cab Pattern

3/4" Dia.

DASH
3/16 × 1 1/2 × 1 3/16"

HOOD
1 1/8 × 1 1/2 × 1 1/4"

CAB
1 1/2 × 1 7/8 × 2"

FRAME
9/16 × 1 1/2 × 6 1/4"

7/16"

3/4"

5/16 × 5/16"
groove

1/4" AXLE

AXLE BLOCK
1/2 × 1 × 1 5/8"

3/16"

1 1/4" WHEEL

FENDER
1/2 × 1 × 3 1/2"

Position bottom edge of
fender flush with frame.

Hood Pattern

1/2" chamfer

Fender Pattern

Full-sized patterns
1 square= 1/4"

Set up for mass production

Straight, square-edged parts like the frame and dashboard can be mass-produced easily by ripping strips, then crosscutting them to length. To produce multiples of other parts, set up different workstations, as shown here. I found that it's best to cut out the cab in pairs, starting with blanks that measure $1\frac{1}{2} \times 2\frac{1}{8} \times 3\frac{1}{8}$". If you've got inexperienced woodworkers on your truck construction crew, put them to work sanding parts or painting them prior to assembly.

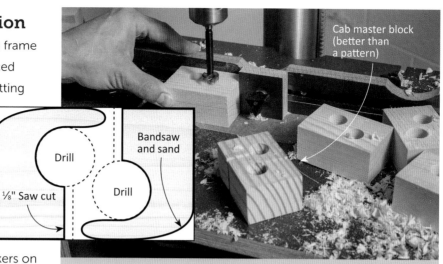

Cab master block (better than a pattern)

Drill

Bandsaw and sand

Drill

$\frac{1}{8}$" Saw cut

STATION 1: Drill Press

Start with boring work. Two cabs can be cut from each blank, as shown in the cutting diagram. The cab begins with a pair of through holes, aligned with a fence and stop, as shown above.

STATION 2: Tablesaw

Tape, then cut. Tape a series of cab blanks together, then adjust the rip fence and blade height to make a pair of vertical cuts. Axle housing strips can also be cut in pairs (far right photo). The grooves for the dowel axles can be cut with a dado head, or by making overlapping kerfs with a standard blade.

Run faces against fence to rip a centered groove.

STATION 3: Bandsaw

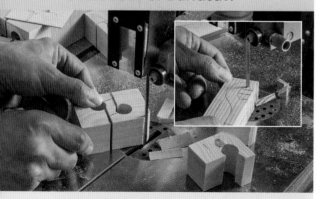

Cut curves for cabs and fenders. Make the final cuts to free the paired cabs, and roughly curve the cab tops. Then cut a bunch of fenders, which include a straight running board.

STATION 4: Sanders

Refine those rough edges. Shaping and smoothing the cabs and fenders can be done by hand-sanding, but the work goes much faster with an oscillating spindle sander and a narrow belt sander.

Super simple flat sander

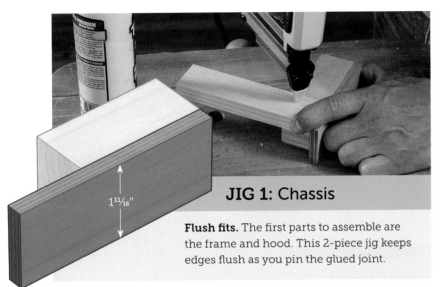

JIG 1: Chassis

Flush fits. The first parts to assemble are the frame and hood. This 2-piece jig keeps edges flush as you pin the glued joint.

1¹¹⁄₁₆"

Speed through assembly with 3 jigs

On this automotive assembly line, yellow wood glue and a headless pinner take the place of welding gear and impact wrenches. Your truck factory should also include the assembly aids shown here, because small parts slip around when coated with glue. These jigs make it easy to maintain your manufacturing tolerances.

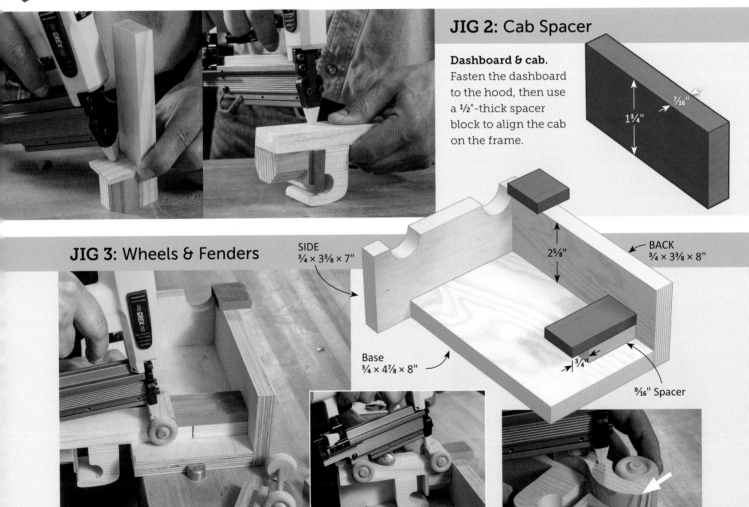

JIG 2: Cab Spacer

Dashboard & cab. Fasten the dashboard to the hood, then use a ½"-thick spacer block to align the cab on the frame.

1¾"

⁷⁄₁₆"

JIG 3: Wheels & Fenders

SIDE
¾ × 3⅜ × 7"

BACK
¾ × 3⅜ × 8"

2⅝"

Base
¾ × 4⅞ × 8"

¾"

⁹⁄₁₆" Spacer

Upside-down alignment. Glue the wheels to axles, then use the jig to establish the correct location for a axle housings on the underside of the frame.

Press up, nail down. Make sure the wheel won't rub on the fender before pinning it.

Stake Side Truck

FRONT PANEL
$\frac{1}{4}$ × $2\frac{3}{8}$ × $1\frac{3}{4}$"

BED
$\frac{1}{4}$ × $2\frac{3}{8}$ × $3\frac{1}{2}$"

$\frac{1}{4}$ × $\frac{1}{8}$"-deep
rabbet

STAKES
$\frac{1}{8}$"D × $1\frac{1}{2}$"

Expand your fleet with customized designs

The basic truck is just the beginning. With a little imagination, you can add features to the core truck platform and create a number of variations. Four different examples are detailed here. Painting your truck parts before assembly and combining contrasting wood species are two other fun options.

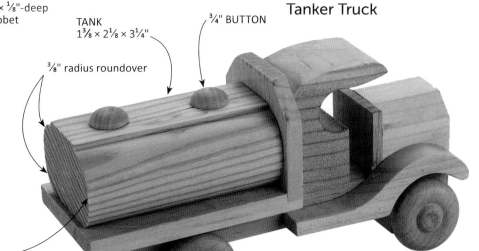

Tanker Truck

TANK
$1\frac{3}{8}$ × $2\frac{1}{8}$ × $3\frac{1}{4}$"

$\frac{3}{4}$" BUTTON

$\frac{3}{8}$" radius roundover

Roundover corners before cutting tank to length.

Pickup Truck

SIDE
$\frac{1}{4}$ × 1 × $3\frac{1}{4}$"

$\frac{1}{4}$ × $\frac{1}{8}$"-deep rabbet
(front and sides)

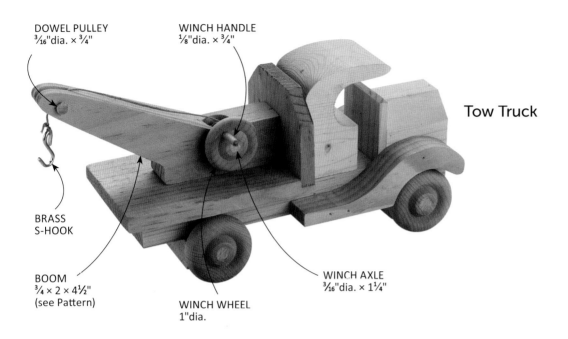

DOWEL PULLEY
3/16"dia. × 3/4"

WINCH HANDLE
1/8"dia. × 3/4"

Tow Truck

BRASS
S-HOOK

BOOM
3/4 × 2 × 4 1/2"
(see Pattern)

WINCH WHEEL
1"dia.

WINCH AXLE
3/16"dia. × 1 1/4"

Figure 2: Tow Truck Boom & Winch Detail

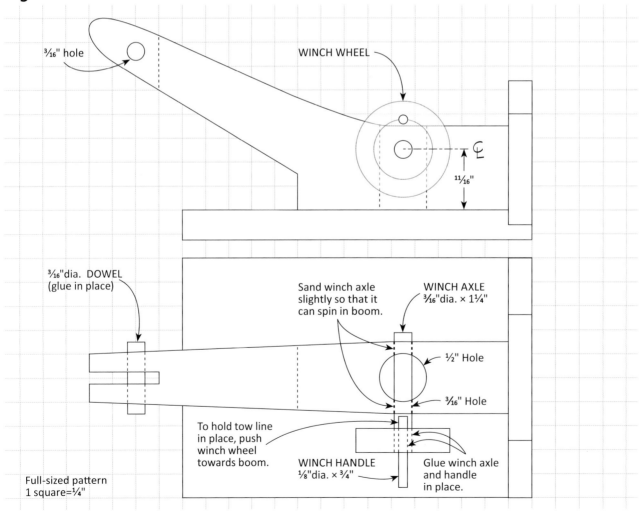

3/16" hole

WINCH WHEEL

11/16"

3/16"dia. DOWEL
(glue in place)

Sand winch axle
slightly so that it
can spin in boom.

WINCH AXLE
3/16"dia. × 1 1/4"

1/2" Hole

3/16" Hole

To hold tow line
in place, push
winch wheel
towards boom.

WINCH HANDLE
1/8"dia. × 3/4"

Glue winch axle
and handle
in place.

Full-sized pattern
1 square=1/4"

TRIO OF TOY TRUCKS

Heirloom quality trucks stand up to rough play

BY KEN BRADY

What is it about little boys and trucks? My grandson has been fascinated with wheels since his eyes first started to focus and, at age two, his preoccupation with all things wheeled is uncanny. Whatever it is, it works on me, too. It got me started back into woodworking after being away from it for over 20 years.

I spotted some small wooden toy trucks in a large retail store (which shall remain nameless except to say that the first letter of their name has a lot of angles in it.) I was intrigued for two reasons: They were very small but still wooden, and they were fairly well designed (though not that well constructed). So I immediately purposed to become a hero to my grandson by producing my own versions of these tiny trucks, and writing about the process.

Here's hoping it worked and that the trucks will be enjoyed for generations.

Setting up

To make these small toys, I needed to think small, so it was only natural to enlist a small arsenal of miniature tools—the Micromot series of bench-top power tools from Proxxon. This German company offers several small machines—table saw, shaper, bandsaw, planer and more—that can be set up on a space the size of a card table. Being a gadget fanatic, I was excited to use these tools, plus I was sure to score some brownie points with my grandson.

A goal of this project was to produce toy trucks in a size not often seen, and in a manner different from methods used in your garden-variety toy plans. I used

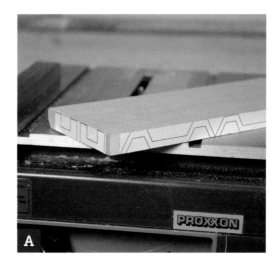

Do whatever is necessary to remove the "non-fender" material. Don't just cut to the line, cut it out.

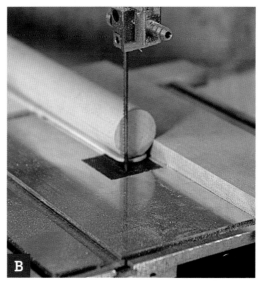

The popsicle sticks helps ensure one flat side. Cut the sticks off with the second cut.

Figure 1: Fender Profiles—Side And Front

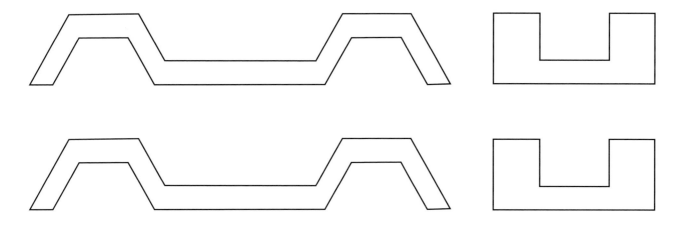

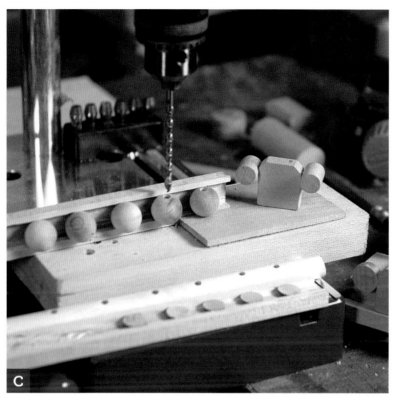

Use a shim to support the glued up "headlights." Drill off-center for a more realistic headlike look when cut off.

The cab offers a chance for variety in design and construction methods. Always consider making multiples.

basswood because it's easy to work, reasonably inexpensive, and comes in a variety of sizes. Another goal was to reduce the need for the use of measurements during the construction process. The directions and visual information offered here are intended to be a general guide through the process, with a large part of the instruction coming from the drawings. You'll probably think of a number of ways to add style and variation to your versions.

A basic foundation

Most of the design time and energy for this project was spent coming up with a way to easily make the fender assembly, because I thought it would be the most difficult part of the truck to make. As it turns out, the fender is the easiest part to make. It's the foundation of the entire truck, and multiple copies are easily cut out of a single piece of ¾" stock.

To start, copy, cut out and glue the fender profiles below to the edges of your ¾" board (Photo A). Do as many on a single board as your equipment can safely and accurately handle. This helps reduce time and waste when making more than one set of fenders. And as a general rule, sanding multiple parts is easier when they are attached together at various stages of construction. Let me say here that I designed the parts and the steps using the Proxxon miniature tools, so using other tools may require different procedures and precautions. Gluing the patterns to the stock should make it easier, no matter what tools you use.

Figure 2: Toy Truck Exploded View

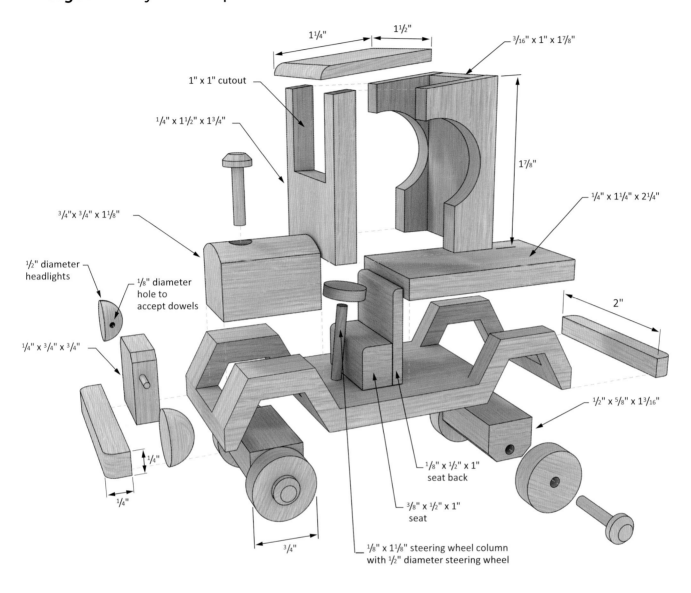

1¼"　　1½"

³/₁₆" x 1" x 1⁷/₈"

1" x 1" cutout

¼" x 1½" x 1³/₄"

1⁷/₈"

³/₄" x ³/₄" x 1¹/₈"

¼" x 1¼" x 2¼"

½" diameter headlights

⅛" diameter hole to accept dowels

2"

¼" x ³/₄" x ³/₄"

½" x ⅝" x 1³/₁₆"

¼"

¼"

⅛" x ½" x 1" seat back

³/₄"

³/₈" x ½" x 1" seat

⅛" x 1¹/₈" steering wheel column with ½" diameter steering wheel

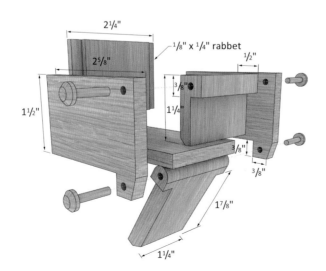

2¼"

⅛" x ¼" rabbet

½"

2⁵/₈"

³/₈"

1½"

1¼"

³/₈"

³/₈"

1⁷/₈"

1¼"

An undercut bevel is a cheap fix for boring design elements. Do one or both sides, depending on the application.

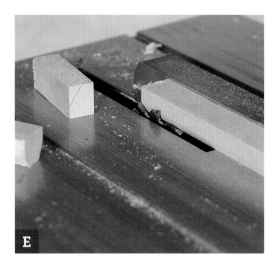

Hood and radiator assemblies

The truck hood is simply a section of 1" dowel with three sides cut off. Follow the pattern on as long a dowel as is comfortable, and just cut off lengths of hood in whatever number you need. To make sure the first cut is flat (the dowel could twist while being cut), glue a couple of large popsicle sticks to the bottom of the dowel to keep it from spinning (Photo B; page 74). The radiator is done in the same fashion: Start with ¾" stock, cut to the pattern specs, and lop off as many as you need. Notice how these processes lend themselves well to mass production.

Henry Ford would be proud.

Headlights and cab

The proportions of the parts of this toy truck are exaggerated for two reasons: sturdiness at a small size, and cuteness. Yes, I said *cuteness*. Just as Mother Nature gives youngsters large eye and head proportions to help elicit nurturing responses from parents, I've given these

Visit old truck enthusiasts on the Web to find ideas for additional truck variations.

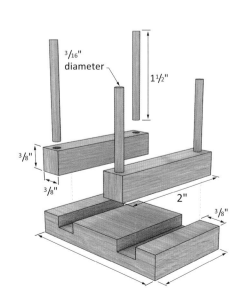

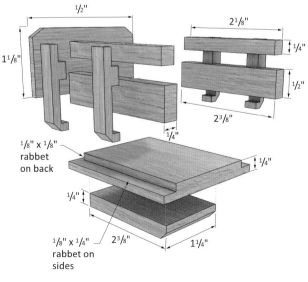

trucks some exaggerated features to give them kid appeal. Even though we're not making these for ourselves (right?), the cuteness factor will be appreciated by kids and adults.

The big "eyes" or headlights can be done in a variety of ways. Drill ⅛" holes in the sides of cylinders cut from dowels (drill a bunch before you cut them off) and in the sides of the radiators (again, more than once before you cut them off), and glue together.

For something a little more challenging, do the same thing with wooden balls. The trick is to drill the sides of the wooden balls: Plow a groove in a piece of scrap deep enough for the wooden balls to just touch on the bottom and sides of the groove, and glue them in. This support allows you to first drill the holes and then cut off the finished headlights (Photo C; page 75).

Once again, since the raw materials here are generally inexpensive, it's a good idea to glue up, cut out, and chop off more parts than you need to allow for the inevitable errors. A general rule of thumb would be, for five or fewer pieces, cut at least twice the number you need.

The cab is simply a box made of cut profiles. You could use a big-boy tool and a 1" Forstner bit, and cut the hole for the "C-cab" window out of solid stock, slice off wall sections and glue up cabs from the pieces. Or use a bandsaw and some sanding – whatever works (Photo D; page 75). Thick walls here (¼") are an advantage because they leave plenty of room to sand away any glueup mistakes. These toys are all about looking good!

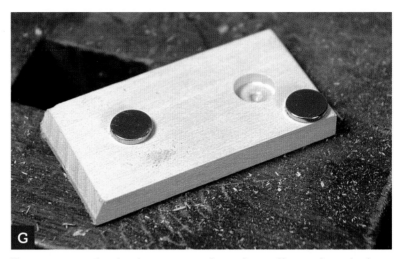

You can conceal or let the magnets show, depending on how devious you are. Be sure to dry fit before fastening.

Axles and other parts

Note that a lot of the measured parts use a ¼" dimension, so using ¼" stock takes you a long way toward completing many of the parts. Shave (curve) the edges of a ¼" x 2" length of stock and lop off as many bumpers as you need. Shape the edge of ⅛" stock for material for seat backs and the top of the cab, according to the illustration.

Rip lengths of ½" stock and cut to length for the axle housings. Adding a bevel to these simple rectangular elements is an easy way to add visual interest without a lot of work. When you set your saw at an angle to undercut for a bevel, you can turn your workpiece around and bevel the other side without changing any blade or fence settings (Photo E; page 77).

Make axles from dowels or buy actual $^5/_{32}$" wooden axles from any craft supplier.

There's no end to efficiencies you can dream up when you're doing these kinds of small projects. Solving problems is a large part of the satisfaction that comes from working in wood.

Making different trucks

Once you've made the basic truck body, it's time to have fun making a variety of beds that will transform the basic body into different kinds of trucks. Three variations are presented here (Photo F; page 77): a utility stake bed, a dump bed and a log truck rack (I used different sizes of dowels for the logs). Use similar construction methods and stock proportions to make these additions. Refer to the exploded drawings for inspiration, or just design your own.

Does the fun ever end?

The intent for this truck and parts was to produce a basic truck body, and differing truck parts to make a variety of trucks. Make a bunch of each. Stain, paint, mix-and-match and start a fleet.

Now how about concealing some ⅜" rare earth magnets (Photo G; page 78) on both the basic truck body and on the parts so you can use one body and just swap parts? Sneaky, huh?

Maybe most kids would rather have three complete trucks, but there's plenty of pleasure in swapping out the beds, especially that satisfying clack when the magnets find each other.

A suggestion: don't do final sanding with steel wool until after you've concealed the magnets.

So have at it, if you're into wheels.And remember, when working at this scale, it's all about fun: for you and the recipient of your labors. Be careful and drive safely!

Overall Dimensions: 6"w × 17"l × 8"h

FRONT-END LOADER

Scoop a bucket-load with this hands-on construction toy

BY CHUCK HEDLUND

Designed to go with the Toy Truck project following this one, this walnut and maple front-end loader features a lift handle for operating the bucket and depositing sawdust, dirt, sand, or gravel into the truck's dump box, as well as a pivoting front end. Here, you'll use the patterns to speed the building time and learn a few tricks for safely cutting small parts. You'll also find out how to make the rugged V-tread tires at the drill press and tablesaw.

First, make the frames

1 From ¾"-thick walnut, cut the rear frame (A) and front frame (B) to the sizes in the Cut List (page 90). Then mark the 1 ⅜"-radius center point which will be used later to bore the centered pivot hole. With your compass draw the radius line on each part. From the radiused end, mark the half-lap shoulder at 2 ¹³⁄₁₆". (See frame parts in Figure 1; page 82.)

2 Lay out the rabbet cuts on the frame parts (A, B) using a marking gauge. Set your tablesaw blade height to cut ¹³⁄₃₂" deep, and then crosscut each part where marked on the bottom face of rear frame (A) and top face of front frame (B). Note that a ¹⁄₁₆"−thick fender washer fits between the two frame rabbets, making up the difference in the pivoting half-lap joint, as shown in Figure 1.

3 Set up your drill press with a fence and bore the ⁷⁄₆₄" pivot hole in rear frame (A) and ⁵⁄₃₂" pivot hole in front frame (B), where shown.

4 Bandsaw to the marked radius line on the rear and front frames (A, B). Then sand to the line, removing saw marks.

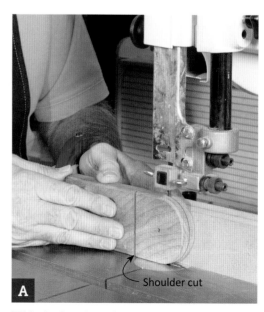

A

Shoulder cut

With the bandsaw fence set, cut the rabbet on a frame part, stopping at the shoulder cut.

Figure 1: Front-End Loader Exploded View

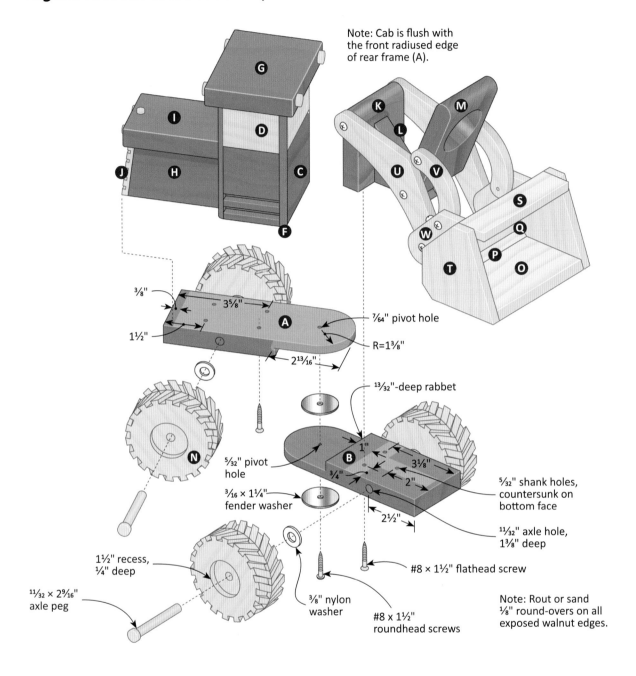

Note: Cab is flush with the front radiused edge of rear frame (A).

3/8"

3 5/8"

1 1/2"

2 13/16"

A

7/64" pivot hole

R=1 3/8"

13/32"-deep rabbet

1"

5/32" pivot hole

3/16 × 1 1/4" fender washer

B

3/4"

2"

3 1/8"

5/32" shank holes, countersunk on bottom face

11/32" axle hole, 1 3/8" deep

2 1/2"

N

1 1/2" recess, 1/4" deep

11/32 × 2 9/16" axle peg

3/8" nylon washer

#8 × 1 1/2" roundhead screws

#8 × 1 1/2" flathead screw

Note: Rout or sand 1/8" round-overs on all exposed walnut edges.

5 Set up your router table with a 1/8" round-over bit, and rout the edges of the rear and front frames (A, B).

6 Set up your bandsaw fence and to make a 13/32"-deep rabbet cut on each frame (A, B), as shown in Photo A (page 81). Sand the sawn surfaces smooth with a sanding block, and test the rabbet-to-rabbet fit, slipping a fender washer in between the parts. The surfaces should be flush.

7 On the side edges of the frames (A, B), lay out the axle peg holes where dimensioned in Figure 1. Set up your drill press with a fence and stop, and bore the 11/32" holes. Then drill and countersink all shank holes where shown.

Figure 2: Cab Blank Cutting Sequence

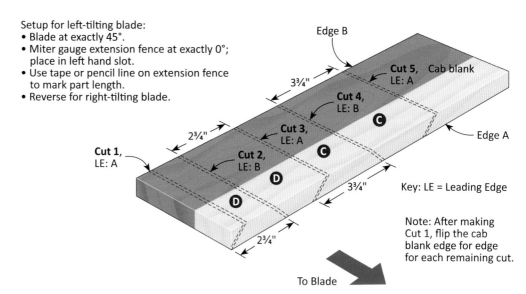

Setup for left-tilting blade:
- Blade at exactly 45°.
- Miter gauge extension fence at exactly 0°; place in left hand slot.
- Use tape or pencil line on extension fence to mark part length.
- Reverse for right-tilting blade.

Edge B

Cut 5, Cab blank
LE: A

3¾"

Cut 4,
LE: B

Cut 3,
LE: A

Edge A

2¾"

C

Cut 2,
LE: B

C

Cut 1,
LE: A

D

D

3¾"

Key: LE = Leading Edge

D

2¾"

Note: After making Cut 1, flip the cab blank edge for edge for each remaining cut.

To Blade

Add the cab

1 Edge-glue a ¾ × 1⅞" piece of maple to a ¾ × 3⅛" piece of walnut to make a 5"-wide by 20"-long blank for the cab front/back (C) and cab sides (D). See Figure 3 (page 84): Cab Exploded View. Remove the squeeze-out and let dry.

2 Miter-cut the cab front/back (C) pieces and the cab sides (D) to the lengths in the Cut List, following the blank cutting sequence in Figure 2. To do this, install a zero-clearance insert and attach an extension fence to your saw's miter gauge, placing it in the left-hand slot. (The blade in my saw tilts to the left. Make the needed changes if your saw tilts to the right.) Angle the blade at 45°. Place the cab blank against the extension fence, and miter-cut one end. Measure in 2¾" from the toe, and lay out the opposing miter-cut for the cab sides on the edges. Flip the blank to place its opposite edge (edge B) against the extension fence, and align the cutline with the blade. Mark the fence with a pencil line or piece of tape to the needed distance

from the blade. Guiding off this mark with the toe of the first cut, make the second cut to free a shorter cab side (D). Flip the blank, align the toe with the mark, and make the third cut, freeing the other cab side. Make a second mark on the fence for the longer cab front and back (C), and similarly cut these pieces to length (here, 3¾" long).

3 To glue up the mitered pieces (C, D), first align the parts end to end with the outside faces up and in the proper order. Apply three strips of tape across the joints with tape tails extending beyond one end part, as shown in Photo B (page 84).

4 Turn over the taped parts (C, D) and spread glue on the mitered ends. Now, starting at the edge with no tape tails, fold the mitered parts together to form a box, securing the open end with the tails (Photo C). Remove any glue squeeze-out at the corners. Let dry.

5 Cut the cab bottom (E) to fit at the inside bottom of the cab box. Apply glue and fit the piece into the box, making it flush with the assembly's bottom edges.

B Straightedge

With the cab parts outside face up and aligned along a straight edge, attach tape to the joints in preparation for the glue-up.

C

Apply glue and then fold the cab front, back, and sides at the mitered ends to form a box. Secure the open corner with the tape tails.

6 Set up a ¼" dado blade at a height of ¼". Cut rabbets at the cab's mitered corners. Also, cut dadoes for the steps on the cab sides (D), where shown in Figure 3.

7 Next, rip a ¼ × ¼" walnut strip 24"-long for the cab corners (F). Measure and cut the cab corners to rough length and glue them in place. After the glue has dried, sand the corners flush with the cab box.

8 Install a ¼" round-over bit in your router table, set up your fence, and rout round-overs on the corners of the cab.

9 From ¾" walnut, cut the cab top (G) to size. Rout a ⅛" round-over on all edges. On the front and back, edge bore ¹¹⁄₃₂" holes for the lights (Figure 3). Then finish-sand the cab parts. Add the lights. Center, glue, and clamp the top onto the cab box.

Make the motor, hood, and grill

1 Laminate three pieces of ¾"-thick walnut together to the size shown for the motor (H) in the Cut List. After the glue dries, bevel one end at the tablesaw using a miter gauge extension fence set at 90° and angling the blade at 7°. Finish-sand the motor. (See Figure 4 for reference.)

Figure 3: Cab Exploded View

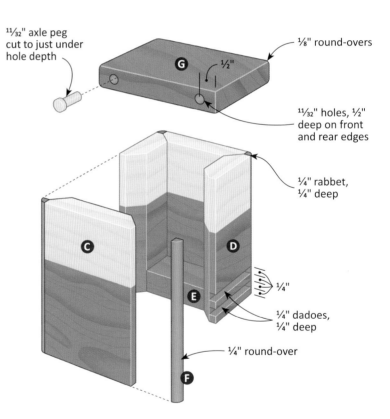

¹¹⁄₃₂" axle peg cut to just under hole depth

⅛" round-overs

G

½"

¹¹⁄₃₂" holes, ½" deep on front and rear edges

¼" rabbet, ¼" deep

C

D

¼"

E

¼" dadoes, ¼" deep

¼" round-over

F

Secure the front frame in a bench vise. Then, using a 1" spacer, locate, glue, and screw the centered brace and bucket support to the frame.

Figure 4: Motor Exploded View

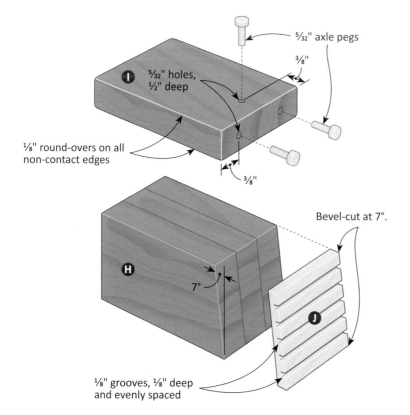

$\frac{5}{32}$" axle pegs

$\frac{3}{8}$"

I $\frac{5}{32}$" holes, $\frac{1}{2}$" deep

$\frac{1}{8}$" round-overs on all non-contact edges

$\frac{3}{8}$"

Bevel-cut at 7°.

H

7°

J

$\frac{1}{8}$" grooves, $\frac{1}{8}$" deep and evenly spaced

2 Next, cut the hood (I) to size. Then rout a $\frac{1}{8}$" round-over on all edges that don't contact the cab when in place. Finish-sand the hood.

3 Bore the $\frac{5}{32}$" holes for the brake lights and radiator cap in the hood (I) and attach. Glue (H) and (I) together, keeping the ends that go against the cab flush.

4 From $\frac{1}{4}$" maple, cut the grill (J), bevel-cutting the edges to match the profile of the motor. To cut the grill kerfs, install a zero-clearance insert in your tablesaw and raise $\frac{1}{8}$". Next, lay out five evenly spaced kerfs on one face. Adjust your saw fence to cut the outside kerfs. Using a pushpad to control the piece, cut one outside kerf, flip the piece end for end, and cut the other. Adjust the fence and similarly cut the neighboring kerfs. Adjust the fence one more time, and cut the center kerf. Glue the grill to the motor and hood (H/I).

5 Glue the cab (C/D/E/F/G) to the motor assembly (H/I/J). Remove squeeze-out, with a moistened rag, rinsing it in clean water as needed. Let the assembly dry, and then sand it flat to fit the rear frame (A). Now, glue and screw the combined assemblies to the rear frame with #8 × 1½" flathead screws, keeping the front of the cab flush with the frame's radiused end.

Bucket support, brace, and handle

1 From $\frac{3}{4}$" walnut cut the bucket support (K), brace (L), and handle (M), referring to the Cut List and Figure 5 (page 86). (Cut the end of a 2½" × 6"-long piece at 45°, and then cut 2½" in for the brace.)

2 Using a drill press and circle cutter or Forstner bit, bore a 2" hole in the handle (M), where shown in Figure 5 (page 86).

Figure 5: Bucket Exploded View

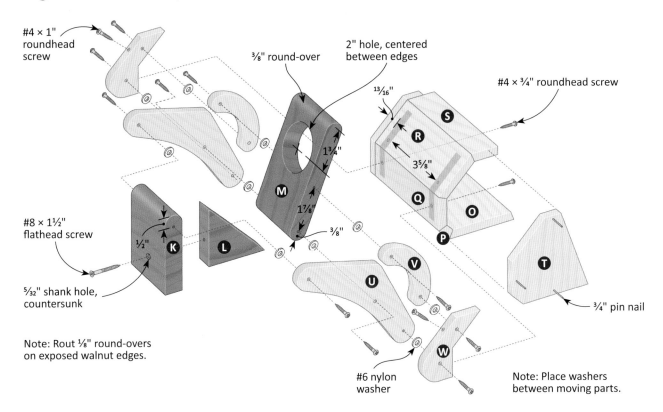

#4 × 1" roundhead screw

⅜" round-over

2" hole, centered between edges

#4 × ¾" roundhead screw

¹³⁄₁₆"

S

R

M

1¾"

3⅝"

#8 × 1½" flathead screw

½"

K

L

1⅛"

⅜"

Q

O

P

⁵⁄₃₂" shank hole, countersunk

V

U

T

¾" pin nail

Note: Rout ⅛" round-overs on exposed walnut edges.

W

#6 nylon washer

Note: Place washers between moving parts.

3 Set up your router table with a fence and a ⅜" round-over bit, and rout one end of the bucket support (K) and both ends of the handle (M).

4 Change over to a ⅛" round-over bit and rout where shown.

5 Set up your drill press with a fence, and drill centered pilot holes in the edges of the bucket support (K) and handle (M), where dimensioned. Switch bits and drill the countersunk shank hole in the bucket support.

6 Attach the bucket support (K) and brace (L) to the front frame (B) with screws in the countersunk shank and pilot holes, where shown in Figure 1 and as shown in Photo D. Note that the bucket support is 1" in from the front frame shoulder.

Make the tires

1 Lay out the center points for ten 3½"-diameter halves for tires (N) on two ¾ × 4½ × 22½" maple blanks. One blank will be for the inside tire halves and the other for the outside halves. (While you only need four complete tires [four inside and four outside halves glued together], use the extra inside and outside tire halves as test pieces).

2 Install a 1½" Forstner bit in your drill press, adjust the fence to center the bit on the tire half center points, and bore a ¼"-deep recess at each center point in the maple blank for the outside halves. (The other blank containing the inside halves will not be recessed.) Switch to an ¹¹⁄₃₂" brad-point bit, and drill a ⅛"-deep starter hole below the ¼" recess. Next, switch to a circle cutter set to make a 3½"-diameter cut. (Orient the cutter's bevel to face away

Cut out the outside tire halves with a circle cutter at the drill press using a low RPM.

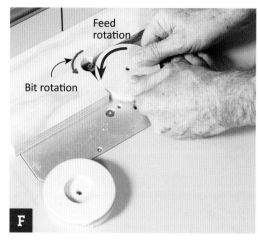

Feed rotation

Bit rotation

Fit the tire half—outside face down—in the L-shaped jig and round over the edge as shown.

from the center; the point of the cutter should be on the inside.) Clamp the maple blank to the drill press fence. Then, using a slow speed for safety (about 300 RPM), cut out the tire halves, as shown in Photo E, drilling a centered ¼" axle hole at the same time. Use the circle cutter to cut the inside tire halves out of the remaining blank.

3 Install a ⅛" roundover bit in the router table. Then make a simple L-jig out of ¾" scrap, drilling a 1" hole in the jig's inside corner. Adhere the jig to the table with double-faced tape, locating the bearing at the jig's inside corner. Round over all of the outside edges of the tire halves, rotating them, as shown in Photo F.

4 Next, referring to Figure 6 (page 88), make ten copies of the tire Kerfing Template, and cut them out. Adhere the paper templates to the inside face of each tire half. Make two groups of tire halves, one for the left tires (N), and one for the right tires (N). Later, when cutting the kerfs, you'll use the miter gauge in the right or left slot. Each group will have two inside tire halves and two outside halves. Keep the tires in separate groups to avoid confusion.

5 Make the Half-Tire Kerfing Jig in Figure 6, as shown, using a ¾"-thick × 3"-wide extension fence. (Check to see if the tire halves will turn on the dowels; if not, sand the dowels down.)

6 Install a ¼" dado set, and raise it to cut ³⁄₁₆" deep. Now, place the miter gauge to the left of the blade. Set it at 60°, as shown in Photo G (page 89). Position the jig fence on the miter gauge, aligning the marked alignment line with the inside edge of the dado set, and attach it with screws. Slip a test half tire onto the dowel, aligning the pattern start line with the alignment line on the top edge of the jig. Use a small clamp to hold the half tire to the fence. Turn on the saw and cut the half tire's tread. Repeat by rotating and aligning the template lines for each kerf cut, making the final cut at the red stop line. Check the tread. The kerfs should be evenly spaced. Finish cutting the "right" group. To cut the "left" group of half tires, move the miter gauge to the left of the blade, and angle it to 60° in the other direction. Reposition the jig fence. Then cut a kerf in the "left" group of half tires.

7 Remove the paper templates from the tire halves while keeping them in right and left groups. To bond the tire halves together, spread glue sparingly on the inside (unrounded) faces. You don't want glue squeeze-out at the joint lines. Next, insert a ¼ × 3" bolt through a washer, the hole in the tire halves, through second washer, and tighten the halves together with a nut, as shown in Photo H. (Doing this keeps the halves flush.) As you tighten, adjust the halves to create an offset V-tread pattern. Similarly glue and clamp the remaining tires for two left-hand and two right-hand tires (N).

8 After the glue dries, install the bolt of a tire assembly into the drill press chuck. Turn on the drill, and sand away any burn marks on a tire (N), using a sanding block with 80-grit sandpaper. Repeat for the remaining tires.

9 Install an 1¹⁄₃₂" brad-point bit in the drill press and, using the tool's fence and stopblock, align it with a tire's ¼" hole and ⅛"-deep recess hole made previously. Widen the hole so an axle peg can slip through it. Repeat for the remaining tires and finish.

Make the bucket

1 From two ⅜" maple blanks measuring 6" wide × 5¼" long, cut the bucket bottom (O), small angle (P), bucket back (Q), large angle (R), and Top (S), referring to the Cut List, Figure 5 (page 86), and the Bucket Patterns. Note that all the parts except the top have two bevel cuts at 22½°. The top has one 0° (or 90°) edge and one 22½° edge. To make the cuts, use a miter gauge and extension fence, sawing similarly to how you cut the cab parts earlier by flipping

Kerfing Template: 100% size

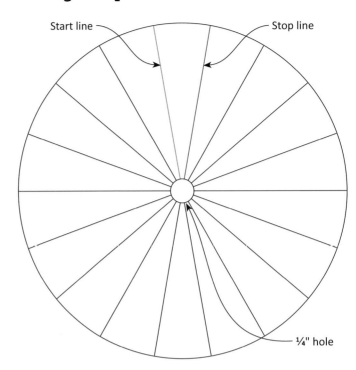

Figure 6: Half-Tire Kerfing Jig

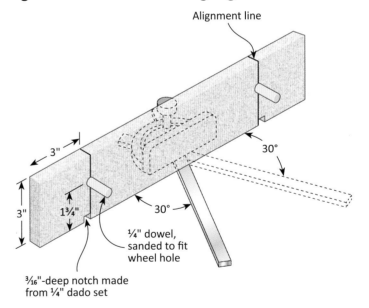

the blanks. Here, lay out the edges of each cut to the needed toe-to-toe widths. (I laid out and cut the parts as follows: S, Q, R from the first blank and P and O from the second blank.)

Dado-cut the treads in the tire halves, using an angled kerfing jig. Align the template lines with the alignment line (Inset) for evenly-spaced cuts.

Use a pair of wrenches to tighten the nut and washers on the glued-up tire halves. Make sure the treads create an offset V-pattern.

Clamp the taped and glued bucket parts to the custom spacers to create the bucket shape.

2 To form the bucket shape, you'll need to make two spacers that will be cut to the bucket's interior size and shape, starting with a ½ × 2¾ × 3¾" piece of MDF. Make the cuts shown in the Bucket Parts End View in the Bucket Patterns. Tape the bucket parts (O, P, Q, R, S) edge to edge. Then fold them around the spacers to check their fit. Glue up the assembly (Photo I).

3 To make the bucket sides (T), place the assembly (O, P, Q, R, S) on end on a ⅜"-thick piece of maple and trace around it. Repeat the process on for a second side shape. Draw a diagonal line on each shape, where shown in the Bucket Parts End View. Bandsaw the sides, cutting just outside the lines.

4 Attach the bandsawn sides (T) to the bucket assembly (O, P, Q, R, S) with glue and ¾" pin nails. Sand the proud bandsawn edges of the sides flush with the bucket assembly, and break the edges.

5 From two ⅜"-thick maple blanks, make the arm (U), knuckle (V), and bracket (W). To do this, make two copies of each full-sized pattern in the Bucket Patterns, and adhere them to the blanks. Then bandsaw or scrollsaw the parts to shape. When cutting the brackets to shape, double-check for a tight fit against the bucket shape. Sand or recut if needed. Drill the shank and pilot holes where indicated. Remove the patterns, and sand the sawn edges smooth, breaking any sharp corners.

6 Make an L-shaped spacer using two pieces of ½ × 2½ × 3⅝" MDF. Glue and pin-nail the pieces together to form the "L." Center and place the spacer on the bucket between the ends. Now, apply glue, position, and clamp the brackets (W) to the spacer, ensuring they're snug to the bucket. Drill pilot holes into the edges of the brackets, where shown in the pattern, and screw them in place (Photo J). Add two more screws from inside of the bucket. (See Figure 5 on page 86.)

Finish-sand, apply finish, and assemble

1 Finish-sand all of the parts and assemblies to 220 grit. Wipe clean, and apply finish to the assemblies and unassembled parts. (I used Watco Satin Lacquer.) Apply finish to just the exposed ends (not the shanks) of the axle parts. Let the finish dry.

2 Assemble the two frames (A, B). To do this, place a fender washer between the two frames and on the #8 × 1½" roundhead screw before you drive it in place. Tighten or loosen the screw to get the right pivoting action.

3 Orient the left and right tires (N) so the recessed faces are on the outside. Place a small amount of glue in the axle peg holes, and then push the axle pegs through the tires. Fit nylon washers on the pegs, and then tap them into the frame holes, leaving a clearance equal to the thickness of a business card for the tires to turn freely. Pin-nail the pegs to the frames (A, B).

4 Attach the bucket parts with roundhead screws and washers, as shown in Figures 1 and 5 (Pages 82 and 86). Do not overtighten.

3⅝"-long L-shaped spacer

Center the brackets between the bucket sides, and glue and screw them in place, using a 3⅝"-long L-spacer.

Cut List: Front-End Loader

	Part	Thickness	Width	Length	Qty.	Mat'l
A	Rear frame	¾"	2¾"	7¼"	1	W
B	Front frame	¾"	2¾"	7¼"	1	W
C	Cab front/back	¾"	5"	3¾"	2	M/W
D	Cab sides	¾"	5"	2¾"	2	M/W
E	Cab bottom	¾"	1¼"	2¼"	1	W
F	Cab corners	¼"	¼"	5"	4	W
G	Cab top	¾"	4½"	3½"	1	W
H*	Motor	¾"	2¼"	3¾"	3	W
I	Hood	¾"	2½"	4"	1	M
J	Grill	¼"	2⁵⁄₁₆"	2¼"	1	M
K	Bucket support	¾"	2¾"	3⅜"	1	W
L	Brace	¾"	2½"	2½"	1	W
M	Handle	¾"	2¾"	5"	1	W
N≠	Tires	1½"	3½" dia.		4	M
O	Bucket bottom	⅜"	3"	5¼"	1	M
P	Small angle	⅜"	¾"	5¼"	1	M
Q	Bucket back	⅜"	1½"	5¼"	1	M
R	Large angle	⅜"	2⅛"	5¼"	1	M
S	Top	⅜"	1¼"	5¼"	1	M
T*	Bucket sides	⅜"	4"	5"	2	M
U**	Arms	⅜"	2¾"	12"	2	M
V**	Knuckles	⅜"	2¾"	12"	2	M
W**	Brackets	⅜"	2¾"	12"	2	M

*Indicates parts are initially cut oversized. See instructions.
**Indicates parts are cut from two pieces of ⅜ × 2¾ × 12" maple.
≠Indicates tires are made up of two opposing halves.
See instructions.
Materials: W=Walnut, M=Maple
Hardware/Supplies: (16) #4 × ¾" roundhead screws; (2) #4 × 1" roundhead screws; (1) #8 ×1½" roundhead screw; (8) #8 1½" flathead screws; (4) ⅜" nylon washers; (10) #6 flat nylon washers; (2) ³⁄₁₆ × 1¼" fender washers; ¾" pin nails.

Patterns: Bucket

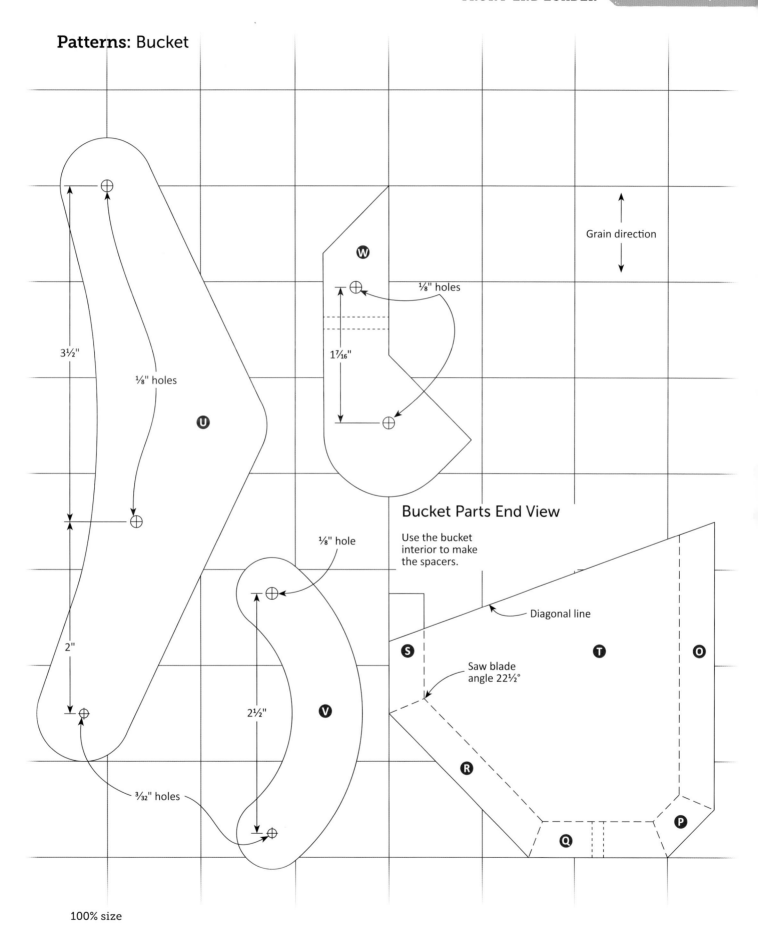

Grain direction

3½"

⅛" holes

U

W

⅛" holes

1⁷⁄₁₆"

Bucket Parts End View

Use the bucket interior to make the spacers.

⅛" hole

2"

2½"

V

Diagonal line

S

T

O

Saw blade angle 22½°

R

P

Q

³⁄₃₂" holes

100% size

Overall Dimensions: 6"w × 15"l × 7"h

TOY TRUCK

A rugged but refined design built for play and display

BY CHUCK HEDLUND

This wooden truck design aims at giving kids a fully functional toy for either the sandbox or carpet. You'll enjoy building the laminated cab and rugged wheels. And once complete, the vehicle's good looks will seem right at home in any kid's room. Young truck drivers will wear out the knees of their jeans hauling sand, stones, and wood scraps.

Walnut and maple serve as the primary woods, while maple axle pegs in two sizes provide realistic accents. During construction, you'll learn how to machine small parts safely and discover a kerfing jig for making grooved tire treads.

First, make the lower cab assembly

Note: Two designated parts in the lower cab assembly consist of glue-ups of more than one piece of wood. See Figure 2.

1 Mill one 4'-long piece of 1×6 walnut to ¾" thick and a 2'-long piece of 1×6 to ⅜" thick.

2 Cut one piece of ¾" walnut and one piece of ⅜" walnut to 5⅝" wide by 6" long. Glue the pieces face to face, and then trim the lamination to the size in the Cut List (page 103) for the cab motor hood (A).

3 Strike a line across the top face of the cab motor hood (A) blank 2¼" from one end and another line along the front end, where shown in Figure 2 (page 95). Connect the lines on both edges to establish the tapered hood. Using a ¾" blade with at least 3 TPI at the bandsaw, bevel-cut the blank (Photo A).

4 Use a random-orbit sander and 80-to 120-grit sandpaper to sand to the cutlines and remove saw marks.

Use a handscrew clamp to safely bevel-cut the cab motor hood blank at the bandsaw.

Figure 1: Truck Exploded View

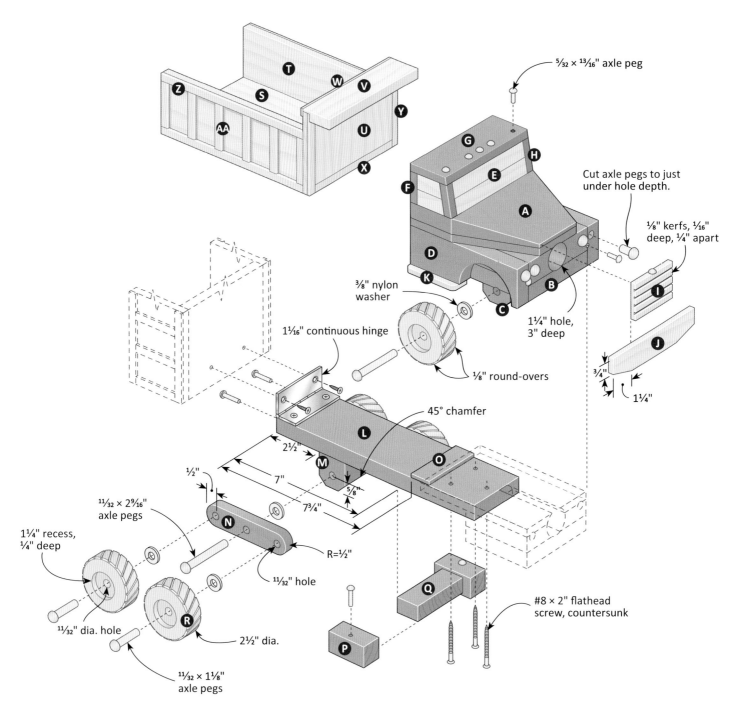

⁵/₃₂ × ¹³/₁₆" axle peg

Cut axle pegs to just
under hole depth.

⅛" kerfs, ¹/₁₆"
deep, ¼" apart

1¼" hole,
3" deep

¾"

1¼"

⅜" nylon
washer

1¹/₁₆" continuous hinge

⅛" round-overs

45° chamfer

2½"

7"

7¾"

⅝"

½"

¹¹/₃₂ × 2⁹/₁₆"
axle pegs

R=½"

¹¹/₃₂" hole

1¼" recess,
¼" deep

¹¹/₃₂" dia. hole

2½" dia.

¹¹/₃₂ × 1⅛"
axle pegs

#8 × 2" flathead
screw, countersunk

Note: The ¹¹/₃₂" (or .344") diameter
axle pegs actually measure .338,
allowing the tires to turn easily.

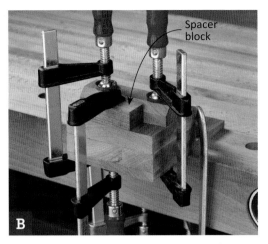

Clamp on a spacer block to the front of the lower cab assembly to locate the front axle support.

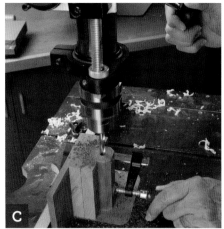

Bore into both ends of the front axle support to complete the through axle hole.

5 Mark the angled cuts on the cab motor hood blank for part (A), where shown in Figure 2.

Bandsaw off the waste, cutting just outside the line. Now, sand to the line at the disc sander.

6 To form the cab bottom (B), cut two pieces of ¾" walnut stock to 4 × 3⅜". Laminate them together, flushing the edges and ends. Now, from ⅜" stock, cut a 4 ×

5⅞" piece, and glue it to the top of the laminated walnut block, flushing the edges and one end, as shown in Figure 2. Sand the cab bottom as needed.

7 From ¾" stock, cut the front axle support (C) to size. Bevel-cut the edges at 45°, where shown in Figure 2.

8 Cut a 1"-wide spacer and clamp it flush along the front edge of the lower cab assembly (A/B). Now, apply glue to the top

Figure 2: Lower Cab Exploded View

To Make Part B:
1. Cut top piece to size.
2. Cut and laminate two ¾" pieces to size.
3. Glue top piece to lamination.

To Make Part A:
1 Laminate hood blank
2 Bevel-cut hood blank
3 Angle-cut hood blank

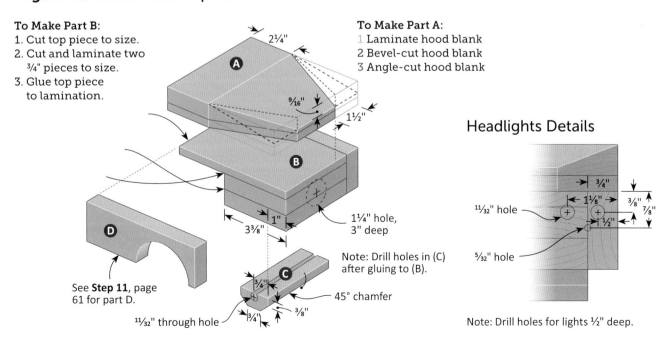

2¼"

9/16"

1½"

1¼" hole, 3" deep

1"

3⅜"

Note: Drill holes in (C) after gluing to (B).

See **Step 11**, page 61 for part D.

¾"

45° chamfer

11/32" through hole

¾"

⅜"

Headlights Details

11/32" hole

5/32" hole

¾"

1⅛"

⅜"

⅞"

½"

Note: Drill holes for lights ½" deep.

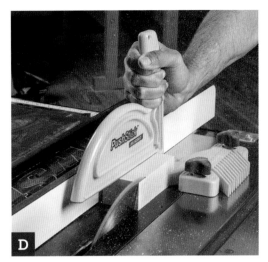

D

Bevel-cut the windshield block, using a shoe-style pushstick with an abrasive edge or rubber sole to keep it down on the table and snug to the fence.

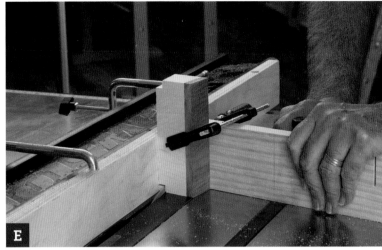

E

With the beveled edge of the windshield block against the saw fence, make several passes at the proper angle to cut the rabbets.

face of the front axle support (C), and clamp the part against the spacer, flushing its ends with the lower cab assembly (Photo B; page 95).

9 After the glue dries, bore an 1¹/₃₂" through hole in the front axle support (C), where shown in Figure 2 (page 95) and as shown in Photo C (page 95).

10 Apply glue to the mating surfaces of the cab hood (A) and lower cab (B), and clamp the parts together, carefully flushing the edges and front ends. Later, remove the clamps and sand smooth.

11 Cut a ¾" piece of walnut to 3⅞ × 5⅞" for the fender (D) blank. Mark a centered hole 1¾" from one end. To drill the hole, use a circle cutter.

Note: Position the cutter so its tip faces outside. At the drill press, clamp the workpiece in position, and then use the circle cutter to bore a 2⅞"-diameter hole. Sand the hole with an oscillating spindle sander to remove burn marks.

12 Ripcut the blank for the fenders (D) to create two 1⅞"-wide parts. Now glue the fenders to the uncompleted lower cab

assembly (A/B/C), where shown in Figure 2, flushing the ends and edges. Sand the completed lower cab assembly smooth.

13 Switch to a 1¼" Forstner bit, secure the lower cab assembly (A/B/C/D) to the drill press table and fence, and bore a 3"-deep hole into the front to remove waste, where shown in Figure 1 (page 94). (Hollowing out the cab makes it lighter.) Later, you'll cover the opening with the grill (I) and bumper (J).

Add the cab top, bumper, and grill

1 Mill one 3'-long piece of 1 × 6" maple to ¾" thick, a second 3'-long piece to ½" thick, a 30"-long piece to ⅜" thick, and a 1'-long piece to ¼" thick.

2 Cut and laminate two pieces of ¾"-thick maple to create a blank that measures 1½" thick × 5⁹/₁₆" wide × 2¼" long for the windshield block (E).

3 From ⅜" walnut, cut the cab back (F) ¹/₁₆" long. Now, glue and clamp the piece to one edge of the windshield block (E). Let dry, and then trim the assembly to 5½" wide. With the tablesaw blade angled at 10° from

F

Cut 1/16"-deep kerfs to create the grill face, using pencil erasers to move the piece safely over the blade.

vertical, bevel-cut the front maple edge of the assembly, as shown in Photo D.

4 Adjust the tablesaw fence to 3/8" from the outside edge of the blade, and raise the blade to 3/8" high. Lock in a mitersaw extension fence at 90°. Now, with the front face of the windshield block assembly (E/F) face down, cut a kerf at one end. Flip the piece and kerf the other end. Next, adjust the miter gauge to 80°, and, with the windshield block on end, complete the rabbet cut where shown in Figure 3. Adjust the miter gauge to 80° in the opposite direction and repeat the process to complete the remaining rabbet, as shown in Photo E. (A 3/8" dado set would let you cut the rabbets on one pass.)

5 From 3/8"-thick walnut, cut the cab top (G) to size, plus 1/16" wider than the final dimension. Glue and clamp it to the windshield block assembly (E/F), flushing the piece at the ends and along the back edge of the cab back. (The piece should extend slightly over the front edge of the windshield block.)

Figure 3:
Cab Top Exploded View

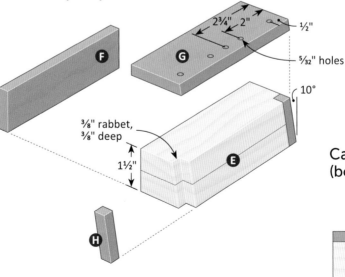

QUICK TIP

Use pin nails of various lengths when gluing parts together to ensure proper positioning and to prevent slippage.

Cab Top Boring Detail (bottom face)

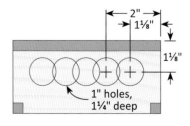

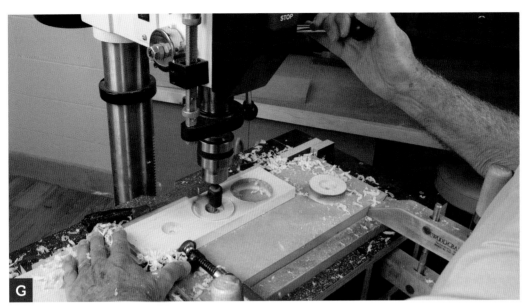

Align the blank with the circle cutter, centering its ¼" bit in the ¹¹⁄₃₂" recess; clamp it in position, and cut out the tire.

6 Cut a ⅜ × ⅜ × 12" strip of walnut. Measure the length of the rabbets in the uncompleted windshield block assembly (E/F/G) for cutting the cab front corners (H) to length. Using a mitersaw or tablesaw and a miter-gauge extension fence adjusted at 10° from square, bevel-cut the cab front corners. Test their fit in the windshield block, and then glue them in place. Sand their bottom ends flush with the assembly.

7 Similar to Step 3, angle the saw blade 10° from vertical, and make a fine bevel skim cut across the front face of the cab top assembly, flushing the cab top (G) with the beveled face of the windshield block. As an alternative, you could sand the pieces flush on a sheet of sandpaper adhered to a flat surface.

8 Mark the locations of the cab top lights, referring to the Cab Top Boring Detail in

Figure 4: Tire Kerfing Jig

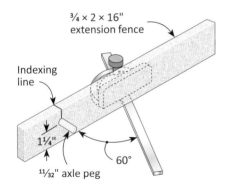

Note: To make kerfs on left and right tires, angle the extension fence at 60° to the left of 90°, and then at 60° to the right. Adjust the fence location so the tire (when on the peg tenon) centers over the blade.

Kerfing Template: 100% size (make 7 copies)

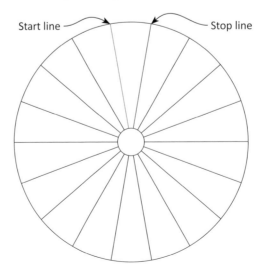

Fit a sanded tire into the jig's corner, and turn it against the bit's rotation to safely round the edges.

Align the template's start line with the jig line, and then cut, rotate the tire, and cut again, making evenly spaced kerfs. Stop at the stop line.

Figure 3. Drill the 5/32" holes 1/2" deep at these locations.

9 Using a 1" Forstner bit, bore out the waste in the cab top assembly, drilling overlapping holes 1¼" deep into its bottom face, where shown in the Cab Top Boring Detail in Figure 3.

10 Next, apply glue to the bottom of the cab top assembly (E/F/G/H), and clamp it in place to the lower cab assembly (A/B/C/D),

flushing it along the back edge and ends. Remove any glue squeeze-out with a moistened rag.

11 Hand-sand 1/8" round-overs on all exposed edges on the cab assembly (A/B/C/D/E/F/G/H). Do not round over mating edges for the grill (I), and bumper (J) at the front end of the cab hood or the bottom edges of the cab assembly.

12 From ¼" maple, cut the grill (I) to size. Referring to Figure 1 (page 94), adjust the tablesaw fence, and cut the four kerfs (Photo F; page 97). Glue the grill to the front of the cab and flush with the hood.

13 From ¼" maple, cut the bumper (J) to 1⅛ × 5½" at the tablesaw. Referring to Figure 1, lay out the angled cuts along the bottom edge. Bandsaw along the angled cutlines and sand smooth. Glue the bumper to the cab, flush with the fenders (D) and grill (I).

14 Cut the running boards (K) to size, rounding the outside corners. Glue and pin the running boards to the cab, where shown in Figure 1, flushing their inside edges with the fenders (D).

Build and add the frame

1 Cut the frame (L) to size, checking its fit within the assembled cab. Drill centered ½"-deep holes for the taillights 3/8" in from the edges.

2 Glue two pieces of ¾" walnut face to face, and then trim the laminate to the size in the Cut List for the rear axle support (M). Bevel-cut chamfers on the edges, where shown in Figure 1. Then glue the axle block to the bottom face of the frame 2½" from its rear end, using a spacer similar to Photo C (page 95). Now, drill the centered 11/32" through hole 5/8" from the bottom face.

3 Cut the wheel pivots (N) to size. Mark and drill the three centered $^{11}/_{32}$" peg holes, where shown in Figure 1. Then mark the ½" radii, and sand them to shape at the disc sander.

4 Cut the spacer block (O), gas tanks (P), and gas tanks bracket (Q) to size. (Note that the spacer block thickness equals that of the hinge.) Drill the holes for the gas caps in the gas tanks, and round over their edges. Center and edge-glue the tanks to the bracket. Let dry, and then secure the assembly (P/Q) to the frame, where shown in Figure 1, with glue.

5 Fit the front end of the frame (L) into the opening of the cab assembly, and secure it in place with glue and three #8 × 2" countersunk flathead screws. With the cab secure, glue and pin-nail the spacer block (O) in place.

Make and install the tires

Note: You can make 2½"-diameter tires using the method described here, or save time by buying tires from an online supplier (there are many). To ensure free movement of the tires, drill an $^{11}/_{32}$" test hole in scrap and fit an axle peg into it.

1 Lay out the centerpoints for seven 2½"-diameter tires (R) on a ¾ × 3½ × 24" maple blank. (While you only need six tires, use the seventh as a test piece.)

2 Install a 1¼" Forstner bit, adjust the fence to center the bit on the tire (R) center points, and bore a ¼"-deep recess at each one. Switch to an $^{11}/_{32}$" brad-point bit, and drill a ⅛"-deep starter hole below the recess. Next, switch to a circle cutter and adjust it to make a 2½"-diameter cut. Clamp the workpiece to the drill-press fence. Then, use a slow-speed (about 300

rpm), cut out the tires (Photo G on page 98) drilling a ¼" axle hole at the same time.

Note: Be sure to orient the cutter to face the center of the opening.

3 Insert a ¼" bolt or length of all-thread through a tire's axle hole, locking it in place between a washer and jam nut. Then, install the bolt into the drill chuck. Turn on the drill and sand away any burn marks. Repeat for the remaining tires.

4 Switch to the $^{11}/_{32}$" bit and, using a stopblock and fence, widen the ¼" axle holes, guiding off the ⅛"-deep starter hole drilled earlier. This will allow the axle peg to slip through the tires.

5 Install a ⅛" round-over bit in the router table. Then make a simple L-jig out of ¾" scrap, drilling a 1" hole in the jig's inside corner. Clamp the jig to the table or fence, locating the bearing at the jig's inside corner. Now, round over the tires, as shown in Photo H.

6 Make the Tire Kerfing Jig in Figure 4 (page 98), gluing in a sawed-off tenon from an axle peg in a wood extension fence. Strike an alignment line on the top edge of the fence, directly above the tenon. Attach the fence to the miter gauge, aligning the tire's center with the saw blade when the fence is angled at 60° to the left or right of 90°. Next, make seven copies of the Kerfing Template and adhere a paper template to the inside face of each tire.

7 Angle the miter gauge kerfing jig at 60° to the left of 90°. Slip a test tire onto the peg tenon, aligning the indicated start line on the template with the line on the top edge of the jig, clamping it to the fence. Raise the saw blade $^1/_{16}$", and, cut the tire's tread, rotating and aligning the template lines as you go. Check the tread after

Cut a spacer block, and use it to evenly space the box ribs when gluing and pinning them in place.

For clearance, use a long shank screwdriver to drive the screws and fasten the remaining leaf of the dump box hinge to the frame.

QUICK TIP

Test the pin-nail depth by shooting through a piece of ⅛" maple and into a ⅜"piece. You want to sink the pin-nail below the surface to hide it. Fill the holes with a color-matching filler prior to finishing.

washer onto an axle peg and glue and pin-nail the peg to the front axle support (C). (I used ¾" pin nails, shooting through the axle support and into the peg.) Do the opposing tire. Similarly, secure the rear tires to the rear axle support (M). Test-fit the rear tires, washers, and axle pegs into the wheel pivots. Mark the protruding axle pegs and cut them to length. Glue and pin-nail the rear wheel axle pegs in place.

9 Finish-sand the cab and then glue in the headlights, signal lights, running lights, rear brake lights, and gas tank and radiator caps, cutting the peg tenons to length as needed.

Build the dump box

1 From the ⅜" and ½" maple stock, cut the dump box bottom (S), box sides (T), box front (U), and cab protector (V) to the sizes in the Cut List. Cut a ⅜ × ⅜" rabbet on one edge of the cab protector. Cut ⅜" rabbets ⅛" deep on the outside face of the box front. Sand the faces of box parts.

2 Drill the countersunk holes, where shown in Figure 5 (page 102), and then assemble the box with #4 × ¾" screws and glue, checking all corners for square.

3 Drill countersunk holes and glue and screw the cab protector (V) to the box front (U). Before adding the strips, finish-sand the box.

4 Install a zero-clearance insert in your tablesaw with a 50- or 60-tooth blade to make a glue-line cut. Then, adjust the square end of your miter gauge extension fence to be ⅛" from the outside face of the blade. Pull the miter gauge back toward the front of the saw, and use the extension fence end to serve as a stop. Now, joint both edges of a 2' long piece of ⅜"-thick maple stock having straight grain. With the

reaching the stop line. The kerfs should be evenly spaced. Now, cut three tires this way for one side of the truck, as shown in Photo (page 99). Adjust the jig at 60° to the right of 90°, move the fence as needed, and similarly cut the tread on the opposing three tires. Sand and finish the tires.

8 Note the tread orientation in Figure 1 (page 94), and then slip a tire and nylon

Figure 5: Dump Box Exploded View

Note: See Step 4 below to safely cut the strips.

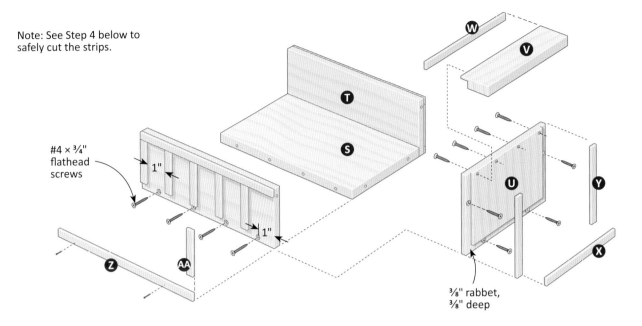

#4 × ¾"
flathead
screws

1"

1"

⅜" rabbet,
⅜" deep

piece against the fence, adjust the fence so the opposite edge contacts the end of the extension fence. Turn on the saw and rip a ⅛"-thick strip. Flip the piece, adjust the fence again, and rip a second ⅛"-thick strip. Joint both edges of the workpiece, and repeat the process to rip two more ⅛"-thick strips.

5 Mark and cut the box front top rail (W), box front bottom rail (X), and box front stiles (Y) to fit. Now apply them, where shown in Figure 5, using glue and ⅜" pin nails. Note that the strips provide a realistic detail and cover up the screw heads.

6 Cut the box side rails (Z) to length. Glue and pin-nail the top box side rails (Z), where shown on Figure 5. Temporarily place a bottom side rail in place, and

measure the distance between the top and bottom rails. Now, cut the box ribs (AA) to length. Remove the bottom rails, and starting at the box front, glue and pin the box ribs, as shown in Photo J (page 101). Finish-sand the dump box.

7 Cut a 3"-long piece of ¹¹⁄₁₆"-wide continuous hinge. Now, hold the hinge on the end of the frame (L), and mark and drill the pilot holes. Center the hinge on the bottom face of the box bottom (S), ¼" from the back end, and mark and drill pilot holes. Finally, attach the dump box to the truck frame (Photo K). Use a grinding wheel to shorten the hinge screws so they don't poke into the dump box.

8 Remove the dump box and finish the box with finish.

Cut List: Toy Truck

	Part	Thickness	Width	Length	Qty.	Mat'l
A*	Cab motor hood	1⅛"	5½"	5⅞"	1	W
B*	Cab bottom	1⅞"	4"	5⅞"	1	W
C	Front axle support	¾"	4"	1½"	1	W
D*	Fenders	¾"	1⅞"	5⅞"	2	W
E*	Windshield block	1½"	5½"	1⅞"	1	M
F	Cab back	⅜"	5½"	1½"	1	W
G*	Cab top	⅜"	5½"	2"	1	W
H*	Cab front corners	⅜"	⅜"	1⅝"	2	W
I	Grill	¼"	1¾"	2½"	1	M
J	Bumper	¼"	1⅛"	5½"	1	M
K	Running boards	¼"	1"	2⅝"	2	M
L	Frame	¾"	3"	11¼"	1	W
M*	Rear axle support	1½"	3"	1½"	1	W
N	Wheel pivots	½"	1"	4½"	2	W
O	Spacer block	3/16"	1"	3"	1	W
P	Gas tanks	1"	1"	2"	2	W
Q	Gas tanks bracket	¾"	3"	1⅛"	1	W
R	Tires	¾"	2½" dia.		6	M
S	Box bottom	½"	5"	8¼"	1	M
T	Box sides	⅜"	3"	8¼"	2	M
U	Box front	⅜"	6"	4"	1	M
V	Cab protector	½"	1½"	6"	1	M
W*	Box front top rail	⅛"	⅜"	6"	1	M
X*	Box front bottom rail	⅛"	⅜"	5¼"	1	M
Y*	Box front stiles	⅛"	⅜"	4"	2	M
Z*	Box side rails	⅛"	⅜"	8¼"	4	M
AA*	Box ribs	⅛"	⅜"	2¼"	12	M

*Indicates parts are initially cut oversized. See instructions.
Materials: W=Walnut, M=Maple
Hardware/Supplies: (8) ⅜" nylon flat washers; (1) ¼ × 3" hexhead bolt; (3) ¼" nuts; (2) ¼" washers; (1) continuous hinge, nickel, 11/16 × 30"; (12) #4 × ¾" flathead screws; (3) #8 × 2" flathead screws.

Overall Dimensions:
9"w × 18⅛"l × 7⅜"h

ROAD GRADER

Paving the way to playtime adventure

BY TOM WHALLEY AND MARLEN KEMMET

Add to your tough-enough toy collection with this rugged grader. The wheels pivot and the blade rotates, allowing young tykes to create their own perfect sandbox roadways and construction sites. Discover a safe and effective way to make off-road tires for gripping the rough terrain.

Start with the frame

1 Cut and laminate two pieces of ¾"-thick maple face to face to form a blank for the frame (A) for a finished size of 1 ½ × 2 ⅛ × 17". (See Figures 1, 2, and 3 on pages 106, 107, 108.) Lay out the opening in the blank as shwon in Figure 2 and cut the frame profile to shape. (Use a dado blade and tablesaw to create the square-cornered notches and a bandsaw to complete the cuts.)

2 Cut the blade pivot (B), axle support (C), and front (D) to the sizes in the Cut List (page 115) from maple. Drill countersunk mounting holes and screw (A) to (B).

3 Drill the ¹¹⁄₃₂" holes in (C) and (D). Using an ¹¹⁄₃₂ × 2⁹⁄₁₆" axle peg inserted through (D) and into (C) to maintain alignment between the two holes, glue and screw these parts to the frame (A). Cut the frame top (E) to size from walnut and glue it to the frame (A).

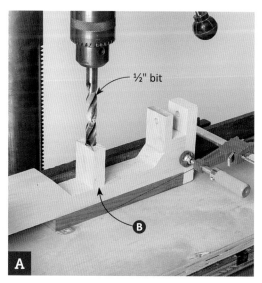

Center the bit over the centerpoint, clamp the frame assembly to your drill-press table using spacers, and complete the blade pivot hole.

4 Mark the centerpoint, and then drill the ½" blade pivot hole through the assembled frame parts (A), (B), and (E). If your bit is not long enough to bore through, flip the assembly bottom edge up and complete the centered hole, as shown in Photo A.

5 Lay out the cutline on the side of frame parts (D) and (E), where dimensioned in Figure 2. Bandsaw the frame's top edge to shape, as shown in Photo B (page 107). Sand the sawn edge smooth.

Figure 1: Road Grader Exploded View

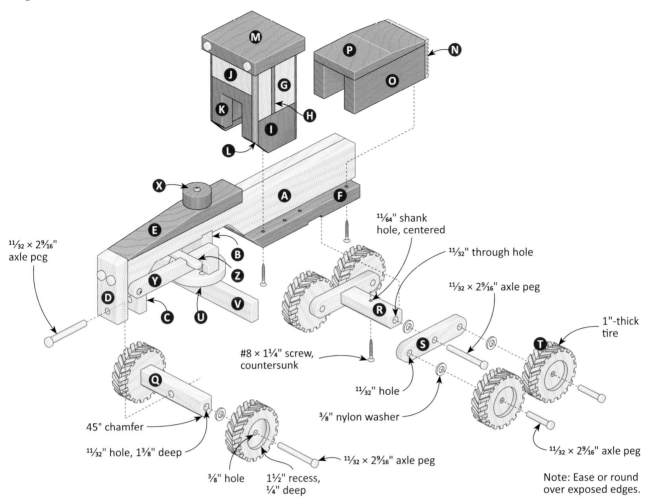

$\frac{11}{32} \times 2\frac{9}{16}$" axle pcg

$\frac{11}{64}$" shank hole, centered

$\frac{11}{32}$" through hole

$\frac{11}{32} \times 2\frac{9}{16}$" axle peg

1"-thick tire

#8 × 1¼" screw, countersunk

$\frac{11}{32}$" hole

⅜" nylon washer

$\frac{11}{32} \times 2\frac{9}{16}$" axle peg

45° chamfer

$\frac{11}{32}$" hole, 1⅜" deep

⅜" hole

1½" recess, ¼" deep

$\frac{11}{32} \times 2\frac{9}{16}$" axle peg

Note: Ease or round over exposed edges.

6 Cut the rear frame bottom (F) to size, as shown in Figure 3. Lay out and cut the 1½" dado, ⅛" deep, across the piece on the top surface. Cut a 1" dado, ⅛" deep, for the rear axle (R) on the bottom. Drill the screw mounting holes. Screw the part to the frame assembly, where shown in Figure 2, aligning the back edge with the ⅛" notch.

Add the cab

1 To form the cab side windows (G), cut a piece of ¾" stock to 2¾" wide by 8" long. Cut a ¼" groove, ¼" deep, where shown in Figure 4 (page 109). Cut a window divider (H) to fit into the groove, and glue it in place. Crosscut two G/H assemblies to 3" long from the blank.

2 Cut the cab side bottoms (I) to size, and glue one to each side assembly (G, H) with the edges flush, creating a "left" and a "right" cab side by positioning the parts, as shown in Figure 4.

3 Using a dado set, miter gauge, and an auxiliary fence for support, cut a ¾" rabbet ½" deep along the bottom end on the inside face of each side assembly (G/H/I). Cut the cab sides to the finished length of 5".

4 For the cab front and backs, cut the cab end windows (J) and cab end bottoms (K) to size, plus ½" in width and 2" in length.

Figure 2: Frame and Blade Assembly Exploded View

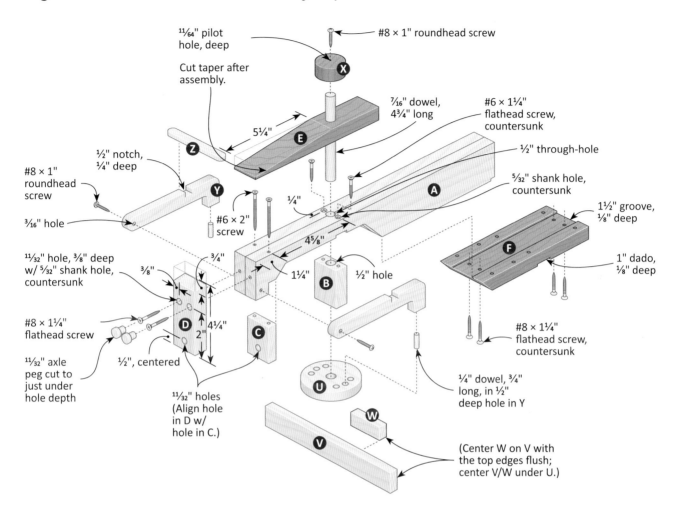

¹¹⁄₆₄" pilot hole, deep

Cut taper after assembly.

#8 × 1" roundhead screw

5¼"

⁷⁄₁₆" dowel, 4¾" long

#6 × 1¼" flathead screw, countersunk

½" through-hole

Z

E

X

½" notch, ¼" deep

A

⁵⁄₃₂" shank hole, countersunk

1½" groove, ⅛" deep

#8 × 1" roundhead screw

Y

¼"

#6 × 2" screw

4⅝"

F

1" dado, ⅛" deep

³⁄₁₆" hole

¾"

1¼"

½" hole

B

¹¹⁄₃₂" hole, ⅜" deep w/ ⁵⁄₃₂" shank hole, countersunk

⅜"

4¼"

2"

#8 × 1¼" flathead screw

¹¹⁄₃₂" axle peg cut to just under hole depth

½", centered

D

C

#8 × 1¼" flathead screw, countersunk

¼" dowel, ¾" long, in ½" deep hole in Y

U

W

¹¹⁄₃₂" holes (Align hole in D w/ hole in C.)

V

(Center W on V with the top edges flush; center V/W under U.)

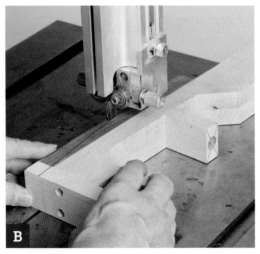

B

Bandsaw the angled top edge of the frame to shape, cutting just outside the cutline.

The extra length is needed for safely cutting the rabbets in Step 5. Glue the pieces end to end. Trim the edges flush for a finished width of 3".

5 Using a dado set at the saw table and a pushblock, cut a ½" rabbet ½" deep along both inside edges of each cab side assembly (J/K).

6 Trim the (J) part of the assembly (J/K) to 1½" long. Then, crosscut the overall assembly length to 4¼". Lay out the notches in the cab end bottoms (K) to slip over the frame (A). Bandsaw and sand the parts to shape.

7 Dry-fit the cab sides to the front and back. There should be a ¼ × ¼" rabbet

Figure 3: Parts View and Turret Template

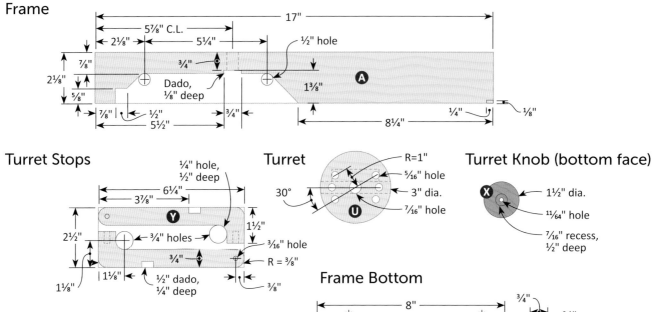

Frame

Turret Stops

Turret

Turret Knob (bottom face)

Rear Wheel Pivot

Frame Bottom

Stretcher

along each corner. Also check that the cab assembly fits snugly over the frame (A) and frame bottom (F). Glue and clamp the cab assembly together keeping the top and bottom ends flush.

8 To form the rounded-over cab corner (L), cut a piece of ¾" walnut to 2" wide by 11" long. Rout a ¼" round-over along two edges of the blank. At your tablesaw, rip two corner pieces for (L) from the blank. Crosscut four cab corners to length, and then glue them in place, as shown Photo C.

9 Drill the mounting holes, and screw the cab assembly to the assembled frame (A), as shown in Photo D.

Align the quarter-round cab corners with the ends of the cab, and then glue and clamp them into the cab's rabbets.

Position the cab assembly on the frame, and screw it in place.

Assemble the motor

1 Cut the motor's grill (N), sides (O), and top (P) to size, as shown in Figure 5 and noted on the Cut List.

2 To cut the grill kerfs, install a zero-clearance insert in your tablesaw, and raise the blade ⅛" above the table. Lay out the kerf locations shown on Figure 5 (page 110), keeping in mind you'll trim the top end of the grill when bandsawing the motor top to shape in Step 3. Cut the kerfs in the grill.

3 Dry-clamp the motor assembly (N, O, P) and test-fit it on the frame. Adjust if necessary; then glue and clamp the motor assembly together. Mark the tapered cutline and bandsaw the top rear of the motor to shape. Glue and screw the motor to the frame and cab.

4 Mark the cutline, and cut the bottom front corners of the cab flush with the tapered front edge of the frame (A), as shown in Photo E (page 110). Sand smooth.

10 Cut the cab top (M) to size. Rout a ⅛" round-over on all edges. Drill a pair of ¹¹⁄₃₂" holes for the lights in the front and back edges. Finish-sand the cab and add the lights. Set the top aside; we'll add it later.

Figure 4: Cab Exploded View

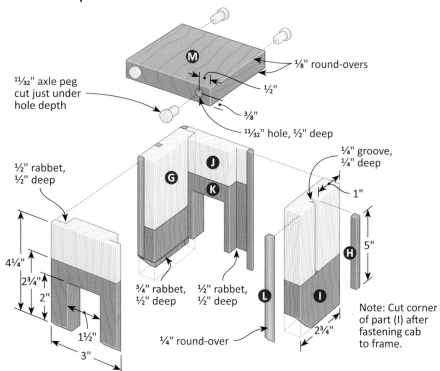

¹¹⁄₃₂" axle peg cut just under hole depth

⅛" round-overs

½"

³⁄₈"

¹¹⁄₃₂" hole, ½" deep

¼" groove, ¼" deep

1"

5"

½" rabbet, ½" deep

4¼"

2¾"

2"

1½"

3"

¾" rabbet, ½" deep

½" rabbet, ½" deep

¼" round-over

2¾"

Note: Cut corner of part (I) after fastening cab to frame.

Add the axle supports

1 Cut the front and rear axle supports (Q, R) to size from ¾" stock. Bevel-cut or sand the bottom edges at 45°. Secure the pieces to the fence with stops, and drill ¹¹⁄₃₂" axle holes in each support to the depth shown in Figure 1 and in Photo F.

2 Use an axle peg to pin the front axle support (Q) to the frame assembly. Glue and screw the rear support (R) to the bottom of the frame bottom (F).

3 Cut the rear wheel pivots (S) to size. Mark the three centered ¹¹⁄₃₂" peg holes and ½" radii, where shown in Figure 3. Drill the peg holes, and then cut and sand the radii to shape. Add the finish to the rear wheel pivots, and set aside to add later.

Make and install the tires

1 To make the 3"-diameter tire halves for the six grader tires (T), extra halves for testing setups, and the two kerfing templates, lay out eight centerpoints on each of two ½ × 4 × 28" maple blanks.

2 Insert a ⅜" brad-point bit in your drill press, adjust the fence to center the bit on the centerpoints, and drill ¼"-deep starter holes at seven centerpoints in one of the maple blanks. These will become the outside faces of the inside tire halves. Switch to a 1½" Forstner bit, and bore a ¼"-deep recess at seven centerpoints in the other maple blank. These will become the outside faces of the outside tire halves.

3 Next, switch to a circle cutter adjusted to make a 3"-diameter cut. (Orient the cutter's bevel to face away from the center; the point of the cutter should be on the inside). Adjust the fence on your drill press, and clamp a maple blank to the fence. Then, using a slow speed for safety (about 300 rpm), cut through the centerpoints of each

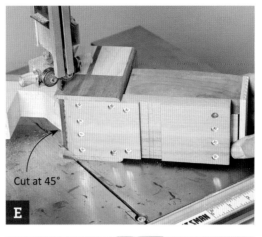

Bandsaw the bottom front corners of the cab flush with the beveled front end of the frame.

Cut at 45°

E

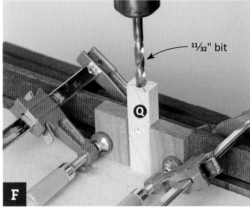

¹¹⁄₃₂" bit

Q

F

With the workpiece held vertically to the fence, drill into both ends of the axle supports for the axle pegs.

Figure 5: Motor Exploded View

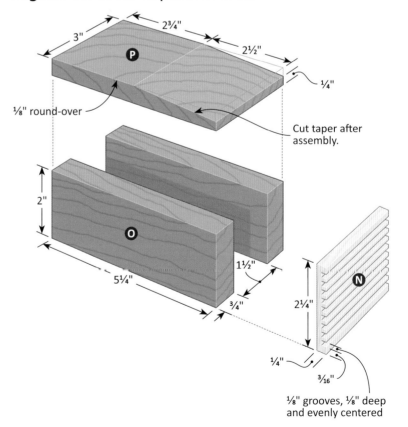

3"
2¾"
2½"
¼"
P
⅛" round-over
Cut taper after assembly.
2"
O
1½"
5¼"
¾"
2¼"
¼"
³⁄₁₆"
N
⅛" grooves, ⅛" deep and evenly centered

Use a slow rpm to cut out the tire halves with a circle cutter at the drill press.

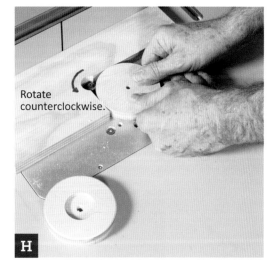

Rotate counterclockwise.

Fit a tire half in the L-shaped jig, and round over the outside edge, rotating it against the bit's bearing.

5 Make and clamp the drilling jig in Figure 6 (page 112) to the drill-press table and drill a ¼" hole. Insert a ¼"-diameter dowel to act as a centering pin.

6 Chuck a ³⁄₁₆" bit into the drill press and reposition the jig so the ³⁄₁₆" bit is 1" from the center of the centering pin. Position a tire half on the centering pin with the rounded outside edge down, and drill a ³⁄₁₆"-deep hole. Repeat for all tire halves and the two kerfing templates.

7 Divide the 12 tire halves into two groups: one for the left tire halves and one for the right tire halves. Each group will have three tire halves with the 1½" recess cut in them and three without. Mark and keep the tire halves in separate groups to avoid confusion.

8 Next, make two copies of the Kerfing Pattern shown in Figure 6. Cut out the patterns, and glue one to the face of each kerfing template, making sure the kerfing pattern is on the face opposite the ³⁄₁₆" hole. Highlight two adjacent lines on the paper kerfing pattern indicating a starting and stopping point for cutting the kerfs in the kerfing template. Insert a ³⁄₁₆" dowel ³⁄₈" long into both kerfing templates in the hole on the back side.

9 Make the kerf-cutting jig shown in Figure 6. Mark an alignment line on the front face, and drill a ¼" hole through the line. Insert a ¼"-diameter dowel 1" long into the ¼" hole. Install a ¼" dado set, and raise it to cut ³⁄₁₆" deep. Adjust the miter gauge to 60° to the right for the first group of wheel halves. Screw an auxiliary extension to your miter gauge. Clamp the Kerf-Cutting Jig to the miter-gauge extension, adjusting the jig so the left side of the dado blade aligns with the alignment line.

10 Place one of the kerfing templates on the jig's ¼" dowel. Position a test tire

maple blank, as shown in Photo G, creating 16 discs. As you cut, you will be drilling a centered ¼" axle hole at the same time. The two discs that were not predrilled will be used for the kerfing templates for kerfing the tire halves.

4 Install a ⅛" round-over bit in the router table. Then make a simple L-jig out of ¾" scrap, drilling a 1" hole in the jig's inside corner. Secure the jig to the table with double-faced tape, locating the bearing at the jig's inside corner. With the 14 tire halves and test pieces placed outside face down, round over the outside edges, rotating them as shown in Photo H.

Figure 6: Tire Kerfing Jigs

Kerfing Full-Sized Pattern (2 copies needed)

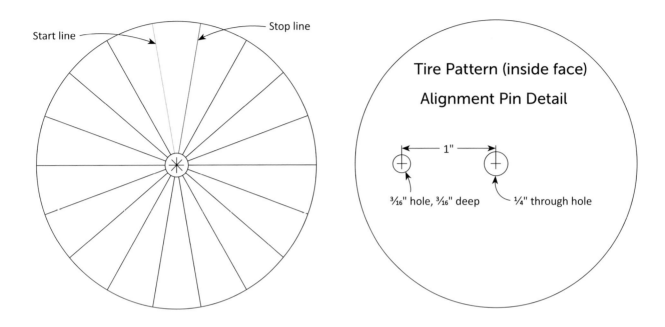

Kerf-Cutting Jig

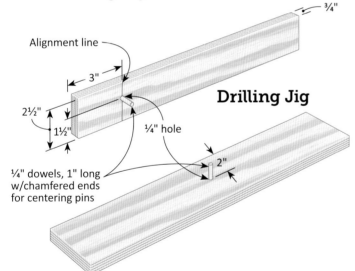

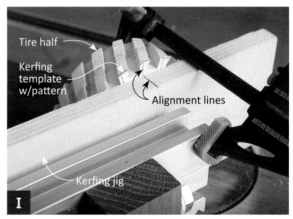

I

Align the kerfing template with the alignment line on the kerf-cutting jig.

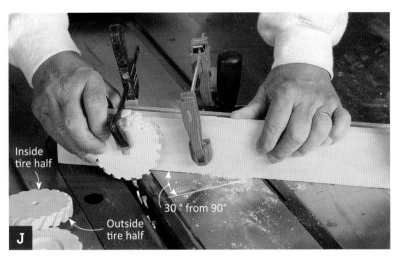

With the miter gauge adjusted to 60°, dado-cut the treads in the tire halves.

With the miter gauge adjusted to 60° in the opposite direction of Photo J, dado-cut the treads in the tire halves.

half with the alignment pin of the kerfing template engaged into the ³⁄₁₆" hole on the tire half. Align one of the highlighted lines on the paper pattern with the alignment line on the Kerf-Cutting Jig as shown in Photo I. Use a small clamp to hold the two pieces to the miter-gauge extension. Turn on the saw and cut the tire tread. Repeat by rotating and aligning the kerfing template lines and tire half for each kerf cut, making the final cut at the other highlighted line. Check the tread. The kerfs should be evenly spaced.

11 Finish cutting the first tire group, as shown in Photo J. To do this, remove the tire half (but not the kerfing template), and repeat the kerf cutting process with the remaining first group tire halves.

12 Remove the Kerf-Cutting Jig from the miter-gauge extension. Reposition the miter gauge to 60° in the opposite direction, as shown in Photo K. Clamp the Kerf-Cutting Jig to the miter-gauge extension, adjusting the jig so the right side of the dado blade aligns with the alignment line. Position the other kerfing template, as described in Step 9. Make the tread cuts, repeating the process with the tire halves from the second group.

13 To bond the tire halves together, select one with the 1½" recess from the first group and glue it to a non-recessed tire from the other group. To eliminate squeeze-out on the treads, spread glue sparingly on the inside (unrounded) faces. Next, insert a ¼ × 3" bolt through a washer, the hole in the tires halves, a second washer, and tighten the halves together with a nut, as shown in Photo L (page 114). (Doing this keeps the halves flush.) As you tighten, adjust the halves to create an offset V-tread pattern. Similarly, glue and clamp the remaining tire halves, resulting in three left-hand and three right-hand tires.

14 After the glue dries, install the bolt of a tire assembly into the drill-press chuck. Turn on the drill press and sand away any burn marks on a tire (T), using a sanding block with 80-grit sandpaper. Finish-sand to 220 grit. Repeat for the remaining tires.

15 Install a ³⁄₈" brad-point bit in the drill press. Using the tool's fence and a stopblock, clamp the tire to the fence, inserting the drill bit into the tire's ³⁄₈" starter hole. Redrill the hole so an axle peg can slip through it. Repeat for the remaining tires, and apply the finish.

Create the adjustable blade assembly

1 Referring to Figures 2 and 3, lay out the turret (U) shape and hole locations. Drill the ⁵⁄₁₆" and ½" holes. Cut the turret to shape.

2 From ⁷⁄₁₆" dowel stock, crosscut the blade rotation pin to 4¾" long. Glue the rotation pin to the turret.

3 Cut the blade (V) and blade support (W) to size. These will be added later.

4 Bandsaw or scrollsaw the rotation knob (X) to shape, and drill a centered ⁷⁄₁₆" hole ½" deep on its bottom side. Then, drill an ¹¹⁄₆₄" shank hole centered inside the ⁷⁄₁₆" hole. Glue the turret (U) to the pin. Slide the pin through the ½" hole in the frame.

5 Cut a pair of turret stops (Y) to shape. Drill a ¼" hole ½" deep in each. Then drill the screw shank holes. The screw shank holes in the turret stops are slightly oversized to allow the turret stops to be adjusted over the holes in the turret. Inset a locking pin (¼" dowel ¾" long) into the hole in each turret stop. Cut the stretcher (Z) to shape. Position and clamp the turret stops against the frame assembly by inserting the locking pins into the center outside holes of the turret (U), as shown in Photo M. Using the holes in the turret stops as guides, drill ⁷⁄₆₄" pilot holes into the frame for the two screws. Screw the turret stops to the frame, so that they can move freely.

6 Center and glue the stretcher (Z) to the two turret stops. Center and glue the blade (V) and blade support (W) to the turret (U). Glue and screw the knob (X) on the top end of the rotation pin.

L

Use a pair of wrenches to tighten the nut and washers on the glued-up tire halves. Make sure the treads create an offset pattern.

M

Screw the turret stops to the frame so the turret stops can move up and down freely.

Complete the assembly and add the finish

1 Glue and clamp the cab top (M) to the cab assembly. Add the lights to the front of the frame assembly.

2 Finish-sand all the parts and assemblies to 220 grit. Wipe clean, and apply finish—a satin laquer works well) to the assemblies and unassembled parts. Apply finish to just the exposed ends (not the shanks) of the axle parts. Let the finish dry.

3 Orient the left and right tires (T) so the recessed faces are on the outside, as shown in Figure 1. Place a small amount of glue in the axle peg holes, and then push the axle pegs through the front tires, a nylon washer, and into the front axle support (Q), leaving a clearance equal to the thickness of a business card for the tires to turn freely.

4 Attach the rear tires (T) to the rear wheel pivots (S) with axle pegs through nylon washers. Flush-trim the axle pegs after attaching to the rear wheel pivots. Attach the rear wheel pivots to the rear axle support (R) with axle pegs through nylon washers.

Cut List: Road Grader

	Part	Thickness	Width	Length	Qty.	Mat'l
A	Frame	1½"	2⅛"	17"	1	M
B	Blade pivot	¾"	1½"	2⅛"	1	M
C	Axle support	½"	1½"	2"	1	M
D	Front	¾"	1½"	4¼"	1	M
E	Frame top	¾"	1½"	8½"	1	W
F	Frame bottom	¾"	3"	8"	1	W
G*	Cab side windows	¾"	2¾"	3"	2	M
H*	Window dividers	¼"	¼"	3"	2	W
I*	Cab side bottoms	¾"	2¾"	2"	2	W
J*	Cab end windows	¾"	3"	1½"	2	M
K*	Cab end bottoms	¾"	3"	2¾"	2	W
L*	Cab corners	¼"	¼"	5"	4	W
M	Cab top	¾"	4"	3¾"	1	W
N	Grill	¼"	2¼"	3"	1	M
O	Sides	¾"	2"	5¼"	2	W
P	Top	½"	3"	5¼"	1	W
Q	Front axle support	¾"	1"	4½"	1	M
R	Rear axle support	¾"	1"	3½"	1	M
S	Rear wheel pivots	½"	1"	4¾"	2	M
T**	Tires	1"	3" dia.		6	M
U	Turret	½"	3" dia.		1	M
V	Blade	½"	1⅛"	8¾"	1	M
W	Blade support	½"	¾"	2"	1	M
X	Rotation knob	¾"	1½" dia.		1	W
Y*	Turret stops	½"	1½"	6¼"	2	M
Z	Stretcher	¼"	½"	4"	1	M

* Indicates parts initially cut oversized. See instructions.
** Indicates tires are made up of two opposing halves. See instructions.
Materials: M=Maple, W=Walnut
Hardware/Supplies: (8) ⅜" nylon washers; (3) #6 × 1" roundhead screws; (2) #6 × 1¼" flathead screws; (2) #6 × 2" flathead screws; (15) #8 × 1¼" flathead screws; ⅛" dowel stock; 3/16" dowel; ¼" dowel; 7/16" dowel.

BULLDOZER

Build an earth-moving playtime favorite

BY TOM WHALLEY AND MARLEN KEMMET

Whether pushing sand in the sandbox or blocks across the playroom floor, this mighty mover does it all. A lifting blade allows for easier maneuvering and the realistic treads lay down tracks just like the real ones. Expect to work with a lot of small parts. That means extra caution is in order. We'll walk you through the part making and assemblies one step at a time.

Note: For the tread, we used ½"-wide tanned and oiled Latigo leather purchased online. It's supple and ideally suited for outdoor uses such as saddle parts.

Start with the frame and motor

1 Laminate two pieces of ¾ × 1¾ × 12" maple together face-to-face to form a blank for the frame (A). Now, joint, rip, and crosscut the part to 1½ × 1⅜ × 10½". (See Figure 1 on page 118 for reference.)

2 Cut the motor sides (B), hood (C), and grill (D) to the sizes in the Cut List (page 127). We used a miter gauge, auxiliary fence, and stopblock, starting with extra long stock for safe cutting.

3 To cut the grill grooves, install a flat-top blade and a zero-clearance insert (ZCI) in

your tablesaw, along with an auxillary fence and miter gauge. Raise the blade ⅛" above the saw table. Lay out the groove locations (Figure 2; page 119), and cut the grooves.

4 Drill a pair of ⁷⁄₃₂" holes in the grill for adding the headlights.

5 Using double-faced tape, adhere the motor sides (B) inside face to inside face, and drill the ⁷⁄₁₆" and ³⁄₁₆" holes where shown on Figure 1 (page 118).

6 First dry-fit the motor assembly pieces (B, C, D), and then glue and clamp them

Position the motor assembly over the frame and screw it in place. Use a block of wood to ensure the bottom edges are flush.

Figure 1: Bulldozer Exploded View

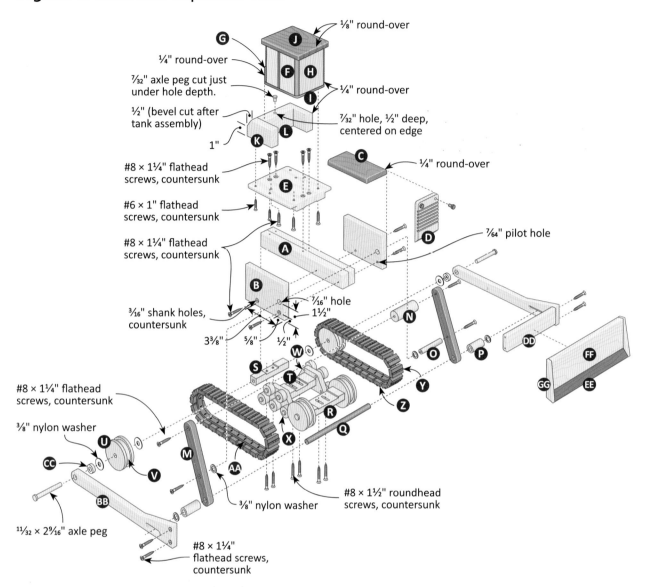

⅛" round-over

¼" round-over

⁷⁄₃₂" axle peg cut just under hole depth.

½" (bevel cut after tank assembly)

1"

⁷⁄₃₂" hole, ½" deep, centered on edge

¼" round-over

¼" round-over

⁷⁄₆₄" pilot hole

#8 × 1¼" flathead screws, countersunk

#6 × 1" flathead screws, countersunk

#8 × 1¼" flathead screws, countersunk

³⁄₁₆" shank holes, countersunk

⁷⁄₁₆" hole 1½"

3⅜"   ⅝"   ½"

#8 × 1¼" flathead screws, countersunk

⅜" nylon washer

¹¹⁄₃₂ × 2⁹⁄₁₆" axle peg

#8 × 1¼" flathead screws, countersunk

⅜" nylon washer

#8 × 1½" roundhead screws, countersunk

together with the edges flush. Rout a ¼" round-over along the top edges of the assembly (C, D). Bevel-rip the tapered bottom edge of the grill at 45° at the tablesaw.

7 Using the shank holes in the motor sides as guides, drill ⁷⁄₆₄" pilot holes into the sides of the frame. Screw the motor to the frame (Photo A; page 117).

8 Cut the platform (E) to size. Drill the 12 mounting holes where shown on Figure 2. Cut the centered groove and rabbets at the tablesaw where shown,

using a dado set, ZCI, and pushblock. Screw the platform to the top of the frame, flushing the back edges.

Add the cab and fuel tank

1 To form the cab sides (F), mill a piece of maple to ½ × 3⅝ × 8". To form the cab (window) dividers and cab corners (G), cut a ¼ × ¼ × 24"-long piece of walnut stock. To cut the cab front and back (H), mill a piece of maple stock to ½ × 3 × 8".

2 Referencing Figure 3 (page 120), cut a ¼" groove, ¼" deep, on one face of the blank

Figure 2: Parts View

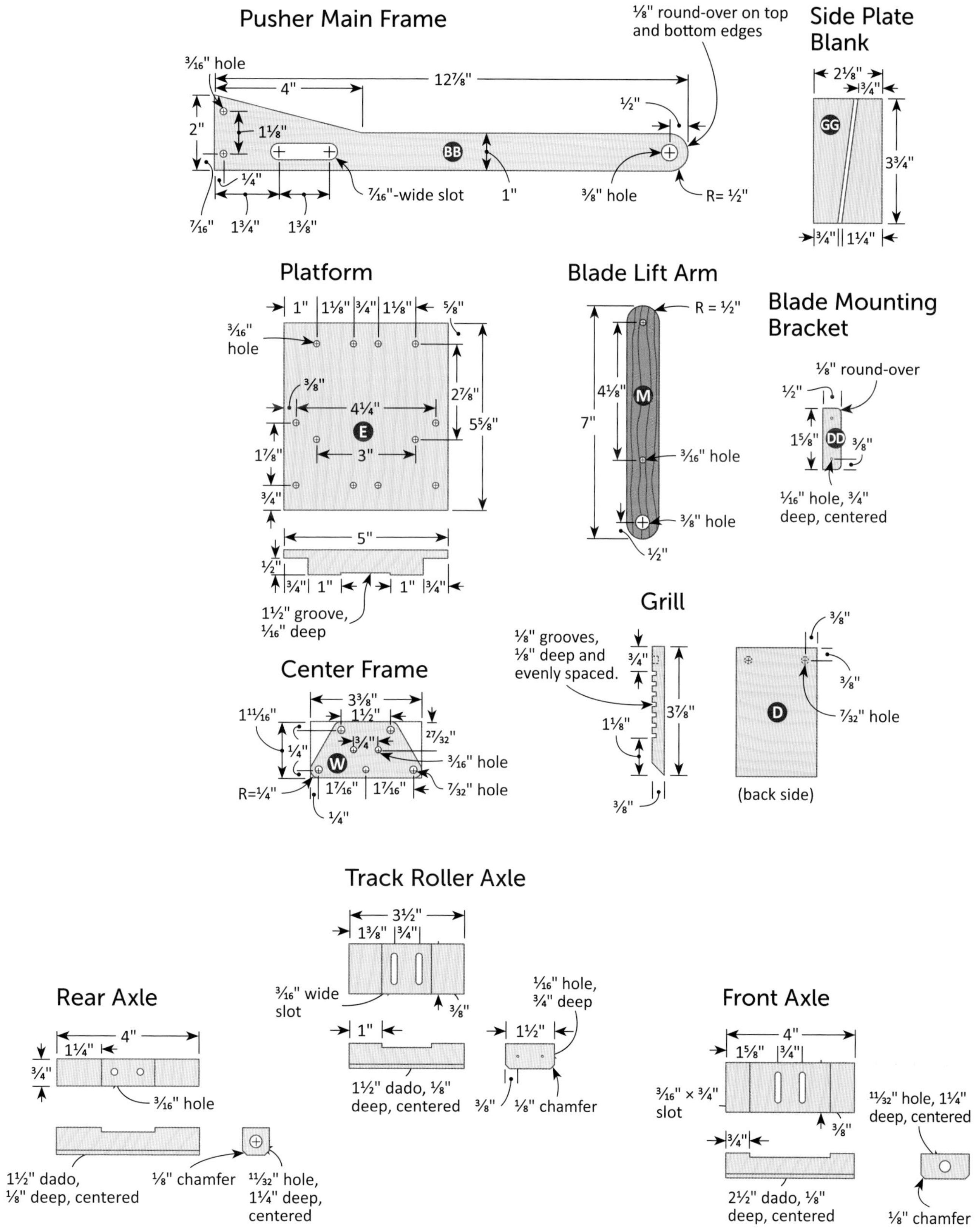
Pusher Main Frame
3/16" hole
12 7/8"
4"
2"
1 1/8"
1/4"
7/16"
1 3/4"
1 3/8"
7/16"-wide slot
1"
3/8" hole
R= 1/2"
1/2"
1/8" round-over on top and bottom edges
BB
Side Plate Blank
2 1/8"
3/4"
3 3/4"
3/4"
1 1/4"
GG
Platform
1"
1 1/8"
3/4"
1 1/8"
5/8"
3/16" hole
3/8"
4 1/4"
2 7/8"
5 5/8"
1 7/8"
3"
3/4"
E
5"
1/2"
3/4"
1"
1"
3/4"
1 1/2" groove, 1/16" deep
Blade Lift Arm
R = 1/2"
4 1/8"
7"
M
3/16" hole
3/8" hole
1/2"
Blade Mounting Bracket
1/8" round-over
1/2"
1 5/8"
DD
3/8"
1/16" hole, 3/4" deep, centered
Center Frame
3 3/8"
1 1/2"
1 11/16"
27/32"
3/4"
1/4"
W
3/16" hole
R=1/4"
1 7/16"
1 7/16"
7/32" hole
1/4"
Grill
1/8" grooves, 1/8" deep and evenly spaced.
3/4"
3 7/8"
1 1/8"
3/8"
3/8"
3/8"
D
7/32" hole
(back side)
Track Roller Axle
3 1/2"
1 3/8"
3/4"
3/16" wide slot
3/8"
1"
1 1/2" dado, 1/8" deep, centered
1 1/2"
1/16" hole, 3/4" deep
3/8"
1/8" chamfer
Rear Axle
4"
1 1/4"
3/4"
3/16" hole
1 1/2" dado, 1/8" deep, centered
1/8" chamfer
11/32" hole, 1 1/4" deep, centered
Front Axle
4"
1 5/8"
3/4"
3/16" × 3/4" slot
3/8"
3/4"
2 1/2" dado, 1/8" deep, centered
11/32" hole, 1 1/4" deep, centered
1/8" chamfer

B

Glue and clamp the cab corners into the rabbets, holding them snugly in place with spring clamps.

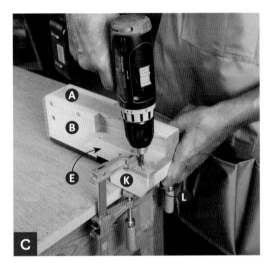

C

Fit the fuel tank assembly onto the platform and flush at the rear end. Screw it in place.

D

Screw the blade lift arm to the pivot pin through the motor assembly.

Figure 3: Cab Exploded View

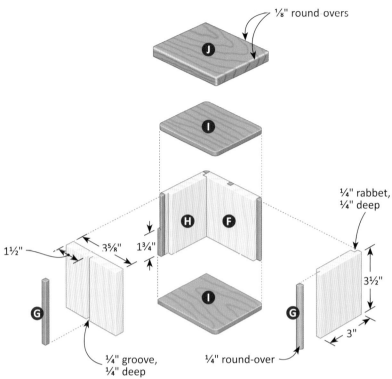

⅛" round-overs

¼" rabbet, ¼" deep

3½"

3"

¼" round-over

1½"   3⅝"   1¾"

¼" groove, ¼" deep

for the cab sides (F). Cut the ¼" rabbets, ¼" deep on the cab front and back (H).

3 Crosscut an 8"-long piece from the dividers and corner blank for parts (G) and glue it in the groove in the cab sides (F) blank. Crosscut two cab sides (F/G) to length from the blank. Cut the remaining walnut stock for the cab corners (G) to 3½". Crosscut the cab front and back blank for (H) to 3½". Now, glue and clamp the assembly together (F, G, H) in the configuration shown in Figure 3 and Photo B. Make sure that the groove is 1½" from the assembly's back side.

4 From ¼"-thick walnut, cut the cab top and bottom (I) to size. Glue these pieces to the cab assembly. Rout ¼" round-overs on the cab where shown. Note where the rear cab corners (G) are not rounded over to accommodate the fuel assembly. Cut the cab roof (J) to size, and rout ⅛" round-overs along all edges.

Figure 4: Axle Assemblies

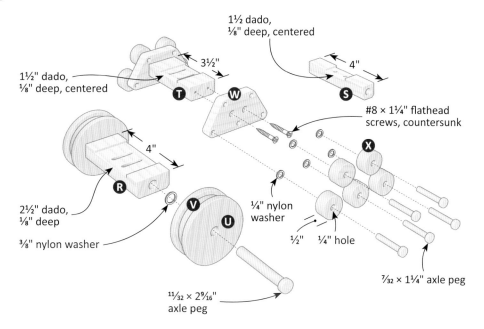

1½ dado, ⅛" deep, centered

1½" dado, ⅛" deep, centered

3½"

4"

4"

#8 × 1¼" flathead screws, countersunk

2½" dado, ⅛" deep

¼" nylon washer

⅜" nylon washer

½"   ¼" hole

⁷⁄₃₂ × 1¼" axle peg

¹¹⁄₃₂ × 2⁹⁄₁₆" axle peg

5 Cut the fuel tank sides (K) and back (L) to size, cutting the length of L to the same width as the assembled cab. (I laminated ¾"-thick stock for the back tank.) Glue-join the parts and let them setup. Then, bevel-cut the top back edge of the assembled tank at the tablesaw using a pushblock. Drill a ⁷⁄₃₂" hole in the back (L) for adding the fuel cap later. At the router table, rout ⅛" round-overs, where shown on Figure 1 (page 118). Edges that touch the cab assembly or platform do not get round-overs. Screw the fuel tank to the platform (Photo C).

6 Finish-sand and apply finish to the frame assembly (A-E, K, L). (We sprayed on Watco Lacquer, Satin.)

7 Center, glue, and clamp the roof (J) to the cab assembly (F-I). Finish-sand the assembly. Screw the cab assembly (F-J) to the platform (E). Sand a ⅛" round-over on the back two corners of the platform to match the fuel tank assembly. Note that the fuel tank fits flush with the end of the platform. Apply finish.

QUICK TIP

After assembling the cab, we taped a sheet of 120-grit sandpaper to a flat surface and rubbed the top and bottom of the assembly on it to even the edges and remove glue squeeze-out.

Build the blade lift assembly

1 Cut the two blade lift arms (M) to the shape shown in Figure 2. Mark the three hole centerpoints on each and drill the holes.

2 Cut the handle (N) and pivot pin (O) to length from dowel stock noted in the Cut List. Drill a ¹⁄₁₆" pilot hole centered in each end of each dowel. (We used a center finder.) Glue and screw the handle and pivot pin to one of the lift arms (M). Apply a finish.

3 Cut the two front spacers (P) from ¾" walnut dowel stock. Drill a ⁷⁄₁₆" hole centered through each. Cut the lift pin (Q) to size from ⅜" dowel stock. Apply finish to the remaining parts (M, P, Q).

4 Slide the lift pin (Q) through the blade lift arms (M). Fit the front spacers (P) onto the ends of the lift pin.

5 Fit a ⅜" nylon washer onto the pivot pin (O). Position the blade lift assembly onto the motor by sliding the pivot pin through the holes in the motor assembly. Fit a nylon washer onto the opposite end of the pivot pin. Screw the remaining blade lift arm (M) to the handle (N) and pivot pin (Photo D).

Cut the axle parts

1 From ¾"-thick maple, cut the front axle (R), rear axle (S), and track roller axle (T) to size. Cut a ⅛"-deep dado in each where shown on Figure 2 (page 119).

2 Mark the locations and cut the adjustment slots and holes in each axle part (R, S, T) to shape. I drilled ³⁄₁₆" holes at each end of each marked slot and scrollsawed the waste between the holes. Sand a slight chamfer on the bottom edges of R, S, T.

3 Mark the locations and drill the axle-peg holes in R and S and a pair of pilot holes in both ends of T.

4 To make the eight 2⁹⁄₁₆"-diameter outer wheels (U), cut a 3½ × 30" blank from ¼" maple. Mark the centerpoints for the eight wheels on the blank. Insert a ⅜" brad-point bit in your drill press, adjust the fence to center the bit on the centerpoints and drill ⅛"-deep starter holes in four of the eight centerpoints. These will become the outer faces of the wheel assemblies. Using a 2¾"-diameter holesaw on your drill press, cut the eight outer wheels to shape.

5 To make the four 2³⁄₁₆"-diameter inner wheels (V), cut a 3 × 15" blank from ⁹⁄₁₆"-thick maple. Mark the centerpoints for the four inner wheels on the blank. Using a 2⅜"-diameter holesaw, cut the four inner wheels to shape.

6 To bond an inner wheel (V) between two outer wheels (U), select one outer wheel with a ⅛" recess and glue it to an inner wheel. Add a non-recessed outer wheel to the other side of the inner wheel. You don't want glue squeeze-out at the joint lines so use a minimal amount of glue. Next, insert a ¼ × 2" bolt through a washer, the hole in the wheels, through a second washer, and tighten the three pieces together with a nut. Repeat for the other three wheel assemblies.

7 Install a ⅜" brad-point bit in the drill press. Using the tool's fence and a stopblock, clamp the wheel to the fence, inserting the drill bit into the wheel's ⅜" starter hole. Redrill the hole so an axle peg can slip through it. Repeat for the remaining wheels, and apply the finish.

8 Cut the center frames (W) to shape. Drill five axle peg holes and two screw shank holes in each, where shown on Figure 2.

9 Working with 1" maple dowel stock, bandsaw the 10 track rollers (X) to ½" thick. Now, drill a centered ¼" hole in each roller. Sand to remove any bandsaw marks.

10 Using the configuration shown on Figure 4 (page 121), assemble the front axle assembly (R, U, V) and the track roller assembly (T, W, X) with axle pegs, screws, and nylon washers.

Construct the tracks

1 From ½" walnut stock, cut the track shoe blank (Y) to 3" wide by 22" long.

2 To cut evenly spaced kerfs, make an auxiliary miter-gauge fence with a protruding ⅛ × ⅛" finger ¾" from the blade. (We used the flat-top blade.) Use scrap stock to verify that the kerfs are cut exactly ¾" apart. Cut extra scrap to verify the test cuts in Step 3. Now, cut ⅛" kerfs, ⅜" deep and ¾" apart, along the entire length of the blank. See Figure 5A.

3 Lower the blade for a ¹⁄₁₆"-deep cut. Slide the auxiliary fence over so that the ¹⁄₁₆" kerfs to be cut for receiving the cleats (Z) will be accurately centered between two ⅜" deep kerfs. Now, using the test pieces made in Step 2, cut ⅛" kerfs, ¹⁄₁₆" deep. Verify and cut the kerfs in the track shoe blank, as shown in Photo E (page 124).

4 Cut enough ⅛ × ⅛" walnut for the 24 cleats (Z). Now, at the bandsaw, crosscut

Figure 5A: Track Shoe Blank Cutting Sequence

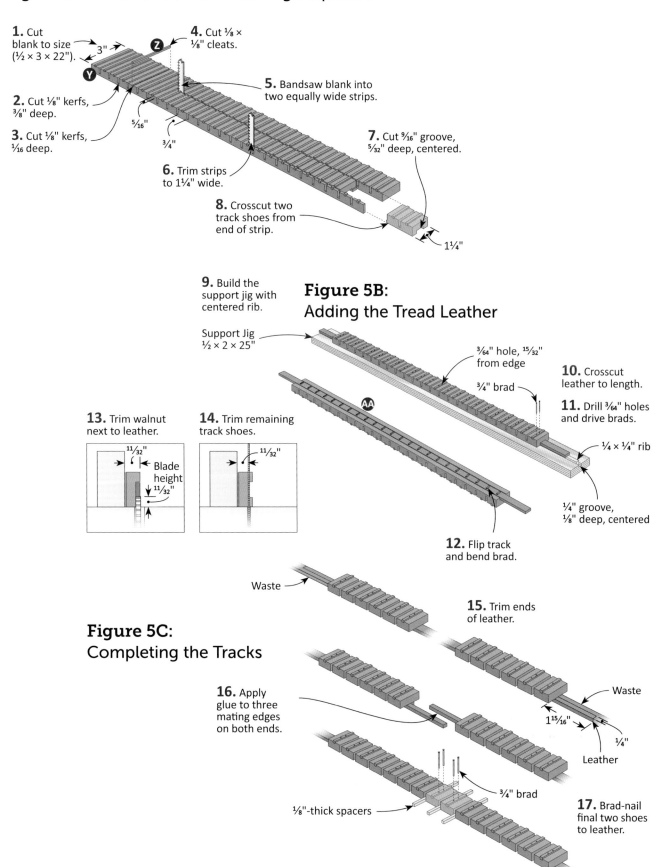

1. Cut blank to size (½ × 3 × 22").
3"

Z

4. Cut ⅛ × ⅛" cleats.

Y

2. Cut ⅛" kerfs, ⅜" deep.

5. Bandsaw blank into two equally wide strips.

5⁄16"

3. Cut ⅛" kerfs, ⅟16 deep.

¾"

7. Cut 9⁄16" groove, 5⁄32" deep, centered.

6. Trim strips to 1¼" wide.

8. Crosscut two track shoes from end of strip.

1¼"

9. Build the support jig with centered rib.

Figure 5B: Adding the Tread Leather

Support Jig ½ × 2 × 25"

3⁄64" hole, 15⁄32" from edge

¾" brad

10. Crosscut leather to length.

11. Drill 3⁄64" holes and drive brads.

AA

¼ × ¼" rib

¼" groove, ⅛" deep, centered

12. Flip track and bend brad.

13. Trim walnut next to leather.

11⁄32"

Blade height

11⁄32"

14. Trim remaining track shoes.

11⁄32"

Waste

15. Trim ends of leather.

Figure 5C: Completing the Tracks

16. Apply glue to three mating edges on both ends.

Waste

1¹⁵⁄16"

¼"

Leather

⅛"-thick spacers

¾" brad

17. Brad-nail final two shoes to leather.

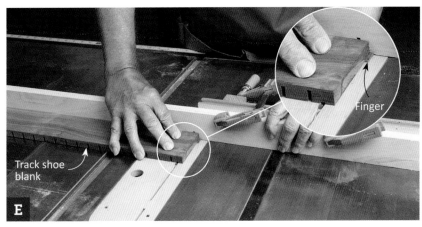

At your tablesaw, use an auxiliary miter-gauge fence and protruding $1/8 \times 1/16$" finger to cut evenly spaced kerfs for the cleats (Z).

Drive brads through the $3/64$" holes and alongside the support strip.

Bend the brads over to secure the treads to the leather strip.

Use a pushblock and sideblock to support the long track shoe strip when cutting.

the cleats to 3", and glue them into the $1/16$"-deep kerfs. Remove any glue squeeze-out.

5 Bandsaw two equally wide strips from the 3"-wide blank, using a fence to ensure accuracy.

6 Bandsaw each strip to $1\frac{1}{4}$" wide, trimming the edges opposite the bandsawn edges from Step 5. Sand the edges of both strips smooth to remove the saw marks.

7 Cut a $9/16$" groove, $5/32$" deep, down the center of each $1\frac{1}{4}$"-wide strip.

8 Drill two rows of $3/64$" holes through the center of each cleat (Z) $15/32$" from the edge of the tread blank. Bandsaw two track shoes from the end of each strip.

9 Cut the support jig base to the size shown on Figure 5B (page 123). Cut a $1/4$"

groove, $1/8$" deep, down the center of the support. Cut a $1/4 \times 1/4$" rib to fit into the groove. Glue the rib in place.

10 Using a sharp utility knife, crosscut two pieces of $1/2$"-wide leather to 24" long for the tread leather (AA).

11 Center the trimmed track shoe blank (Y) onto the leather strip (AA). Using $3/4$" brads, drive a brad through each hole to securely nail the track to the leather strip (Photo F).

12 Flip the track assembly over and bend the brads toward the center of the track (Photo G). Lightly pound the bent ends flat into the leather.

13 Set the saw blade height to cut along the bottom edge of the leather, but not into the leather, to create the track shoes (Photo H).

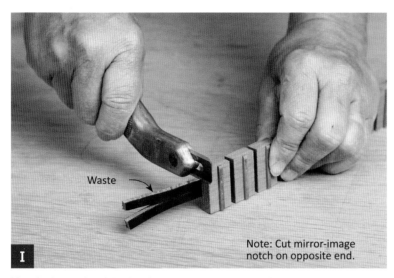

Waste

Note: Cut mirror-image notch on opposite end.

I

Notch the ends of the leather strip to mate together.

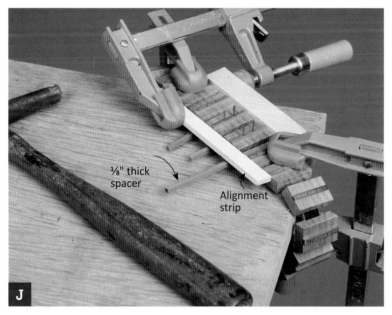

⅛" thick spacer

Alignment strip

J

Using spacers and edge guides, brad the final two tracks to the leather strip.

14 Bandsaw the final four track shoes from the piece cut in Step 8.

15 Using a sharp utility or razor knife, split then notch the mating ends on the leather strip nailed to the walnut tracks, as shown in Figure 5C and Photo I. Note that the notches are mirror images of each other.

16 Using Tanner's Bond Craftsmen Contact Cement, adhere the two mating ends of the leather together using small clamps. Allow the glue to get tacky.

17 Using ⅛"-thick spacers for even tread placement, brad the two remaining track shoes over the notched leather ends (Photo J). Clinch the ends as before.

Blade lift arm

1 Cut the pusher main frames (BB) to shape (Figure 2; page 119). Mark the ⁷⁄₁₆"-wide slot locations, drill holes at each slot end, and cut out the waste at a scrollsaw. Now, drill a ⁷⁄₁₆" axle peg hole and the ³⁄₁₆" shank holes in each. Rout a ⅛" round-over on all but the front edges of BB.

2 From ¾" maple dowel, crosscut the rear spacers (CC) to ¼" thick, and drill a ³⁄₈" hole centered in each (Figure 1; page 118).

3 Cut the blade-mounting bracket (DD) to size. Rout an ⅛" round-over on the top and bottom inside edges. Clamp that part between the main frames (BB), centered top to bottom with the front edges flush. Use the shank holes in each BB to drill mating pilot holes in each end of DD. Part AD will be added later.

4 Finish-sand (BB) and (DD). Apply finish to all but the front surfaces of (BB) and (DD) where the blade will attach later.

Create the blade

1 Cut the blade bottom blank (EE) and blade blank (FF) to the sizes noted in the Cut List and shown in Figure 6 (page 126), bevel-ripping one edge of EE where shown. Glue the two pieces together.

2 Bevel-cut the ends of the blade assembly (EE, FF) at 15°. Cut the side plate blanks (GG) to size (Figure 2). Glue one to each end of the blade assembly. Sand the side plates flush with the front and back of the blade. Finish-sand the blade assembly.

Figure 6: Blade Assembly

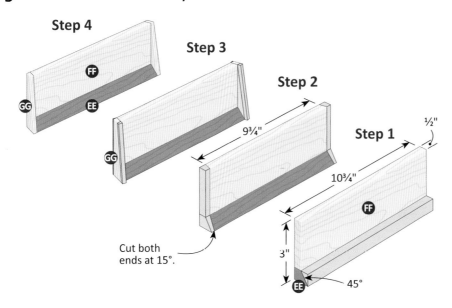

Step 4

FF
GG
EE

Step 3

9¾"
GG

Step 2

10¾"
FF

Cut both
ends at 15°.

½"

Step 1

3"
EE
45°

Final assembly

1 Position the bulldozer upside down on a soft cloth on your workbench to prevent scratching the cab top. Screw the rear axle (S) to the frame bottom ¼" from the back end.

2 Position, but don't screw, the track roller assembly (T, W, X) and front axle assembly (R, U, V) on the frame. Place the two track assemblies over the front axle and track roller assemblies. Slide a ⅜" nylon washer onto each end of the lift pin (Q). Now, add the pusher main frame pieces (minus the blade mounting bracket [DD]) to the rear axle as shown in Figure 1 (page 118), gluing the axle pegs into the rear axle (S). I applied glue into the holes in the rear axles (S) with a cotton swab, making sure the wheel assemblies turned freely.

3 Snug the track assemblies to the front axle assembly (R, U, V) with a small clamp. Then, using the slots in the front axle assembly as guides, drill a pair of 7/64" pilot holes into the bottom of the frame, positioning the bit in the middle of each slot. Drive the two front screws as shown

K

With the tread tightened against the wheels, screw the front axle assembly to the frame bottom.

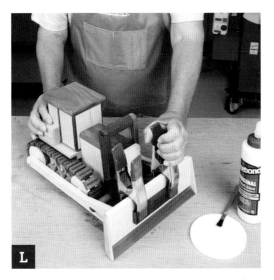

Spring clamps work well to clamp the blade to the blade mounting bracket.

L

(Photo K; page 126). Center the track roller assembly between the front and rear axle assemblies and screw it in place.

4 Screw the blade mounting bracket (DD) between the pusher main frames (BB).

5 With the blade lift assembly vertical, center and glue the blade assembly to the front of the main pusher frame (Photo L).

6 Mask off the front end of the bulldozer and apply finish to the blade. Let it dry and turn the toy over to the up-and-coming builder in the family.

Cut List: Bulldozer

	Part	Thickness	Width	Length	Qty.	Mat'l
A*	Frame	1½"	1⅜"	10⅜"	1	M
B	Motor sides	½"	3⅜"	4⅞"	2	M
C	Hood	½"	2½"	4⅞"	1	W
D	Grill	⅜"	3⅞"	2½"	1	M
E	Platform	¾"	5"	5⅝"	1	M
F *	Cab sides	½"	3⅝"	3½"	2	M
G *	Cab dividers/corners	¼"	¼"	3½"	6	W
H	Cab front and back	½"	3"	3½"	2	M
I	Cab top/bottom	¼"	3½"	4⅛"	2	W
J	Cab roof	½"	3⅞"	4⅝"	1	W
K	Side fuel tanks	¾"	1¾"	3¼"	2	M
L	Back fuel tank	1½"	1¾"	3½"	1	M
M	Blade lift arms	½"	1"	7"	2	W
N	Handle		1" dowel	2⅝"	1	W
O	Pivot pin		⅜" dowel	2⅝"	1	M
P	Front spacers		¾" dowel	1½"	2	W
Q	Lift pin		⅜" dowel	7¾"	1	W
R	Front axle	¾"	1½"	4"	1	M
S	Rear axle	¾"	¾"	4"	1	M
T	Track roller axle	¾"	1½"	3½"	1	M
U*	Wheel outer	¼"	2⁹⁄₁₆" dia.		8	M
V*	Wheel inner	⁹⁄₁₆"	2³⁄₁₆" dia.		4	M
W	Center frames	½"	11¹⁄₁₆"	3⅜"	2	M
X	Track rollers	½"	1" dowel		10	M
Y*	Track shoe blank	½"	3"	22"	1	W
Z	Cleat blanks	⅛"	⅛"	80"	1	W
AA	Tread leather	³⁄₁₆"	½"	24"	2	L
BB	Pusher main frames	½"	2"	12⅞"	2	M
CC	Rear spacers		¾" dowel	¼"	2	M
DD	Blade mounting bracket	½"	1⅝"	6¾"	1	M
EE	Blade bottom blank	¾"	1"	10¾"	1	W
FF	Blade blank	½"	3"	10¾"	1	M
GG *	Side plate blank	¼"	2⅛"	3¾"	1	M

* Indicates parts initially cut oversized. See instructions.
Materials: M=Maple, W=Walnut, L=Leather
Hardware/Supplies: (10) ¼" nylon washers; (10) ⅜" nylon washers; (20) #8 × 1¼" flathead screws; (6) #8 × 1½" roundhead screws; (96) ¾" brads; ⅜" maple dowel stock; ¾" maple dowel stock; ¾" walnut dowel stock; 1" maple dowel stock; 1" walnut dowel stock; 2⅜" holesaw; 2⁹⁄₁₆" holesaw; ⁹⁄₁₆ - 6" medium holesaw mandrel.

TUGBOAT

Get under way with this bandsaw-built telescoping toy

BY RIC HANISCH

When deciding on a toy to make for my grandson, I found myself considering the kind of "pop-up" construction used to manufacture spiral-cut Shaker baskets and the collapsible camping cup I had as a Boy Scout. The technique allows tapered telescoping pieces to lock in place when spread apart, and it worked well for making this toy boat. Although the project won't telescope after it's assembled, the tapered cuts are a quick and easy way to create a boat with curved parts that automatically fit into each other.

Building procedures and patterns are provided here for this specific design, but once you understand the approach, you can take the helm and get inventive. The trick to making any caricature like this is to observe and distill the characteristics that define the subject. For this project,

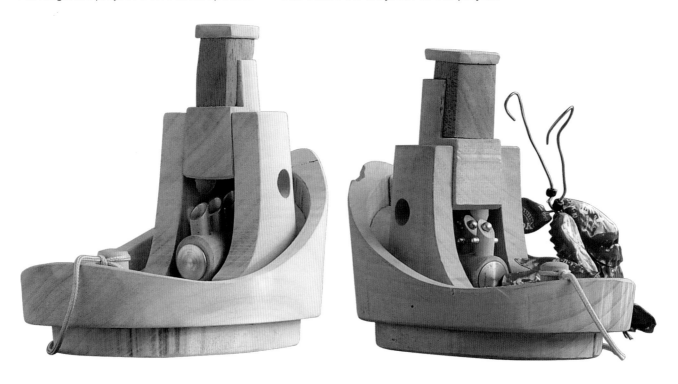

Figure 1: Tug Boat Sections

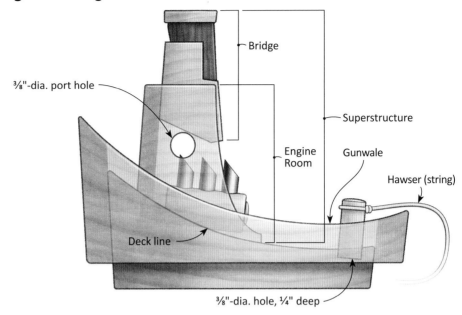

- Bridge
- ⅜"-dia. port hole
- Superstructure
- Engine Room
- Gunwale
- Hawser (string)
- Deck line
- ⅜"-dia. hole, ¼" deep

Wheelhouse Blank

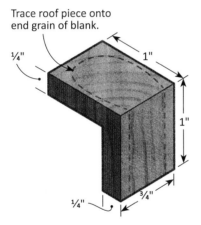

Trace roof piece onto end grain of blank.

¼"

1"

1"

¼"

¾"

Exploded View

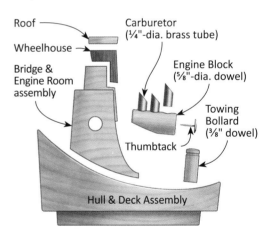

- Roof
- Carburetor (¼"-dia. brass tube)
- Wheelhouse
- Engine Block (⅝"-dia. dowel)
- Bridge & Engine Room assembly
- Towing Bollard (⅜" dowel)
- Thumbtack
- Hull & Deck Assembly

I studied various boats to identify the elements that said "tug," and then exaggerated the forms and curves to arrive at this design.

Creating the engine is particularly fun. Use a cartoonist's eye when looking through your miscellaneous parts boxes or the small parts drawers at the hardware store. Bits of tubing, odd washers, and doohickeys of uncertain provenance can suddenly become intake manifolds, nuclear fusion condensers, and carbuncle pumps!

This supercharged three-banger engine sports carburetors of brass tubing.

After adding any of your own refinements, such as capstans, winches, bumpers, ventilators, ladders, or perhaps a figurehead, it's time to release your tug from dry dock. However, note that this is a DL-class (dry land) tugboat. She'll float beautifully on hardwood harbors where a keel would just get in the way. In water, she'll capsize. Add a weighted keel and some marine varnish if you want a bathtub-worthy version.

Figure 2: Block Layout and Cutting Order

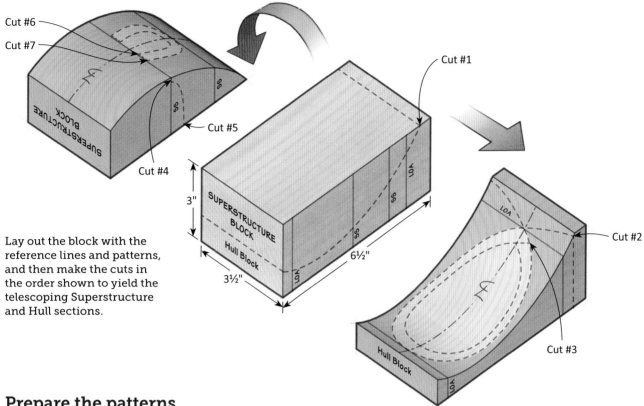

Lay out the block with the reference lines and patterns, and then make the cuts in the order shown to yield the telescoping Superstructure and Hull sections.

Prepare the patterns and block

1 Enlarge and copy the patterns on page 135, use spray adhesive to adhere them to manila folder stock, and then carefully knife them out.

2 Cut a block of wood to 3 × 3½ × 6½". I used poplar, but soft maple, clear pine, basswood, or other mild-grained wood that's not too dense will work well.

3 Place Pattern A (page 135) on a 3" side of your block, aligning the straight sides of the pattern flush with the top and end of the block. Now carefully trace along the gunwale curve while holding the pattern

Blades, Test Blocks, and Pop-Up Construction

Pop-up construction works because tapered telescoping parts lock up when slid apart a certain distance. That distance is determined by both the amount of saw table tilt and the blade kerf width. Therefore, it's wise to make test blocks with your chosen blade, especially if you're experimenting with various designs.

For this boat, I used a ¼" 4-TPI blade that cuts a .050"-wide kerf. (A narrower blade will cut a smaller radius, but it won't sweep curves as smoothly.) Before starting on the project, I used the blade to make two telescoping blocks, as shown in the photo at right. These showed me the amount of projection I could expect using different saw table angles and revealed the smallest radius the blade would cut. Whatever blade you choose, make sure it's very sharp, and take some test cuts in scrap to check the results before committing to your project.

Trace the curve of Pattern A onto the side of the block, marking the Length Overall (LOA) and Superstructure (SS) locations.

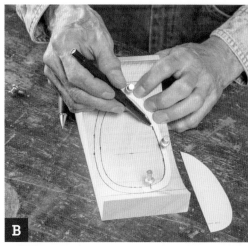

Trace the Hull on both sides of the centerline. Use the Deck Pattern D to check that the pinned Hull Pattern isn't distorted.

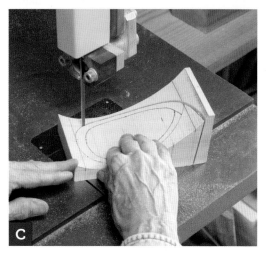

Saw to the outermost Hull line with the bandsaw table tilted at 4°. Aim to leave just the pencil line on the outer perimeter.

Saw as smoothly as possible to the innermost Hull line, leaving just the pencil line on the Hull piece. Don't back up to correct an errant cut.

securely. Mark the Length Overall (LOA) and Superstructure (SS) locations (Photo A), and then use a square to extend the marks fully across the edge of the block.

4 With the bandsaw table set square to the blade, carefully cut the curve. This is cut #1 in the sequence shown in Figure 2, and it will create the Hull and Superstructure blanks. Put the Superstructure block aside for now.

Make the Hull

Note: From this point forward, all angled cuts should be made with the table tilting downward at its outer edge and the part being cut on the lower side of the table.

1 Scribe a centerline on the curved surface of the Hull block. Carry the LOA and SS locations across the curve.

2 Pin Pattern B to the Hull blank so that it abuts the centerline and fits between the LOA lines. Trace the inner and outer Hull lines, and then flip the pattern over and trace the opposite half of the Hull (Photo B).

3 Extend the outer Hull curve to the right-hand edge of the block, where shown in Figure 2 to create a lead-in cutline. Now, tilt your bandsaw table to 4°, and make the outer Hull cut (#2), as shown in (Photo C; page 131). Then sand away any fuzz on the bottom surface.

4 Leaving the table at 4°, make the inner Hull cut (#3), as shown in Photo D. Since a good fit between the Hull and Deck depends on a kerf of consistent width, don't back up to try to correct. At the end of the cut, carefully hold both parts in place while you turn off the saw, and then maneuver the blade free of the kerf.

5 Press the Deck piece downward so that its bottom surface projects about ⅜" from the Hull's bottom edge. The Hull should squeeze the Deck in place when the kerf at the bow is pinched closed. If the kerf doesn't quite close, sand a wee bit off the Deck perimeter (being careful to maintain the cut angle), or plan on gluing in a sliver later to fill the gap. Any offset at the closed kerf can be sanded off after glue-up.

Make the Superstructure

1 Scribe a centerline along the convex surface of the Superstructure block where shown in Figure 2. Then square the SS lines across the block to create intersecting lines for locating the horseshoe-shaped Engine Room Top Profile Pattern C. Align the pattern with the centerline and SS lines, pin it in place, and then carefully trace around the pattern, using your fingers as additional hold-downs, as shown in Photo E.

2 Place Pattern E on the side of the Superstructure block, and trace along the aft curve, as shown in Photo F. Set the saw table square to the blade, and make the cuts (Photo G), beginning with cut #4, and then following up with cut #5, where shown in Figure 2.

Make sure the open end of the centered engine room pattern (C), is aligned with the upper SS line, and carefully trace the shape.

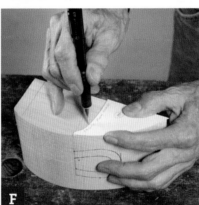

Align the blunt tip of Pattern E with the upper SS line on the Superstructure block, and trace along the Engine Room curve.

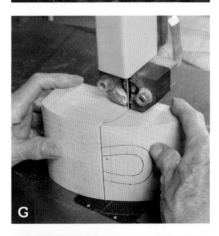

Make the short, straight cut of the Engine Room curve first, and then begin the long curve from the other side of the block.

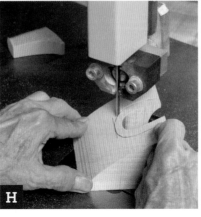

After making the innermost cut to free the Bridge, saw the outer line to shape the Engine Room. In both cases, enter at the side shown.

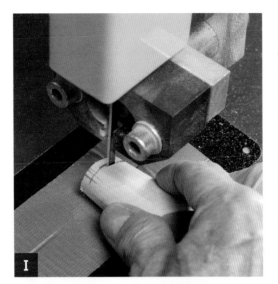

Tape over your saw throat opening to prevent the freed Bridge Roof from falling into it.

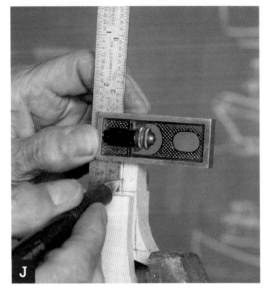

Mark the profile of the Engine Room onto the Bridge, mark a cutline ¼" from the bottom end of the Bridge, and mark the Wheelhouse notch on the top end.

3 Set the saw table to 3°, and make the two U-shaped cuts that will free the Bridge and Engine Room (Photo H). Start the cuts (#6 and #7) where indicated in Figure 2 (page 130) , with the cutouts on the lower side of the table to ensure correct telescoping.

Make the Bridge

1 To make the Bridge Roof, slice about ⅛" off the top of the Bridge section, with the saw table remaining at a 3° angle. Feed the piece, as shown in Photo I, to ensure a Roof of consistent thickness.

2 Raise the Bridge until it's snug within the Engine Room section. Clamp the two

pieces in a handscrew, as shown in Photo J, and then mark the curved profile of the Engine Room onto the rear wall of the bridge, offsetting the line about ⅛". Also mark a cutline about ¼" up from the bottom edge of the Bridge to make room for the Engine below. Finally, lay out a ¼"-deep notch for the Wheelhouse, marking its lower end about ¼" up from the top end of the Engine Room section.

3 Use a handsaw to rough out the cuts, and then sand a slight crown on the aft face of the Bridge.

Make the Wheelhouse

1 Make the L-shaped Wheelhouse block. The dimensions shown in Figure 2 are approximate, so amend them as necessary to match the measurements of your particular Bridge. Use the Roof piece you sliced off the Bridge to mark the shape on the end-grain leg of the Wheelhouse (Photo K on page 134). Then belt-sand the curved face of the Wheelhouse to inset it a bit from the Bridge and Roof, as shown on the boat in Figure 1 and the lead photo on pages 128 and 129.

2 Use a ⅜" brad-point bit in the drill press to bore the portholes in the Engine Room (Photo L). Clamp the piece, keeping its centerline horizontal if you use a drill press. Using the same bit, drill a ¼"-deep hole for the Towing Bollard about ¼" in from the aft end of the Deck.

3 Cut a ⅜"-diameter dowel to length to make the Towing Bollard. When inserted in its Deck hole, it should project about ¼" above the gunwale (the upper edges of the Hull). Chuck it in the drill press, and sand a shallow dome on the top end. Then use a small file to turn a groove for the hawser string.

Sand and assemble the parts

1 Lightly sand the Deck, taking care not to completely remove the SS lines, as you'll need them to locate the Superstructure. (If necessary, use the pattern to reestablish them.) Slide the Hull section up, and mark along its lower edge to demarcate the gluing area on the sides of the Deck section. Apply glue to the section, and clamp the Hull to the Deck with one clamp extending bow to stern, and another clamp perpendicular to the first, pulling the sides in. After the glue cures, sand the top edge and outside of the Hull, easing any corners in the process.

2 Sand the outside of the Engine Room section, and ease any sharp edges on it and the Bridge. Mark the gluing area on the Bridge, apply glue, and slide the Bridge upward into position. If necessary, clamp sideways across the Engine Room to pinch the Bridge in place until the glue dries.

3 Glue the Towing Bollard into its hole in the Deck.

4 Apply glue to the unsanded bottom edge of the Engine Room, and press it onto the Hull between the SS lines. Let the glue cure.

Make the Engine

1 To make the Engine Block, begin with a ⅝"-diameter dowel about 6" long for safe handling. Referring to the Figure 1 Exploded View (page 129), saw off a ¾"-long wedge that approximates the curve of the Deck. Use Pattern A as a rough guide, and then sand and test-fit. Crosscut the dowel to 1¼" long to create the Engine Block.

2 Outfit your drill press with a ¼" Forstner or brad-point bit. Mount the Engine Block and support pieces in a drill press vise (or handscrew), as shown in Photo M, and drill ¼"-deep holes for the brass tubing.

Trace the shape of the Roof onto the end-grain section of the L-shaped Wheelhouse block.

Use a handscrew to support the Engine Room section so its bottom is square to the table for drilling the portholes one at a time.

Bore the holes for the brass tubing with the Engine Block dowel and its waste wedge placed on a support block and clamped in a drill press vise.

Clamp the brass tubing within a slotted hole to hold it while you use a cutoff wheel in a rotary tool to slice the end at an angle.

3 Cut the end of a length of ¼"-diameter brass tubing at 45°, as shown in Photo N. Then crosscut the piece so it protrudes ⅜" from the Engine Block. Repeat to make two more lengths. Finish up with a light sanding to chamfer the sharp edges, and then epoxy the pieces into the Engine Block.

4 Chuck a ½" thumbtack in the drill press, and sand it with 220-grit paper to produce a brushed finish. Then drill a hole in the aft end of the Engine Block, and epoxy the tack in place. Finally, apply glue to the underside of the Engine Block, press it in place, and let the glue cure.

5 Tie one end of a stout string to the Bollard, tie a loop in the other end, and get underway. Something needs towing. Just watch out for giant lobsters!

Patterns: Tugboat

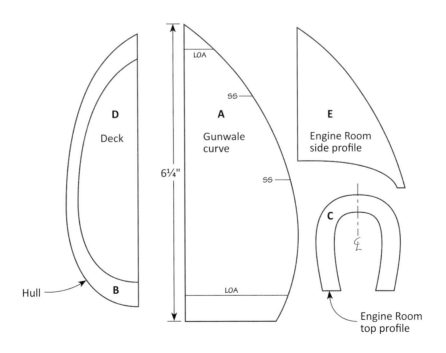

Half-sized patterns; enlarge 200%.

Overall dimensions: 12⅛"l × 6"w × 3¾"h

CHOMPING SHARK

Just when you thought it was safe to go back in the toy box

BY DAVID WAKEFIELD

As a toymaker, I continually strive to make my creations more than what most folks might expect from a block of wood. In order to do so, I often incorporate simple mechanisms to make my playthings come to life. The shark, a favorite subject, is a case in point. My ultimate predator employs hidden pegs that power its toothy chomp when it's rolled about. I've designed several sharks over the years, but this version sports a sculpted–almost fluid–physique.

This toy may look menacing, but fear not: small fingers are perfectly safe. To ensure that your fingers are just as safe during construction, I've provided advice to help keep your digits away from both blades and bits while machining the small parts. Of course, if any step seems too close for comfort, stop and use another, safer method. For example, shaping parts with files and sanding blocks takes more time than using a router or belt sander, but the hand-tool approach is equally effective and can be a suitable chore for young shop assistants.

Make the body

1 Cut out and affix the full-sized body (A) pattern onto a 1½ × 3½ × 11¾" block. (I prefer cherry because it's moderately lightweight, resists splintering, sands to a fine finish, and looks good when oiled. However, any hardwood will do.)
2 Referring to the pattern, use a drill press to bore through holes for the eyes and axles.
3 Outfit your bandsaw with a ¼"-wide, 4-6 TPI blade, and cut out the body profile. Note: You can nibble out the notch for the pectoral fin using your tablesaw and miter gauge, but do this before shaping the body.

4 Edge-sand the body (A) through 120 grit. You can use an oscillating spindle sander, but I prefer using a 1"-wide belt sander. (As you'll see in Photo B, I ripped a 1" dowel in half and screwed it to the platen to better negotiate inside curves.) Hand-sand the faces through 120 grit, and then rout the edges with a ¼" round-over bit.

5 Affix the Body Top View pattern on the body (A). Holding the work firmly against the bandsaw's table, cut away the sides of the sculpted tail (Photo A). Next, refine the curves with a belt or oscillating spindle sander (Photo B). In this instance, a spindle sander is preferable because the abrasive spins with the grain. A belt-sander will create cross-grain scratches that will require additional hand-sanding.

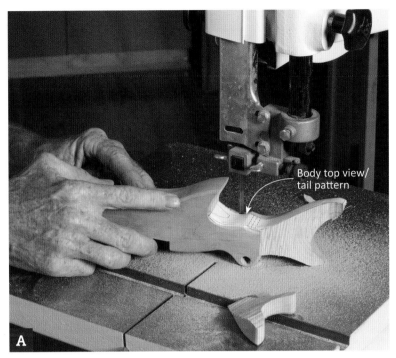

Body top view/ tail pattern

A

Hold the head to ensure that fingers stay a safe distance away from the blade. Affixing the top view to the tail section provides an easy-to-follow cutting guide.

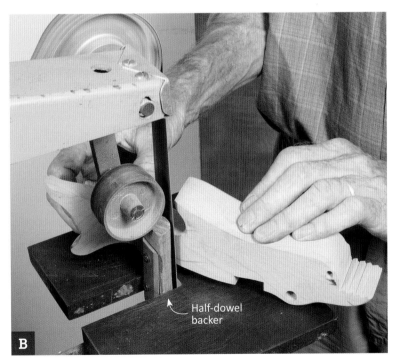

Half-dowel backer

B

Attaching a short half-dowel to the belt sander's platen enables the machine to handle tight curves.

C

Use a short handsaw to make quick work of a tricky cut. Take care not to nip the end of the tail with the saw blade.

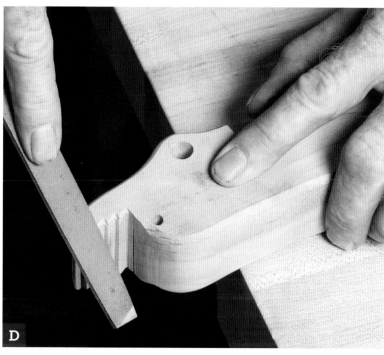

6 Referring to the Body Top View, sketch out the dorsal fin on the top of the body, and then saw away the sides of the fins (Photo C).

7 Clamp the body (A) in a vise with the tail sticking up at about a 45° angle. Using rasps and files, fine-tune the shape of the tail and dorsal fin. When you get the desired shape, switch to 80-grit sandpaper to remove all the cross-grain scratches. Finally, finish-sand the entire body through 120 grit.

8 Using a safe-edged file, define the outside edges of the teeth, as shown in Photo D, to add a bit more menace to your shark's grin.

9 Affix the pectoral fin (B) pattern on a piece of ½" stock, and bandsaw it out. Sand the fin's edges and sides through 120 grit.

Use one half-stroke to establish a small bevel. Next, rest the file's edge against the jaw and finish "sharpening" each tooth.

Figure 1: Shark Exploded View

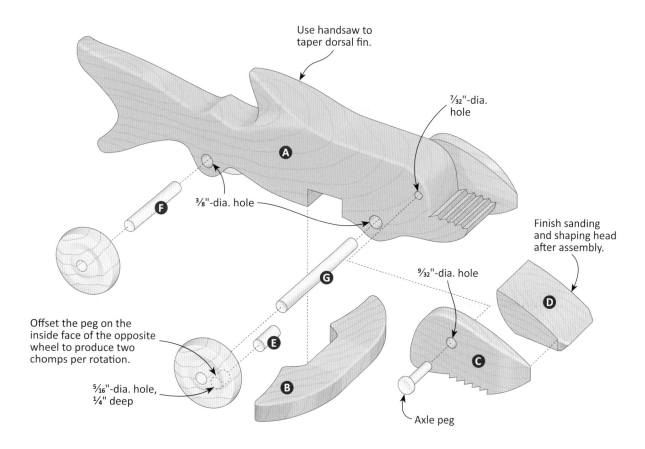

Use handsaw to taper dorsal fin.

⁷⁄₃₂"-dia. hole

³⁄₈"-dia. hole

Finish sanding and shaping head after assembly.

⁹⁄₃₂"-dia. hole

Offset the peg on the inside face of the opposite wheel to produce two chomps per rotation.

⁵⁄₁₆"-dia. hole, ¼" deep

Axle peg

Make the head

1 Attach two ⅜"-thick boards face-to-face with double-faced tape and affix the head side (C) pattern to the stack. Using a drill press, drill the ⁹⁄₃₂" hole for the axle pegs. Now, cut out the pattern, and then sand up to the lines. Don't worry too much about the topmost section; you'll sand that section after gluing in the spacer. Separate the head sides and put them aside.

2 Affix the head spacer (D) pattern on 1⅝"-thick stock (for safer sawing, start with a piece that's a few inches longer than needed). Bandsaw out the piece, as shown in Photo E, and then sand the inner edge of the profile. Set the piece aside.

3 Build the assembly jig shown in Figure 2. Next, apply a little glue on both sides of the head spacer (D). Work it inward from the edges to avoid squeeze-out, and attach the head sides (C). Position the assembly on the jig, as shown in Photo F.

4 After the assembly has dried, edge-sand where the spacer (D) meets the outer edges of the sides (C). Referring to the Head Assembly Top View, lay out a taper on the front, and sand the head to shape. Next, finish-sand the head through 120 grit. Finally, file the teeth as you did on the body (A).

Shark assembly

1 At the drill press, use a ⁵⁄₁₆" twist bit to enlarge the axle holes. Next, drill a ⁵⁄₁₆" hole in a scrap board, and insert a short ⁵⁄₁₆" dowel. Using the axle hole, fit the wheel on the dowel, backside facing up. Position and clamp the board to the drill press table, and then drill a ⁵⁄₁₆" hole for the peg (E), as shown in Photo G. Repeat with the second front wheel.

2 Cut the pegs (E) to length, and lightly chamfer the ends. Put a little glue inside

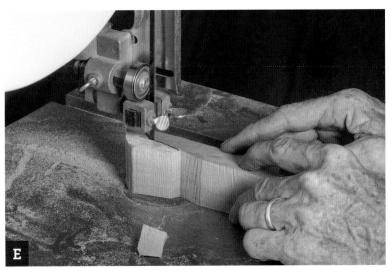

E

Affix the head spacer pattern onto a longer piece to keep fingers a safe distance from the blade.

F

Use the assembly jig to glue the head sides to the spacer to keep the parts aligned. This ensures that the head will pivot freely.

Figure 2: Assembly Jig

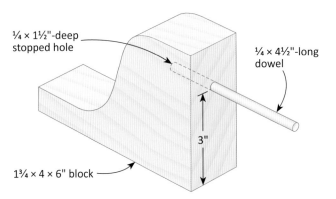

¼ × 1½"-deep stopped hole

¼ × 4½"-long dowel

3"

1¾ × 4 × 6" block

G

Fit the wheel on a dowel to keep it safely positioned while you drill the peg hole.

QUICK TIP

If you're going to use paint or apply a hard finish, do so before assembly; otherwise, excess finish may gum up the inner workings of your toy.

the wheel holes with a toothpick, and then drive the pegs in with a hammer. Make sure that both are inserted perpendicularly.

3 Cut the rear axle (F) to length, and then lightly chamfer both ends. To ensure that excess glue doesn't seize up the axle, put a bit of glue inside the axle hole of one rear wheel, place it outside-face down, and then tap in the axle. Next, apply glue to the axle hole of the opposite wheel, position it under the body, and then insert the axle through the body and drive it into the wheel.

4 Cut the front axle (G) about ¼" longer than finished length, and attach it to a front wheel. As you insert the axle through the body and into the opposite front wheel, take care not to pinch the pegs against the body. Before the glue sets, rotate the wheels so that the pegs are offset 180° to each other. (By doing this, the shark will chomp twice with each rotation of the wheels.) When dry, sand the axle flush with the outside faces of the wheels.

5 Put a little glue inside each of the eye holes in the body (A). Position the head

Cut List: Chomping Shark

	Part	Thickness	Width	Length	Qty.	Mat'l
A	Body	1½"	3½"	11¾"	1	C
B	Pectoral fin	½"	1½"	6"	1	C
C	Head sides	⅜"	1¾	3⅛"	2	C
D	Head spacer	1⅝"	1¼"	1⅞"	1	C
E	Short pegs		5/16" dia.	¾"	2	B
F	Rear axle		5/16" dia.	2¼"	1	B
G*	Front axle		5/16"	5"	1	B

*Indicates that parts are initially cut oversized. See instructions.
Materials: C=Cherry, B=Birch

assembly on the body, and tap in an axle peg, using a shim to ensure adequate clearance for the head to pivot (Photo H). Insert the second peg in the same manner.

6 Glue and clamp the pectoral fin (B) to the body (A). When the glue has dried, set your perfect predator on a flat surface and give him a test push.

Finishing Touches

I finish most of my toys with food-grade mineral oil because it's nontoxic and easy to use. Simply apply it liberally with a rag, let it soak in, and then wipe away any excess. Reapply if the wood begins to look dry.

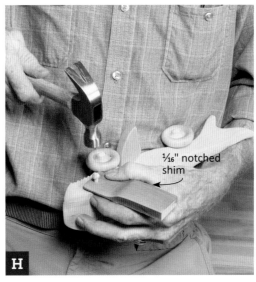

Use a shim when setting the axle to prevent overdriving the peg and pinching the head to the body.

Patterns: Chomping Shark Half-Sized

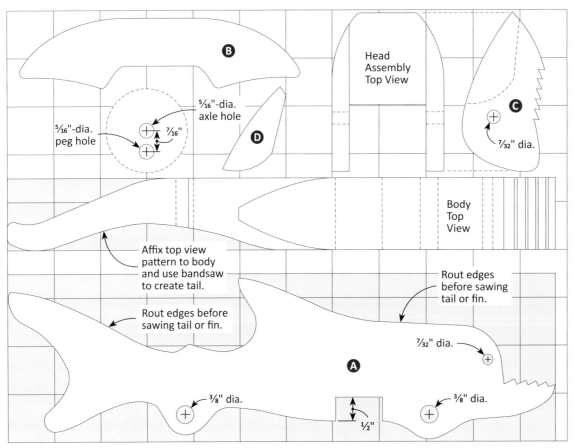

1 square=1"
Half-sized pattern, enlarge 200%

WADDLING WALRUS

Clever toy chomps, waddles and rolls

BY DAVID WAKEFIELD

Since I began designing animated toys three decades ago, I continually strive to make my toys more than what most folks expect from a block of wood. My secret is to incorporate simple mechanisms that make the playthings come to life. This walrus is a case in point. Unlike most other toys that simply roll, this fellow has eccentric wheels that create an ambling gait as he's pushed across the floor. Thanks to a cam and piston hidden within the body, the tusked head rises and falls as he's rolled in either direction.

This toy is easy to make, but requires some patience and precise work to guarantee that the parts operate smoothly. Of course, special care should be taken when machining small parts. I've provided advice to help keep your fingers away from blades and bits, but if any procedure seems too close for comfort, stop and use another, safer method.

Figure 1: Walrus Exploded View

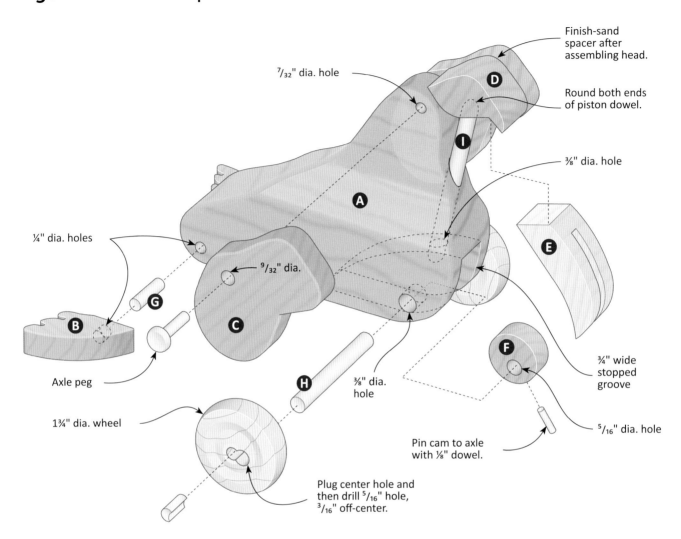

Finish-sand spacer after assembling head.

Round both ends of piston dowel.

⁷/₃₂" dia. hole

¾" dia. hole

¼" dia. holes

⁹/₃₂" dia.

Axle peg

1¾" dia. wheel

⅜" dia. hole

Pin cam to axle with ⅛" dowel.

Plug center hole and then drill ⁵/₁₆" hole, ³/₁₆" off-center.

¾" wide stopped groove

⁵/₁₆" dia. hole

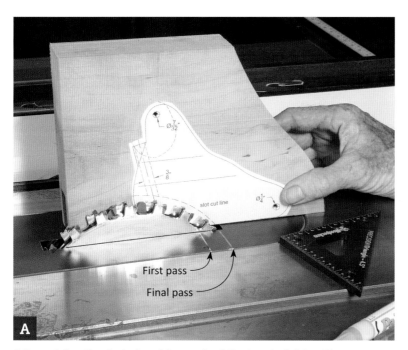

First pass
Final pass

A

After raising the dado head for each of the two height settings, mark the location of the cutter's front edge on the table for your stopping mark.

Stop line

B

Advance the block until the line on the pattern line meets the stop line on the saw. Wait for the blade to stop before removing the block.

Temporary ledge

C

Use a wedge to position the body and a square to verify that the hole layout lines are perpendicular to the table. Then drill the hole.

Make the body

1 Cut out and affix the full-sized body (A) pattern onto a block that's a few inches longer and slightly wider than the dimension in the Cut List (page 149), which will make it safe to hold for initial machining. (I prefer cherry, but any relatively light, strong hardwood will do.) Position the pattern so that its bottom edge is adjacent to the bottom edge of the block.

2 Referring to the pattern, use a drill press to bore the holes for the fins, head, and axle.

3 Referring to Figure 1 and the body pattern, lay out on the block's front edge the entry end of the ¾"-wide × 1½"-deep stopped groove, centering it across the thickness of the body. Next, set up a ½"-wide dado head on your tablesaw, adjust its height to ¾", and strike a line on your saw table indicating where the front of the cutter meets the plane of the table. Adjust the fence to saw to one of the groove shoulder lines, and start the cut. When the trailing end of the groove profile line on the pattern meets the mark on your saw, hold the workpiece in place while you turn off the saw and wait for the blade to stop. Next, adjust the fence to cut to the opposite groove shoulder, and make the second cut in the same manner. Now, using the pattern as a guide, raise the cutter to final 1½" height, mark the table again (Photo A: page 145), and complete the stopped groove using the same two-step approach (Photo B; page 145).

4 Outfit your bandsaw with a ¼"-wide 4-6 TPI blade, and cut out the body profile. Leave the ledge in the front of the head for now, as you'll need it to drill the piston hole.

5 At the drill press, position the body (A) so the piston hole layout lines are perpendicular to the table and drill the hole (Photo C).

6 Saw off the ledge, and then sand the edges and both faces through 120 grit. (You can use an oscillating spindle sander, but I prefer a 1"-wide belt sander. To handle inside curves, I ripped a 1"-diameter dowel in half and attached it to the sander platen. See Photo F, at right.) Now rout the entire profile with a ¼"-diameter quarter-round bit.

7 Referring to Figure 1 (page 144), lay out the shoulder cuts that reduce the thickness of the walrus' neck section. Use your bandsaw's fence when cutting the straight neck sections (Photo D), then remove the fence, prop the body on a ¼"-thick scrap, and saw the walrus' shoulders with a nice sweeping curve (Photo E).

8 Edge-sand the neck/shoulder curves through 120 grit, as shown in Photo F, and then round over all the edges of the sawn area by hand-sanding.

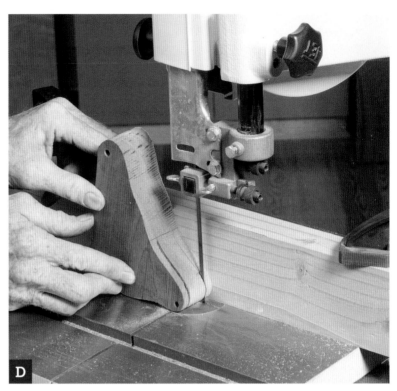

D

Using a fence to guide the initial straight cuts ensures a neck of consistent thickness.

E

Prop the neck section on a ¼"-thick block, and then saw each shoulder with a single, sweeping cut.

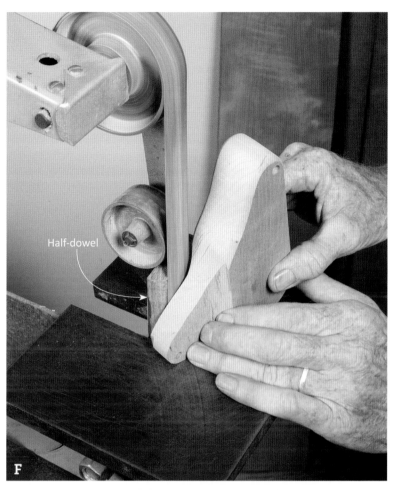

By attaching a short half-dowel to the belt sander's platen, tight curves, such as the shoulders, can be easily sanded to shape.

Use a bandsaw fence to make the initial straight cuts to define the tusks. Then remove the fence to nibble away the waste.

Make the flippers and head

1 Attach two ½"-thick pieces face-to-face with doublestick tape, and then affix the flipper pattern, positioning its inside edge adjacent to the edge of your stock. Using a drill press, drill the ¼"-diameter holes for the flipper dowels into the edges. Next, drill ¹⁄₃₂"-diameter holes through the faces, where shown, to simplify shaping the tight curves.

2 Dry-fit a ¼" dowel into a flipper (B) to provide a hand-hold, and then cut out the pattern on the bandsaw. Finish-sand the edges, then split the flippers apart and sand both faces.

3 Temporarily join two ½"-thick pieces face-to-face and affix the head (C) pattern. Drill the eye/pivot hole, and saw and sand the profile. Separate the twin head pieces, and finish-sand their faces.

4 Affix the head spacer (D) pattern on ⅞"-thick stock. (For safer sawing, use a piece that's a few inches longer than needed.) Saw out the piece, and then sand the inside edges. Set this piece aside for now.

5 Affix the tusk (E) pattern on ⅞"-thick stock. Using a bandsaw, saw out the tusks, but leave a few inches of extra material along the blunt end. Finish-sand the edges and faces, and then cut the notch to create the individual tusks, as shown in Photo G. Clean up by hand-sanding, and then saw off the extra wood on the blunt end.

6 Build the assembly jig shown below. Now apply a little glue on both faces of the head spacer (D) and the mating face of each head piece (C). Position the assembly on the jig, as shown in Photo H (page 148), and glue in the tusks (E). When the assembly has dried, edge sand where the spacer meets the outer head pieces. Be careful not to mar the edges of the tusks. Hand-sand the assembly through 120 grit.

H

Using the assembly jig to align the parts ensures that the head operates when it's attached to the body.

Make the mechanism and assemble the walrus

1 Make the cam (F) by drilling into ½"-thick stock with a 1⅛"-diameter holesaw. Use dowels to plug the center hole in the cam and each wooden wheel, and then drill offset axle holes where shown on the pattern page.

2 Cut the flipper (G) dowels to length, and chamfer their ends to ease insertion. Put a bit of glue in the flipper holes, a little glue on the edge of the flipper (B) where it touches the body (A), and attach the flippers. To avoid smearing glue on the body, twist the flippers in place until they're almost touching the body, then tap them home. Make sure that the flippers are parallel to the bottom of the body and to each other.

3 Cut the axle (H) to length, and chamfer the ends. Apply glue inside one wheel hole, and tap in the axle. Next, insert the cam (F) in the body (A), and twist the axle through both. Now place the remaining wheel beneath the body, and

> **QUICK TIP**
>
> To minimize squeeze-out, apply glue sparingly, particularly near the edges of the parts.

Figure 2: Assembly Jig

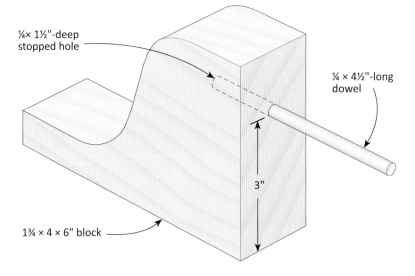

¼× 1½"-deep stopped hole

¼ × 4½"-long dowel

3"

1¾ × 4 × 6" block

I

Use a slotted ⅛"-thick spacer when driving in the eye pegs and wheels so that the parts have adequate clearance to operate smoothly.

set the axle just into the hole. Offset the eccentric holes 180° to create the walrus's waddle, apply a bit of glue on the axle between the body and wheel, and tap the axle into the wheel.

4 Drill a ⅛" hole through the center of the edge of the cam (F) and through the axle (H). Glue a ⅛"-diameter dowel in the hole. When the glue has set up, trim and file the dowel flush so that it doesn't interfere with the smooth movement of the piston (I).

5 Cut the piston (I) to length, and dry-fit the head to test the mechanism. (You may need to adjust the piston length a bit so that the head starts to lift as soon as the cam engages the dowel.) When you have the perfect length, round off both ends of the dowel, reinsert it in place, apply glue into the eye holes, and tap in the axle pegs to attach the head to the body (Photo I).

Finishing touches

I finish most of my toys with food-grade mineral oil because it's nontoxic and easy to use. Simply apply it liberally with a rag, let it soak in, and then wipe away any excess. Reapply if the wood begins to look dry.

QUICK TIP

If you're going to use paint or apply a hard finish, do so before assembly; otherwise, excess finish may gum up the inner workings of your toy.

	Part	Thickness	Width	Length	Qty.	Mat'l
A*	Body	1½"	5"	6½"	1	C
B*	Flipper	½"	1¼"	1¾"	2	C
C*	Head	½"	1⅞"	2⅞"	2	C
D*	Head spacer	⅞"	1⅝"	1⅜"	1	C
E*	Tusks	⅞"	1"	1¼"	1	M
F	Cam	½"	1" dia.		1	C
G	Flipper dowel		¼" dia.	¾"	2	B
H*	Axle		5⁄16" dia.	2¾"	B	B
I	Piston		5⁄16" dia.	3⅜"	1	B

Cut List: Waddling Walrus

*Indicates that parts are initially cut oversized. See instructions.
Materials: C=Cherry, M=Maple, B=Birch

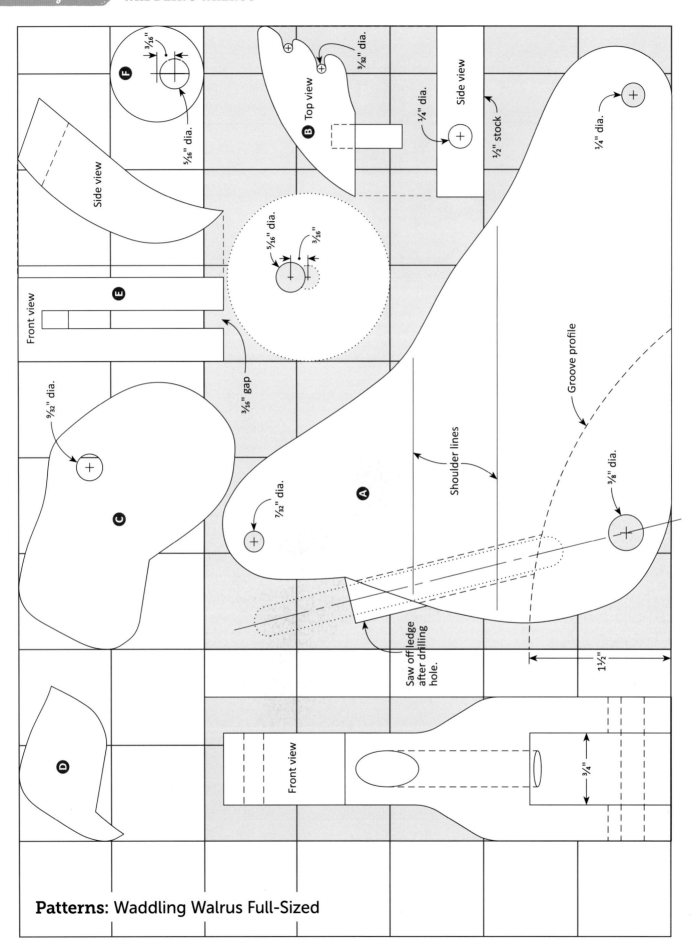

F

3/16"

5/16" dia.

Side view

Front view

E

9/32" dia.

C

3/16" gap

5/16" dia. 3/16"

B Top view

3/32" dia.

1/4" dia.

Side view

1/2" stock

1/4" dia.

Side view

A

7/32" dia.

Shoulder lines

Groove profile

3/8" dia.

Saw off ledge after drilling hole.

1 1/2"

D

Front view

3/4"

Patterns: Waddling Walrus Full-Sized

BEAVER

Build this simple slaphappy push toy

BY DAVID WAKEFIELD

Overall dimensions: 2"w × 9½"l × 4⅝"h

Ever since I designed and built my first animated toy three decades ago, I have strived to make toys that not only capture the look of an animal, but also have a little life of their own. Unlike Pinocchio's Geppetto, the trick to making a toy waddle, chomp, or thump isn't magic, but simple mechanics.

This beaver is one of my easier projects, despite its simplicity, the design still delights both young children and the young at heart. Thanks to a cam hidden within the solid-wood body, the tail rises and falls as it's rolled in either direction. (When the toy is pushed quickly, the tail makes a hard slapping sound, much like the real beavers that I've startled on canoe trips.) You could carve some additional detail into the tail and body sides if you are so inclined, but I prefer not to go overboard with finishing and detail work. I don't want to make toys that are too pretty to play with.

I made this beaver from cherry, but any relatively light, strong hardwood will do. This toy is easy to make, but it does require some precise machine work and careful assembly to guarantee that the moving parts operate smoothly. Machining small parts warrants special attention. I've provided some advice for safe operations, but if any step seems too close for comfort, stop and use another safer method. For example, if you're nervous about routing small parts, feel free to resort to files and sanding blocks. Considering the small amount of shaping involved, completing the parts with hand tools would not add much time to this project.

Make the body

1 Cut out and affix the full-sized body (A) pattern found on page 157 onto a 1½"-thick block that's at least 3½" wide and 6¾" long. (If you can spare the stock, a wider, longer block will be safer to handle on the tablesaw.) Position the pattern so that the groove shown in Figure 1 on page 153 runs parallel with the bottom edge of the block.

2 Referring to the pattern, use a drill press to bore through-holes for the eyes, axles, and tail pivot. Place a scrap of wood beneath the block to prevent tear-out.

3 Referring to Figure 1 and the body (A) pattern, lay out the shoulder lines for the ¾"-wide stopped groove on the beaver's rear end, centering it across the thickness of the body. Next, set up a ½"-wide dado head on your tablesaw, adjust its height to

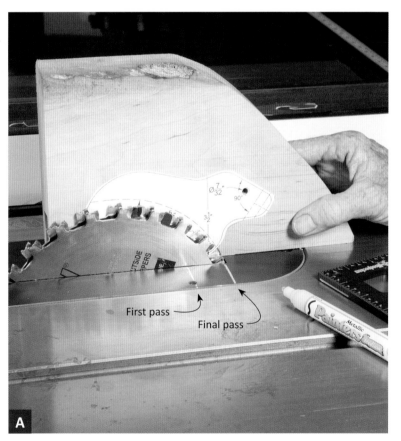

First pass

Final pass

A

Use the pattern to set the dado height, and mark a line on the table to indicate the location of the cutter's front edge to know where to stop the cut.

Figure 1: Beaver Exploded View

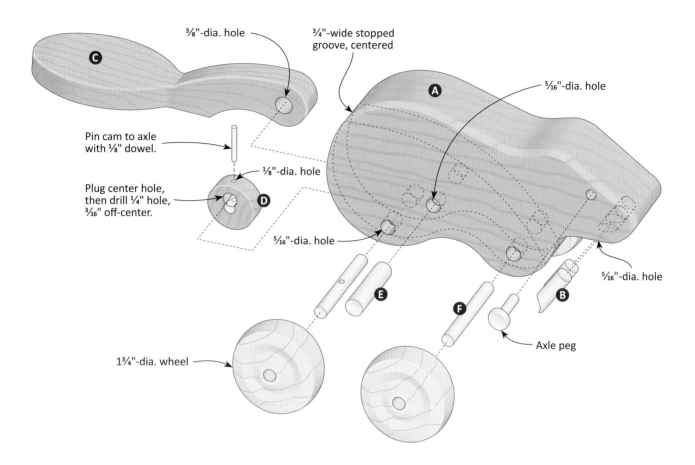

³⁄₈"-dia. hole

³⁄₄"-wide stopped groove, centered

⁵⁄₁₆"-dia. hole

C

A

Pin cam to axle with ¹⁄₈" dowel.

¹⁄₈"-dia. hole

Plug center hole, then drill ¼" hole, ³⁄₁₆" off-center.

D

⁵⁄₁₆"-dia. hole

⁵⁄₁₆"-dia. hole

E

F

B

Axle peg

1³⁄₄"-dia. wheel

1", and then strike a line on your saw table indicating where the front of the cutter meets the plane of the table. Adjust the fence to saw to one of the groove shoulder lines, and start the cut. When the trailing end of the groove's profile line on the pattern meets the mark on your saw, hold the block in place while you turn off the saw and wait for the blade to stop. Next, adjust the fence to cut the opposite groove shoulder, making the second cut in the same manner.

4 Using the pattern as a guide, raise the cutter to final height, mark a second stop line on the saw's table (Photo A; page 152), and complete the stopped groove using the same two-step approach (Photo B).

5 Outfit your bandsaw with a ¼"-wide, 4-6 TPI blade, and cut out the body profile.

6 At the drill press, position the body (A) upside-down with the beaver's forehead resting against the table, as shown in Photo C, and drill two ⁵⁄₁₆" holes for the teeth (B).

7 Remove the pattern, and then sand the edges and both faces of the body (A) through 120 grit. (You can use an oscillating spindle sander, but I prefer a 1"-wide belt sander (Photo D; page 154). To better negotiate inside curves, I ripped a 1" dowel in half and screwed it to the platen.)

8 Rout the entire body (A) with a ¼" quarter-round bit. (When shaping small parts, I prefer to clamp my compact router table to my workbench and use it like a mini router table. See Photo F; page 155.) Lastly, hand-sand the routed edges through 120 grit.

9 Cut two short pieces of ⁵⁄₁₆" dowel for the teeth (B). Lightly chamfer an end of each tooth, and then glue that end into the body (A). Once inserted, use a bandsaw to even out the lengths of the teeth, and then cut the inside curves. Use a round file or sandpaper-wrapped dowel to remove saw marks.

10 Trim the shafts of two axle pegs to ¾" in length to make the eyes, and then glue them into the body (A).

Make the tail

1 Cut out and affix the tail (C) side view pattern to a 1½"-thick block that's 2" wide and at least 6" long. Position the pattern so that the tail's back edge touches the end of the block and its bottom edge touches the bottom edge of the block.

2 Using a drill press, bore the ⅜" through-hole for the tail pivot (E). Now, bandsaw the profile, and then sand the top and bottom faces through 120 grit.

3 Affix the tail (C) top view pattern to the top face of the block, again aligning the pattern's back edge with the corresponding end of the block. Next, attach a fence to the bandsaw, hold the tail firmly against the table and cut the shoulders of the pivoting section (Photo E; page 155) so that the tail can fit into the body (A). Next, saw the round rear section, and then finish-sand the tail through 120 grit.

4 Rout the tail's round section with a ¼" quarter-round bit. The angle of the tail makes routing the top face a little tricky. Using a compact router helps (Photo E; page 155), but the angled section limits the bit's reach, so use a rasp to finish shaping the tail, and then finish-sand through 120 grit.

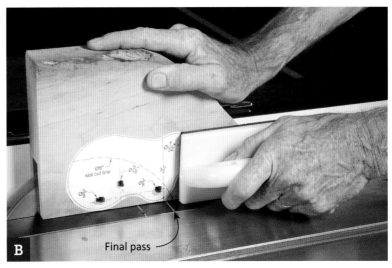

B

Final pass

Advance the block until the line on the pattern meets the final pass stop line. Wait for the blade to stop before removing the block.

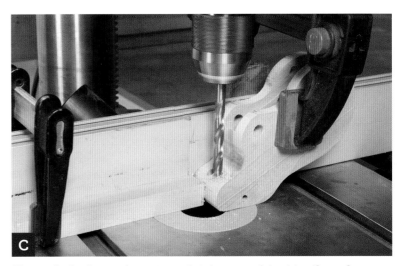

C

Clamp the body to a fence to maintain a consistent tooth angle. Use a scrapwood stop to ensure identical nose-to-tooth spacing.

Half-dowel backer

D

Screwing a short half-dowel to the belt sander's platen enables the belt to shape and smooth tight inside curves.

Securing a compact router in a bench vise turns it into a mini router table. Taping a block to the tail helps keep fingers away from the bit.

Tap the wheel and axle through the body, cam, and free wheel. Support the body with your bench so that the dowel doesn't split the block.

Make the cam and add the wheels

1 From ½"-thick stock, use a 1" holesaw to make the tail cam (D). Plug the hole created by a holesaw with a dowel, trim it flush, and then bore a ¼" through-hole, where shown on the Patterns page.

2 Cut the tail pivot (E) about ⅛" longer than the width of the body (A), and lightly round over one end to prevent it from snagging any edges when inserted through the body and cam. Next, position the body (A) on its side, and fit the tail (C) in the groove. (It may help to position the body so that the tail hangs off the edge of your bench). Begin tapping the tail pivot through the body and tail, and stop when the dowel just enters the hole on the far side of the body. Put a little glue on the inside of the pivot hole, and then drive the dowel home. Wipe off excess glue from the dowel, and then trim both ends flush.

3 Cut the axles (F) to length and again round over one end to prevent snagging. Apply glue inside a front wheel, place it on wax paper, and tap an axle in place. Repeat with a back wheel and axle.

4 Put a dab of glue in the remaining front wheel. Rest the body (A) on its side, place the wheel under the front axle hole, and then insert the front axle from the top. (You may need to tap the axle with a hammer to drive it home.)

5 Insert the rear axle (F) into the body (A), and through the tail cam (D). Set the remaining free wheel under the body (I suggest positioning the assembly directly over a dog hole), and fit the axle about half-way into the wheel (Photo F). Apply glue in the wheel hole, and then drive the axle home. Once the glue has cured, edge-sand the axle ends.

6 Drill a ⅛" hole through the tail cam (D) and rear axle (F), and pin the cam to the dowel with a ⅛" dowel. Afterward, make sure to smooth away any projection, which can interfere with the lifting motion of the tail.

7 Finish the toy and give it away. Enjoy the show as your youngster figures out how the beaver seems to move on its own.

Finishing Touches

I finish most of my toys with food-grade mineral oil because it's non-toxic and easy to use. Simply apply it liberally with a rag, let it soak in, and then wipe away any excess. Reapply if the wood begins to look dry.

QUICK TIP

If you're planning to use paint or a hard film-building finish, do so before assembly; otherwise, excess finish may gum up the inner workings of your toy.

Cut List: Beaver

	Part	Thickness	Width	Length	Qty.	Mat'l
A*	Body	1½"	3¼"	6½"	1	C
B*	Teeth		5⁄16" dia.	1"	2	B
C*	Tail	1½"	2"	6"	1	C
D	Tail cam	½"	1"-dia.		1	C
E*	Tail pivot		5⁄16" dia.	1½"	1	B
F*	Axles		¼" dia.	2⅝"	2	B

*Indicates that parts are initially cut oversized. See instructions.
Materials: C=Cherry, B=Birch

Patterns: Beaver Full-Sized

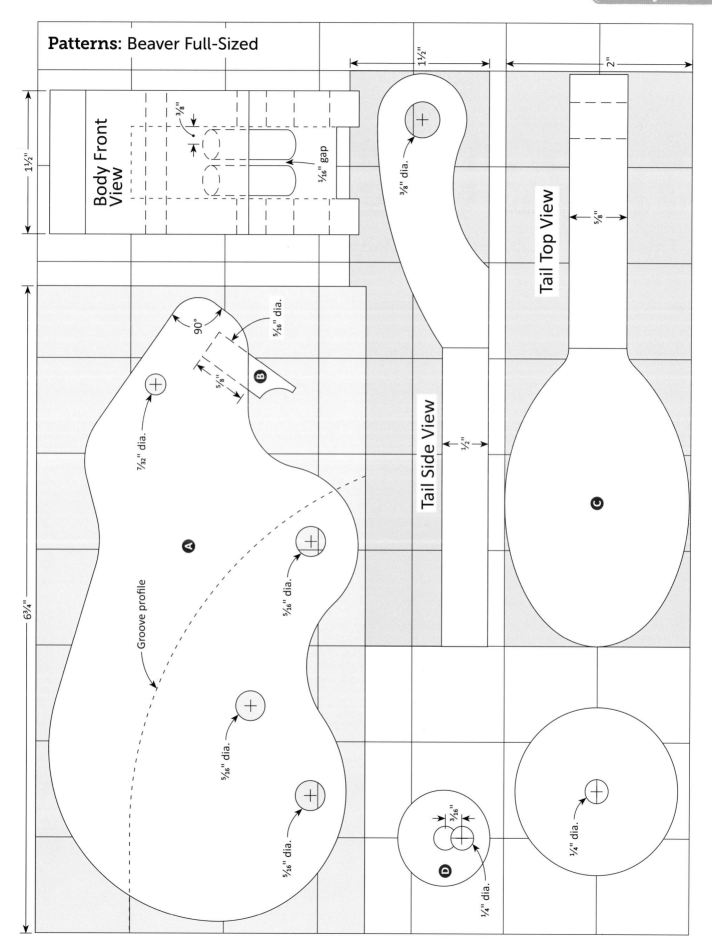

Body Front View

1½"

3/8"

1/16" gap

1½"

6¾"

90°

5/16" dia.

5/8"

B

7/32" dia.

A

Groove profile

5/16" dia.

5/16" dia.

5/16" dia.

D

3/16"

¼" dia.

¼" dia.

3/8" dia.

Tail Side View

½"

Tail Top View

5/8"

2"

1½"

C

TREASURE CHEST

This toy box "matures" into a blanket chest with a flip of its panels

BY ANDY RAE

Every kid loves a toy chest to stow treasures in, and this design provides delight. With its colorful exterior and curved lid, it makes a fun, bold statement in any child's room. But the real magic here happens when it's time to put the toys in the attic and move on to more grown-up gear. In less than five minutes, you can transform a brightly colored playroom piece into a stately blanket chest that will be at home in any bedroom, den, or living room. All it takes is a quick flip of the panels. (See sidebar, page 160.)

This is a deceptively easy chest to build. At its core, it's just a plywood box. The classy looking faux frame-and-panel construction is created by gluing solid wood trim to the faces of the box. Although the lid mimics a fancy coopered panel, there's no fussy edge-beveling here. Instead, the slats are glued to curved plywood ribs before attaching battens that accept the narrow reversible panels. And don't worry about pinched li'l fingers: the lid lifts easily, stays open securely, and closes slowly and safely.

Build the plywood box

1 Cut the sides (A, B) to the dimensions shown in the Cut List (page 171). Leave the bottom (C) about 1/16" oversized in both width and length for now; you'll trim to final dimensions once the sides are assembled.
2 Smooth all inside faces through 220 grit, and then mask off all the glue areas with removable tape. Apply three to four coats of 2-lb.-cut shellac, wiping on each coat with long, overlapping strokes. (I use shellac inside the chest because it leaves a neutral scent.)

After each coat dries, scuff-sand it with 320-grit sandpaper, except for the next-to-last coat, which gets rubbed out with 0000 steel wool. After applying the final coat, let it dry, and then rub with the grain using generous amounts of paste wax on a 0000 steel wool pad. After aggressively wiping away the excess with a clean, soft cloth, your finish should shine and feel silky to the touch.

3 To ease final assembly, first dry-clamp the four sides (A,B) together, and drill 2"-deep pilot holes through the long sides and into the edges of the short sides. Then disassemble the box, enlarge the pilot holes in the long sides with a 7/64"-diameter bit, and countersink them for #8 screws. Add glue, reclamp the parts, and screw them together with #8 × 2" screws (Photo A on page 161). (Before you set the box aside, measure for square.)
4 Measure the outside dimensions of the assembled sides (A, B), and cut the bottom (C) to fit. Attach it as before with clamps, glue, and screws (Photo B; page 161). Because the bottom is squared, it will automatically square up the box.

Figure 1: Treasure Chest

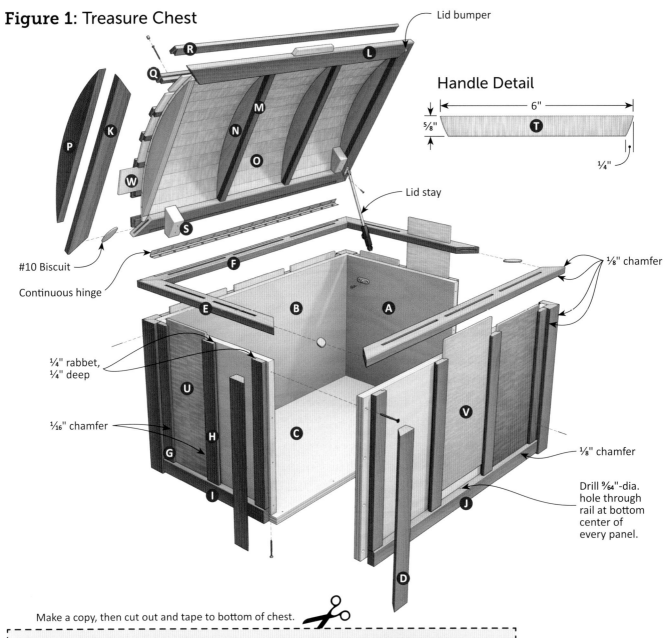

Lid bumper

Handle Detail

6"

⅝"

T

¼"

Lid stay

#10 Biscuit

Continuous hinge

⅛" chamfer

¼" rabbet, ¼" deep

⅛" chamfer

1/16" chamfer

⅛" chamfer

Drill 9/64"-dia. hole through rail at bottom center of every panel.

Make a copy, then cut out and tape to bottom of chest. ✂

Flipping the Panels

When toys go by the wayside, it's time to update your kid's décor. Reverse the outer panels of this toy box and— Presto!—it matures into adult furniture.

Raise the panels in the main box section by poking through the access holes in the lower rails using a bamboo skewer or other ⅛"-diameter implement. To reverse the lid panels, push each one out, flip it end for end, and slide it back in its slots. Magnets buried in the panel and frame automatically align the parts.

Push panel out of slots, flip end for end, and reinsert.

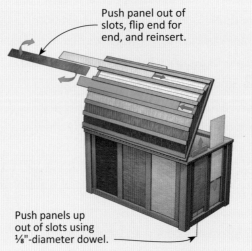

Push panels up out of slots using ⅛"-diameter dowel.

A Add glue to the joints, clamp the box, and drive the screws home. You can remove the clamps as soon as the screws are in.

B With the box upside down on shop-made risers, add glue, and then clamp the bottom even with the box sides before adding the screws.

Make the box trim

1 Mill the leg pieces (D) to the thickness and length shown in the Cut List, leaving them slightly oversized in width. Bevel one edge to 45° on the tablesaw, setting the fence so the ripped stock will be 2" wide at the tip of the bevel. Check the joint fit by holding two mitered leg pieces together against a corner of the chest.

2 Next, you'll make the short and long top rails (E, F), creating their panel slots by ripping each oversized rail blank into three strips, crosscutting the center strip into sections, and then regluing the pieces back together, as shown in Figure 2. Start by initially sawing $^{13}/_{16}$"-thick stock into rail blanks that are at

least $^3/_8$" wider and a couple of inches longer than the finished sizes for the top rails (E, F) shown in the Cut List.

3 Draw a triangle across the face of each rail blank to allow reassembling the pieces in the same orientation for the best grain match after ripping. Then rip each blank into three pieces that are each slightly wider than the finished widths shown in Figure 2. Use a thickness planer to clean up the saw marks, and bring the strips to finished width.

4 Crosscut the center strips to the lengths shown in Figure 2, again marking the strips for reorientation later.

5 Glue each three-piece top rail (E, F) together using scrap wood spacers to

Figure 2: Top Rail Construction

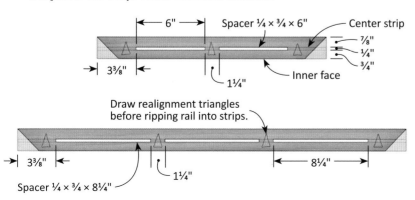

6" — Spacer $^1/_4 \times ^3/_4 \times$ 6" — Center strip
$^7/_8$"
$^1/_4$"
$^3/_4$"
3$^3/_8$"
1$^1/_4$"
Inner face

Draw realignment triangles before ripping rail into strips.

3$^3/_8$"
1$^1/_4$"
8$^1/_4$"
Spacer $^1/_4 \times ^3/_4 \times$ 8$^1/_4$"

QUICK TIP

For aesthetics, I chamfer the edges of the trim pieces before assembly. Cut the widest chamfers, like those on the legs and top and bottom rails, on the router table using a chamfer bit. For smaller chamfers, a block plane does the job. For tricky grain or hard-to-reach areas, use 180-grit sandpaper glued to a flat block of MDF.

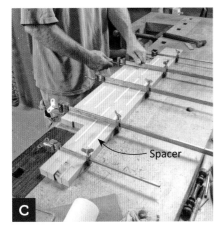

C Glue the four rails together at the same time, using scrapwood spacers to establish the panel slots. Wax the spacers to ensure easy release.

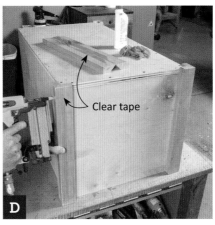

Clear tape

D Tape along the leg bevels, add glue, and fold the leg over the corner of the chest. Pin nails will clamp the leg until the glue sets.

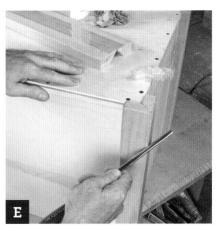

E While the glue is still wet, remove the tape and rub a burnisher along the joint to close any gaps.

establish the panel slots (Photo C). After the glue dries, remove the spacers, and plane the rails to final thickness. (For efficiency and accuracy, now is a good time to mill the short and long lid rails (K, L) to final thickness and width, leaving them oversized in length for now.)

6 Make the side and center stiles (G, H) to the thickness and width shown in the Cut List, but leave the pieces slightly oversized in length for now. Rout a ¼" × ¼" rabbet in one edge of each side stile (G) and in both edges of each center stile (H).

7 Mill the short and long bottom rails (I, J) to the thickness and width shown in the Cut List, but leave them slightly oversized in length for now.

Apply the trim

1 Join each pair of legs (D) with clear tape along their show faces. With the box upside down on the bench, spread glue on the bevels and along the inside faces of the legs, fold each assembly square, and press it over the corner of the box. I used six 1⅜" pin nails to hold each leg assembly in place while the glue dried (Photo D).

2 Close up any gaps by rubbing a burnisher or other smooth, round piece of metal over the miters to squash the adjacent fibers together (Photo E).

3 Mark the center of a long rail (F), measure outward to half of the finished length shown in the Cut List, lay out the miter, and cut it. Then clamp the rail to the

Figure 3: Mitering the Box Rails

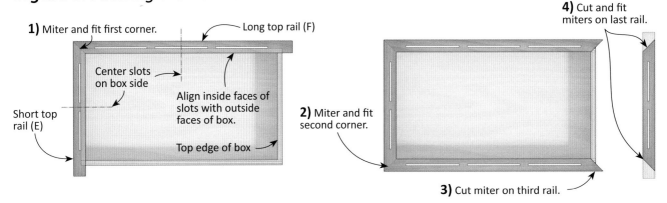

1) Miter and fit first corner.

Long top rail (F)

Center slots on box side

Align inside faces of slots with outside faces of box.

Short top rail (E)

Top edge of box

4) Cut and fit miters on last rail.

2) Miter and fit second corner.

3) Cut miter on third rail.

Figure 4: Miter Assist Jig

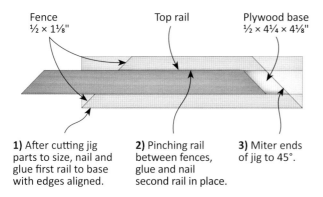

Fence
½ × 1⅛"

Top rail

Plywood base
½ × 4¼ × 4⅛"

1) After cutting jig parts to size, nail and glue first rail to base with edges aligned.

2) Pinching rail between fences, glue and nail second rail in place.

3) Miter ends of jig to 45°.

F

You can either trim an errant miter to a perfect 45° angle with this jig or adjust the angle in small degrees.

box, aligning the inside walls of the panel slots with the outside walls of the box, as shown in Figure 3 (page 162). This ensures your panels will slide in and out easily.

4 Cut the mating miter on the adjacent short rail (E), and check the fit of the joint, again with the rail slots flush to the box walls. If necessary, adjust the fit of the miter. I typically fine-tune miters with a block plane, holding the work in a simple jig clamped in a bench vise (Figure 4 and Photo F).

5 When satisfied with the fit of the joint, clamp the short top rail (E) in place, and

mark for the miters on the opposite ends of both rails (Photo G). Then cut to your marks.

6 As shown in Figure 3, miter and fit the other long top rail (F) in the same manner. Set the remaining unmitered top short rail (E) aside for the moment.

7 Cut #10 biscuit slots in all the miters you just cut. To make the job easy, clamp your miter-assist jig to your benchtop with the end of a rail flush with an end of the jig. Attach a ½"-thick plywood sub-base to your biscuit joiner, and you're ready to go (Photo H).

G

Clamp the mitered ends of the rails to the chest, and mark the opposite ends by pressing a square against the inside of the chest.

H

Plywood subbase

The miter-assist jig will solidly hold each rail in place for accurate, safe biscuit slotting.

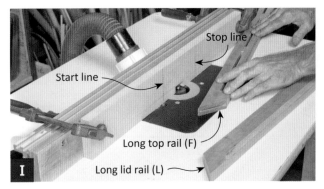

Start and stop lines on the router table fence register the ends of the rail travel when mortising for the continuous hinge.

With all but the last two miters fitted, glue and clamp the three mitered rails to the box, and pin them in place.

8 Rout a ¹⁄₃₂"-deep × ½"-wide stopped mortise in the rear long top rail (F) to accept the continuous (piano) hinge. Set a ½" rabbeting bit to project ¹⁄₃₂" from your router tabletop, and mark the fence for the beginning and end of the cut. Mark the start line 2¹⁄₁₆" to the left of the bit perimeter and the stop line 2¹⁄₁₆" to the right of the perimeter. (This setup stops the cut ¹⁄₁₆" shy of each mortise end as a safety measure.) Begin the cut by pivoting the work into the bit so the tip of the miter contacts the start line (Photo I). When the trailing miter tip meets the stop line, pivot the work away from the bit.

9 While the router table is set up for the job, also rout the mating mortise in the lid's rear rail (L) after mitering the rail's ends.

10 Square the ends of the mortises with a chisel, and check the fit of the hinge on the box and lid rails.

11 Glue and clamp the three mitered top rails (E, F) to the chest (Photo J). Again, it's not critical that the inside surfaces of the rail and box are flush with each other; what is important is that the inside walls of the panel slots are flush with the outside of the box.

12 As shown in Figure 3 (page 162), fit the remaining short top rail (E), making trial miter cuts until the joints mate perfectly.

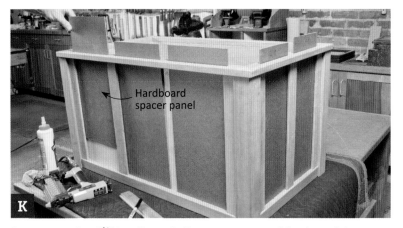

Spacer panels of ⅛" hardboard allow accurate positioning of the center stiles, which will ensure a perfect fit of the finished panels you'll make later.

Then cut the biscuit slots, and glue and clamp the piece in place.

13 Crosscut the bottom rails (I, J) to fit between the legs. Lay out the locations of the ⁹⁄₆₄"-diameter access holes on the rails between each pair of stiles (G, H), where shown in Figure 1 (page 160), and then drill the through-holes on the drill press.

14 With the box upside down, glue and clamp the bottom rails (I, J) in place without nails.

15 Crosscut the side and center stiles (G, H) to fit tightly between the top and bottom rails.

16 Attach the side stiles (G) with glue and 1" pins.

17 Glue and pin the center stiles (H) in place. To ensure accurate positioning, place

Figure 5: Ripping the V-notch

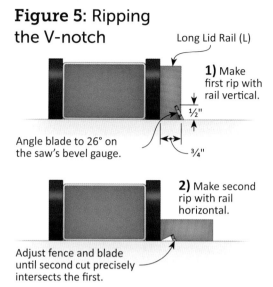

Long Lid Rail (L)

1) Make first rip with rail vertical.

½"

Angle blade to 26° on the saw's bevel gauge.

¾"

2) Make second rip with rail horizontal.

Adjust fence and blade until second cut precisely intersects the first.

Use loosely set F-style clamps to position the lid rails on the box rails while pulling the miters tight with a band clamp.

After assembling the frame, use a chisel to extend the V-notch ¾" into each adjacent rail.

A ⅛" straight bit in a laminate trimmer lets you rout closely into the corners of the cross rail notches before finishing up with a chisel.

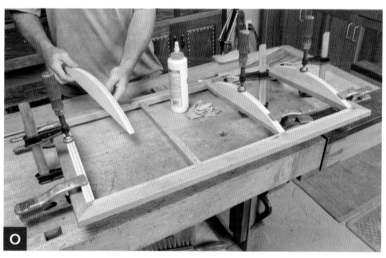

Center the two small middle ribs on the cross rails, and glue the two small outer ribs flush with the inside of the frame.

QUICK TIP

To conceal small cracks and holes, mix sanding dust with enough 2-lb.-cut shellac to make a wet (but not runny) mixture. Spread the filler into the recess, and then sand it flush after it dries. The repair will disappear after applying a few coats of finish.

Figure 6: Cross Rail Connection

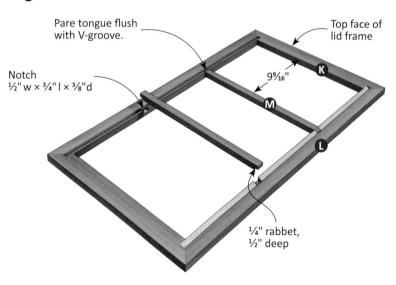

Pare tongue flush with V-groove.

Top face of lid frame

Notch ½" w × ¾" l × ⅜" d

9⁹⁄₁₆"

K

M

L

¼" rabbet, ½" deep

Pattern-Sawing On The Bandsaw

Making multiple identical parts on your bandsaw is easy with this jig and a plywood pattern of your desired shape. Make the jig, and outfit your saw with a ½" 4-tpi blade (which provides a better cutting sight line than a narrower blade.) Temporarily tack or tape the plywood pattern to your stock, and clamp the jig to your bandsaw fence. Locate the nose block about ⅛" above the work, and adjust the fence so the block's contact point sits even with, or slightly past, the blade.

Then position the jig fore or aft until the block sits about ¹⁄₁₆" in front of the blade's teeth.

To make the cut, press the pattern against the nose block while steering the work so that the edge of the pattern remains parallel to the blade at all times. Don't be surprised if you unwittingly saw into the nose block. That's why it's removable. Just make a new one and keep on sawing.

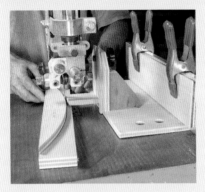

Pattern-Sawing Jig

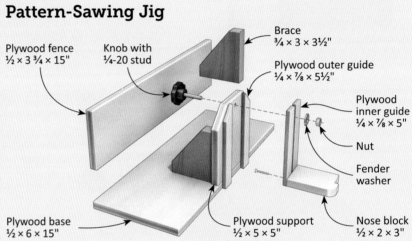

Plywood fence ½ × 3¾ × 15"
Knob with ¼-20 stud
Brace ¾ × 3 × 3½"
Plywood outer guide ¼ × ⅞ × 5½"
Plywood inner guide ¼ × ⅞ × 5"
Nut
Fender washer
Plywood base ½ × 6 × 15"
Plywood support ½ × 5 × 5"
Nose block ½ × 2 × 3"

them against the edges of carefully squared spacer panels made of ⅛" hardboard (Photo K; page 164).

Make the spacer panels wide enough to fit precisely between each opposing pair of stile rabbet shoulders, using the panel (U, V) widths shown in the Cut List as a starting reference. However, make the spacer panels 18" long for easier handling.

Make the lid

1 Notch the lid's long rails (K, L) on the tablesaw with the blade tilted to 26°, as shown in Figure 5 (page 165). Make sure to saw into the top face of the rear rail—not into the face with the hinge mortise.

2 To ensure that the lid aligns with the box, test-fit the lid rail miter joints while the

Figure 7: Rib Layout

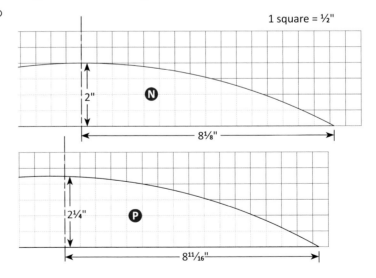

1 square = ½"

2" Ⓝ 8⅛"

2¼" Ⓟ 8¹¹⁄₁₆"

Figure 8: Rabbeting and Beveling the Battens

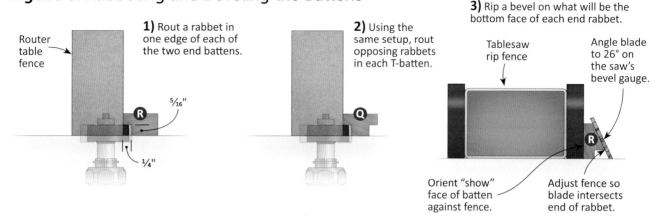

Router table fence

1) Rout a rabbet in one edge of each of the two end battens.

⁵⁄₁₆"

¼"

R

2) Using the same setup, rout opposing rabbets in each T-batten.

Q

3) Rip a bevel on what will be the bottom face of each end rabbet.

Tablesaw rip fence

Angle blade to 26° on the saw's bevel gauge.

R

Orient "show" face of batten against fence.

Adjust fence so blade intersects end of rabbet.

P

Add a spot of glue to each rib, and then drive two pins through each slat into each rib.

Q

Use hardboard spacers to position the battens parallel and equidistant to each other, and then glue and screw them to the underlying ribs.

rail pieces sit atop the assembled box rails. When everything aligns well, cut the biscuit slots in the miters.

3 Unlike the box top rails (E, F), the lid rails (K, L) must come together all at once. Use the box top rail frame as a platform for gluing up the lid frame. Apply wide tape over the box frame joints to prevent gluing the two frames together. Use F-style clamps to initially position the frame members, and then weave a band clamp through the clamps to draw the miters tight (Photo L; page 165).

4 Lengthen the V-notch in each long rail (L) so it extends ¾" into each short rail (K), as shown in Photo M (page 165). I penciled the outline and then pared to it with a chisel. Don't fuss—the ribs and the battens will eventually cover up your handiwork.

5 Use a knife to lay out the cross rail (M) notches in the long rails (L). Rout the notches to depth, staying inside your knifed lines (Photo N; page 165). Then clean up to the lines with a chisel.

6 Make the cross rails (M) as shown in the Cut List on page 171, and cut a ¼"-deep × ½"-long rabbet in each end. Glue and clamp the cross rails (M) to the lid frame. After the glue dries, pare the ends of each cross rail flush with the adjacent V-groove wall.

7 Make the small plywood ribs (N), pattern-sawing them on the bandsaw.

8 Attach the small ribs (N) to the frame using glue and clamps as shown in Photo O (page 165).

9 Mill the slats (O) to the thickness and length shown in the Cut List, selecting straight-grained stock for stability. Rip them about 1/32" oversized in width for now.

10 Tuck the outermost slats in their respective notches, and then dry-fit all of the slats in place, butting their edges tight to each other. Trim the edges of each one a bit, if necessary, to seat them all firmly on the ribs. Then attach them to the ribs (Photo P; page 167).

11 Pattern-saw the large ribs (P) from solid stock. Test-fit them to ensure they align with the highest points on the slats without extending any further, which could cause the panels to bind going in.

Figure 9: Lid Stay Block

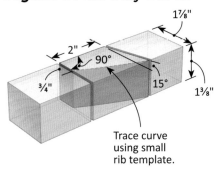

Trace curve using small rib template.

Figure 10: Lid Stay Mounting

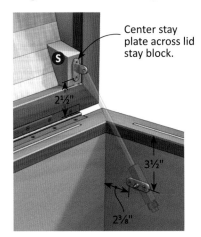

Center stay plate across lid stay block.

Color To Dye For

Dyes are available in solvent (liquid) form or as a powder that you mix with a solvent. Several recently developed powder dyes can be mixed with either water or alcohol. I prefer water-based dye for wiping because its longer dry time helps prevent lap marks, which often occur when wiping or brushing on faster-drying alcohol-based dyes. (When spraying, it doesn't matter much.) Plus, water-based dyes resist fading better. Keep in mind that many dyes–especially the powder type–are caustic, so wear gloves, eye protection, and a respirator rated for vapors.

Follow these guidelines when using water-based dye:

- Prepare the surface by sanding through 220 grit to ensure clear color and grain and to prevent muddiness. Then "pre-raise" the grain by wetting the surface with clean water and sanding again with 220 grit after the water evaporates.
- Flood the surface with dye using a foam brush. Work in the direction of the grain, overlapping your strokes and pulling the brush completely off the end of the work. Avoid puddles.

- Once the dye has dried, apply the first coat of your favorite clear finish. When that's dry, rub lightly with the grain using 0000 steel wool or a white synthetic abrasive pad. Don't fret if the color looks dull and blotchy; successive coats will add depth, luster, and clarity.
- Apply the second, third, and fourth coats of finish, rubbing with 0000 steel wool or a white pad between coats, but not after the final coat. Four to six coats should do it, depending on the thickness of each coat. More coats add depth, but too many can diminish that "close-to-the-wood" look.

Figure 11: Aligning the Magnets

1. Arrange lid panels (W) for pleasing grain.
2. Drill ⅜"-dia. × ³⁄₁₆"-deep holes for magnets.
3. At one end of lid, install all magnets with north pole faces oriented upward.
4. At opposite end, install all magnets with south pole faces oriented upward.

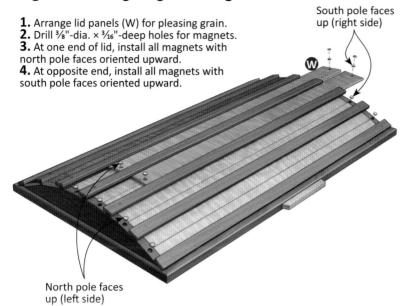

South pole faces
up (right side)

North pole faces
up (left side)

Fine-tune the curve if necessary, shaping and smoothing the ribs with a disc or belt sander. Then hand-sand through 220 grit.

12 Glue and pin the large ribs (P) to the outermost small ribs (N) and the frame.

13 Mill the T-battens and end battens (Q, R) to the dimensions in the Cut List.

14 Rout the edge rabbets in the battens (Q, R) on the router table using a rabbeting bit adjusted for a ⁵⁄₁₆"-deep cut. (See Figure 8 page 167.) Make sure to rout only one edge of each end batten (R). Then rip the 26° bevel on each end batten on the tablesaw.

15 Cut the end rabbets on all the battens using the bandsaw. First, set the fence ⁵⁄₁₆" from the blade, and make a ³⁄₁₆"-long rip cut with the top of the batten pressed against the fence. Then mark one of the battens ³⁄₁₆" from the end, use the piece to reset the fence to this cutline, and saw away the remaining waste on all the battens while supporting the workpiece on edge against a squared block.

16 Finish-sand the battens (Q, R) through 220 grit, and sand or plane a ¹⁄₁₆" chamfer on the top edges and ends. Drill

¼"-diameter counterbores, ⅛"-deep, as well as clearance holes for #7 × 1⅝" trim-head screws in the T-battens (Q), locating them at the small rib intersections. Don't drill the end battens (R).

17 Use glue and pin nails to attach the two end battens (R) to the front and back rails (L), aligning each until the lower edge of its rabbet contacts the lowest slat.

18 It's crucial to align the T-battens (Q) parallel to each other and at the same distance apart. To do this, rip six 30"-long spacers of equal width from ⅛" hardboard, test-fitting them between the battens until all fit tightly. (You'll have to experiment with the correct rip setting for your saw, but a good starting point is 2⅝".) When everything fits well, glue and screw the battens to the lid (Photo Q; page 167).

19 Cut ¼"-diameter plugs on the drill press using a plug cutter, and then glue them into the counterbores. When the glue is dry, pare and sand the plugs flush with the battens.

20 Cut the handle (T) to the shape shown in the Figure 1 Handle Detail (page 160), gently curving the ends on the bandsaw. Invert the lid, and glue the handle to the front rail (L), centering the handle across the rail's length and thickness.

Attach the lid to the box

1 Place the continuous hinge in its mortise in the rear lid rail (L). Temporarily attach it with three equidistantly placed screws driven into ³⁄₃₂"-diameter pilot holes.

2 Mark *box* on the back of the free hinge leaf, and remove the hinge from the lid. Then attach the hinge to the box in the same manner.

3 Elevate the inverted lid on a platform next to the box (or have a helper hold it)

while you reattach the hinge leaf to the lid with the three screws. Close the lid and check the fit. Make any necessary adjustments by lengthening the hinge mortise and drilling for screws in new locations. Once everything checks out, drill and install the remaining screws in the lid and box.

4 Make the lid stay blocks (S), as shown in Figure 9 (page 168), bandsawing and sanding the curve, as necessary, to match the curve of the lid.

5 Screw the lid stay plates to the box and the lid stay blocks, locating them, where shown in Figure 10 (page 168).

Make and install the panels

1 Mill the box and lid panel (U, V, W) stock to thickness, using scrap to check for a sliding fit through the top rail (E, F) slots and their respective stile (G, H) rabbets, as well as the rabbets in the lid battens (Q, R).

2 Cut the panels a bit narrower than the width of the space and about ½" longer than the size shown in the Cut List. Don't ease over any of the edges yet, as a sharp edge helps restrain dye from migrating to an adjacent edge.

3 Mark the magnet locations, centering them across the thickness of the large ribs (P), and between the battens (Q, R). Also mark the corresponding locations at the ends of one face of each lid panel (W).

4 Drill the ³⁄₁₆"-deep magnet holes in the ribs using a hand drill and a ³⁄₈" Forstner or brad-point bit (Photo R).

5 Drill the ³⁄₁₆"-deep magnet holes in the lid panels (W) using a ³⁄₈" Forstner or brad-point bit in the drill press. (Warning: If your bit has a long center point that may poke through the opposite panel face, grind or file it down before drilling.)

R

Drill the ³⁄₁₆"-deep magnet holes using a ³⁄₈" Forstner bit marked ³⁄₁₆" up from its cutting edge. Stop drilling when the mark disappears.

6 Spin a ³⁄₈" plug cutter on the drill press to make face-grain plugs in matching stock for the holes in the lid panels (W) and the large ribs (P). Saw them to a thickness of about ³⁄₈".

7 Dab epoxy into each hole before inserting a ³⁄₈" rare-earth magnet. To ensure correct polarity for panel reversal, orient the magnets, as shown in Figure 11 (page 169). (To keep track of their polarities, first mark all 24 magnets on the same polarized face with a permanent marker.) Before the epoxy sets, spread some yellow or white glue into the holes and onto the plugs before tapping the plugs home (Photo S).

QUICK TIP

For perfectly fitting thin plugs, use a tapered plug cutter on the drill press, drilling only 1/4" or so into your stock to keep the plugs fat enough to ensure a snug fit.

With each magnet marked for polarity, install it with a dab of epoxy, and then glue in the wood plug.

Cut List: Treasure Chest

	Part	Thickness	Width	Length	Qty.	Mat'l
Box						
A	Short sides	3/4"	16 5/16"	16 5/16"	2	BP
B	Long sides	3/4"	16 5/16"	31 3/4"	2	BP
C*	Bottom	3/4"	17 3/4"	31 3/4"	1	BP
Box trim						
D*	Legs	15/16"	2"	17 1/4"	8	C
E**	Short top rails	3/4"	1 7/8"	20"	2	C
F**	Long top rails	3/4"	1 7/8"	34"	2	C
G*	Side stiles	9/16"	1 1/2"	15 9/16"	8	C
H*	Center stiles	9/16"	1 3/4"	15 9/16"	6	C
I*	Short bottom rails	3/4"	1 1/2"	15 5/8"	2	C
J*	Long bottom rails	3/4"	1 1/2"	29 5/8"	2	C
Lid						
K	Short rails	3/4"	1 7/8"	20"	2	C
L	Long rails	3/4"	1 7/8"	34"	2	C
M	Cross rails	5/8"	3/4"	17 1/4"	2	C
N	Small ribs	3/4"	2"	16 1/4"	4	BP
O	Slats	1/4"	1 1/2"	31 3/4"	12	M
P	Large ribs	3/4"	2 1/4"	17 3/8"	2	C
Q	T-battens	5/8"	1"	33 5/8"	5	C
R	End battens	5/8"	1"	33 5/8"	2	C
S	Lid stay block	1 3/8"	1 7/8"	2"	2	M
T	Handle	7/16"	5/8"	6"	1	M
Panels						
U*	Small box panels	1/4"	6"	16 1/4"	4	M
V*	Large box panels	1/4"	8 1/4"	16 1/4"	6	M
W*	Lid panels	1/4"	2 5/8"	33 7/16"	6	M

* Indicates parts are initially cut oversized. See instructions.
** Indicates parts were made of more than one piece.
Materials: BP=Birch Plywood, C=Cherry, M=Maple

8 After the glue cures, trim the plugs flush and sand the surfaces through 220 grit.

9 Dye one side of all the panels. (See sidebar on page 168 for a few helpful hints.)

10 Crosscut the panels (U, V, W) square and to finished length.

11 Rip the box panels (U, V) about 1/16" narrower than the width of the rail slots and the lid panels about 1/32" narrower than their openings.

12 Apply your preferred finish. Remember to use an odorless finish, such as shellac, for the inside of the lid.

13 Once the finish is dry, stick a couple of bumpers on the underside of the front lid rail (L), and turn the knurled knobs on the stays to adjust their resistance for a soft lid closure.

KID-FRIENDLY TOYBOX

An Arts & Crafts toy box that works for any age

BY DEWAYNE BAKER

As a new dad, I've learned that a toy box is a necessary piece of furniture in a child's room. The one I designed for my own son soon after he was born is not only a great place for toys, but also an attractive piece of fine furniture

that doubles as a bench seat. The sturdy construction ensures this small chest will be passed down for generations. As the child grows, the chest can become a souvenir or keepsake chest, a hope chest or even a blanket chest.

The first thing I considered in my design was the potential for small fingers to get pinched. The lid rests on a ledge on the interior side walls and a 1" gap below the lid allows for its safe operation. Another safety feature I added is a weight-rated lid support that prevents the lid from slamming down.

I also wanted handles on the sides to make the box easy to move. Routed finger pulls fit the bill, and they can never break off.

Getting started

There are several options to consider for the frame-and-panel assemblies that make up the front and sides of this chest. Options include solid raised panels, plywood, and veneered substrate panels. However you make it, the panel thickness will determine the tongue-and-groove size and the router bit or bits needed to make the joints.

Careful stock selection can make a good-looking project a great-looking project. I used quartersawn white oak and purpleheart for mine, hand-picking a few boards with some interesting figure. The purpleheart I used will turn a brownish purple color with time.

A word of caution: some woods can bleed and transfer color to the contrasting wood during the first coat of finish. This can be somewhat controlled by pre-sealing the contrasting panels with shellac. (See the sidebar on page 182.)

Prepare the panels and templates

The width of the tongue-and-groove joinery for the front and side frame-and-panel assemblies will be determined by the thickness of your panel stock. If you plan to veneer your panels, that should be the first step. Other options include using plywood or solid wood milled between ½" and ⅜" thick.

For my panels, I veneered ¼" plywood with shop-sawn purpleheart veneers thicknessed to ¹⁄₁₆" at the drum sander. The resulting panels are ⅜" thick when veneered on both sides. No need to cut the panels to size at this time; we are just establishing the thickness of the finished panels to be used as a guide for milling the joinery later.

Make templates for parts F, M and upper C, and for the recessed finger pulls, from ½" MDF or comparable material. Refer to the illustrations on page 174. Cut the template material a little oversize and lay out the shapes with a pencil. Rough-cut the shapes at the bandsaw, staying ¹⁄₁₆" or so outside the line. Sand to refine the template shapes.

To make the router template for the finger pull, calculate the radius of the cut with the dimensions of your router base. Measure the width of your handheld plunge router base. Add ⅜" to this measurement and divide the total by two. For example:

$$\text{router base} = 7"$$
$$7" + \tfrac{3}{8}" = 7\tfrac{3}{8}"$$
$$7\tfrac{3}{8}" \div 2 = 3\tfrac{11}{16}"$$

Lay out center lines and the radiuses as shown in the pull template illustration.

To cut out the template interior, I used an adjustable circle cutter in the drill press, then cut the straight portions of the template interior with a jigsaw. A scroll saw also works. Smooth the interior edges of the template by sanding and filing, as needed.

Mill the hardwood stock

Take a little extra time to plan your cuts by laying them out on your rough stock with a pencil or chalk. Paying attention to color and figure will be well rewarded in the finished piece. Rough-cut your stock a couple inches over length prior to milling. Mill your stock flat, straight, and square by a process of jointing, planing, and ripping. Cut and mill project parts A through G to final dimensions.

Glue up parts L and M. You can use biscuits to align the boards and help ensure flat glue-ups. Another helpful hint is to leave the glue-up pieces a bit over final thickness and glue them in sections within the capacity of your planer. The sections are then planed to thickness and joined in one final glue-up.

Part M will later be glued to ¾" plywood to form the rear panel, so mill it to the same thickness as your plywood stock for a seamless joint. Leave the parts oversize for now; we'll trim them later.

Front

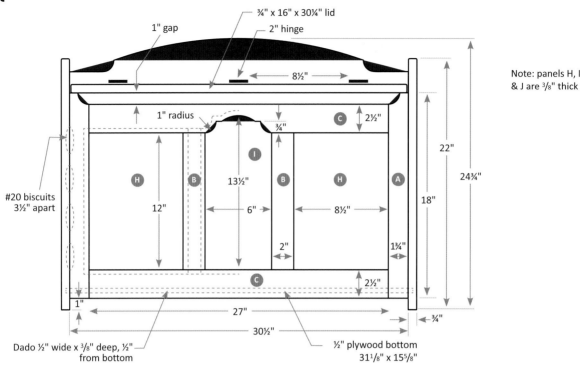

¾" x 16" x 30¼" lid

1" gap

2" hinge

8½"

Note: panels H, I & J are ⅜" thick

1" radius

¾"

2½" C

22"

24¾"

18"

H

B

I

13½"

B

H

A

12"

6"

8½"

2"

1¾"

#20 biscuits 3½" apart

C

2½"

1"

27"

¾"

30½"

Dado ½" wide x ⅜" deep, ½" from bottom

½" plywood bottom 31⅛" x 15⅝"

Back

Side

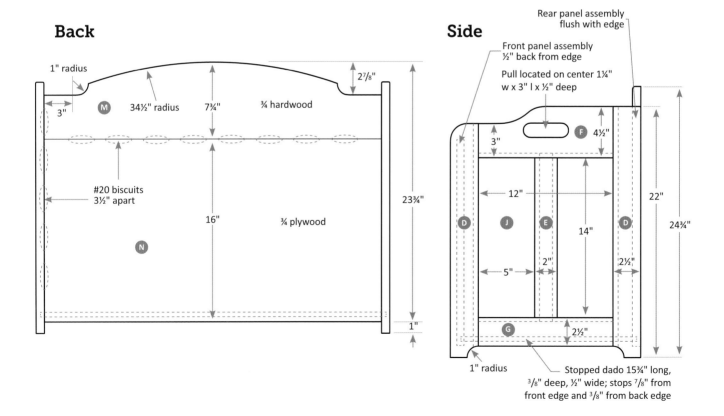

1" radius

M

34½" radius

7¾"

2⅞"

¾ hardwood

3"

#20 biscuits 3½" apart

23¾"

16"

¾ plywood

N

1"

Rear panel assembly flush with edge

Front panel assembly ½" back from edge

Pull located on center 1¼" w x 3" l x ½" deep

F

4½"

3"

12"

22"

24¾"

D

J

E

14"

D

5"

2"

2½"

G

2½"

1" radius

Stopped dado 15¾" long, ⅜" deep, ½" wide; stops ⅞" from front edge and ⅜" from back edge

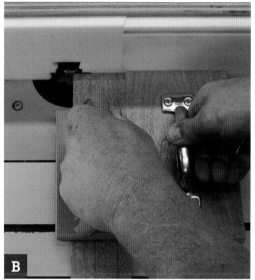

Rout the finger pulls

Before you rout the finger pulls in parts F, make some test cuts in ¾" MDF or other inexpensive material. Lay out horizontal and vertical center lines, line up the center lines of the template and clamp the template securely to your bench. Use additional stock of the same thickness to help support the template if necessary (Figure 1). Install a ½" straight bit in your router and set the plunge/cut depth to a little less than ½". Rout out the material, following the template edges with the router base as well as the remaining material in the center. Use only the round portion of the router base; if your router has a straight portion, be sure not to align this portion with the template edges, or the cut will be ruined.

Now install a finger-pull bit (sometimes called a drawer pull bit) and set the plunge/cut depth to ½" or according to the bit manufacturer's recommendation. When you plunge this bit, you will need to position the router in one of the radius centers, not against the template edge, or the cut will be ruined. Once the bit is plunged to its set depth, rout the profile, following the template edges and center

area as before. When the cut is finished, power down the router and wait until it stops before lifting. The resulting finger pull is shown inset in Photo A.

Rout the frames and panels

Using a ¼"-wide, ½"-deep slot-cutting bit, rout test cuts for the tongue-and-groove joinery on the stiles and rails of the frame-and-panel assemblies. Set up the bit to first rout a slot that accommodates the panel thickness. Two passes are required to complete the slot. For a ⅜"-wide slot, set the bit height to ⁹⁄₁₆". After routing the first pass, flip the workpiece and make a second pass. This will produce a ⅜" groove that is perfectly centered.

Test-fit the groove to the panel stock and make adjustments and further test cuts until a slightly loose—but not sloppy—fit is achieved. Save and mark this test piece as a setup block.

Next, make test cuts to rout a tongue that fits the slot. The fit should be a slight friction fit. Mark this test piece as a setup block as well.

Now you can begin routing the stiles and rails themselves. First, rout the tongues on

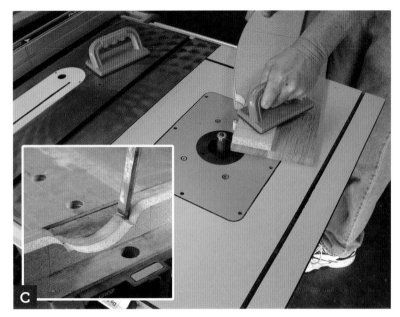

the ends of parts B, C, E, F and G. Feed the narrow stock with a square chaser block or sled (Photo B; page 175).

Next, trace the template outline on the top front rail (C) and rear crest rail (M). M should be left a bit over final length and the template referenced on its center. Rough-cut the shapes of parts C and M at the bandsaw, staying just outside the line in preparation for flush trimming. Save the offcut for part M to use as clamping cawls during the rear panel glueup. Attach the templates with double-stick tape and flush-trim the shapes on the router table using a flush-trim bit (Photo C). Some careful chisel work is required to complete the inside square detail on the upper part C.

Set up your slot-cutting bit in the router table using the setup block you made during the test cuts. Rout the groove in one side only of parts A, C, D, F and G. Parts B and E receive a groove in both sides.

To complete part C, you must remove the fence (Photo D). Use a starting pin to safely start the cut.

Dry-fit the completed parts.

Assemble the panels

Cut the panel stock to final size. For the front center panel (I) you will have to cut the curve detail to match the upper rail. Use the template for part C, referenced on center with the crest of the curve at the finished panel height. Trace the shape and cut it out at the bandsaw. The square portion of the curve detail will have to be rounded over slightly to fit the slot.

Dry-fit the frame-and-panel assembly as well as the side assemblies. Note that the lower rails are referenced 1" up from the bottom of the adjoining stiles for the side assemblies. For the front assembly, the top rail is referenced 1" down. Mark these, and lay out center lines for proper alignment of the center stiles to the adjoining rails.

I recommend sanding the panels now, but the remaining curves in the side assemblies and top of the front assemblies will be cut and shaped after they are glued up.

Glue up the side frame-and-panel assemblies, working from the center out. Align and clamp the center stiles, slide the panels in place and add the outer stiles

(Photo E; page 178). The clamping procedure is similar for the front assembly, with the center panel placed between the center stiles first.

When the glue has cured, scrape and sand the stiles and rails. Note that the groove in the front assembly's outer stiles is visible at the top end. Most of this will be removed after cutting the 1"-radius curve in the top of the stiles. Cut off the tongue from one of your test cut pieces to fill a ½"-long section of the groove where the upper rail and stile meet. Test the fit and glue the filler pieces in place.

Glue up the rear panel assembly

Part M (rear crest rail) and part N (plywood back panel) are joined with #20 biscuits and glue. Lay out and cut biscuit slots 3½" apart. Dry-fit the pieces and check the assembly height, which should measure 23¾" at the top of the crest. The parts are left overlong and glued up with biscuits in place. Use the crest rail offcut you saved earlier to help with clamping (Photo F; page 178).

When the glue has cured, scrape and sand the assembly. The back can now be cut to its final width of 30½" to match the front assembly. It's helpful to use the front as a guide. Placing it on top of the rear panel assembly, line up your center reference lines and mark your cuts (Photo G; page 178). Use table saw sled to make the cuts.

Cut the biscuit joinery

The sides are joined to the front and back with #20 biscuits spaced 3½" apart, aligned with the lower rails on the side assemblies. Lay out four biscuit slots on each side of the front assembly and five on each side of the back. The back will be flush with the side frame edges, and the front assembly will be stepped ½" back from the side assembly edges.

To ensure accurate biscuit slot placement, I prefer to reference from the base rather than the fence. To cut the biscuit slots in the back, place the back face-up on a flat surface and cut the slots with the biscuit joiner on its base. To cut the slots on the side frames, I stand the biscuit joiner on end and use a 90° fence jig made from scrap butted against the side frame edge (Photo H; page 178). I use the same jig for the front slots with a ½" shim taped to the biscuit joiner base.

Templates

Note: templates extend 1" longer than workpiece where indicated by dotted lines.

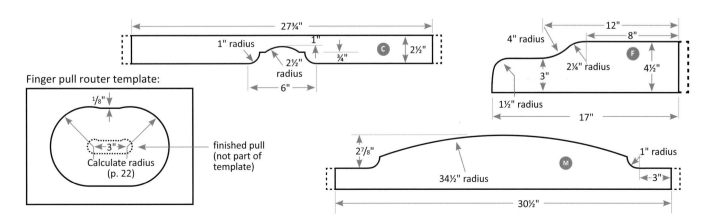

Finger pull router template:

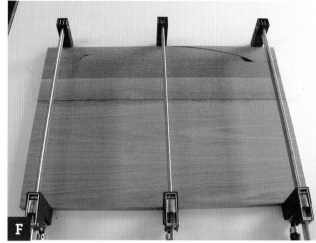

Shape the profiles

Place the side frame profile template at the top of each side assembly and trace the shape with a pencil. Use a compass to lay out a 1" radius from the bottom inside edge of each side frame stile. This radius should meet the lower rail. Lay out a 1" radius in the inside top corner of the front frame assembly in the same manner and rough-cut all these curves at the bandsaw.

Attach the template for the upper side frame profile and flush-trim the shape at the router table. For the small corner curves, I used an oscillating spindle sander with a 1" spindle to smooth and complete the curves. Rout a roundover profile on the front and top edges of the side frames using just a portion of a ¾" roundover bit, creating a gentle arc. The top of the front assembly receives the same profile. For the rear crest rail, I used a classic ogee bit. The completed side, front and rear assemblies are shown in Photo I.

This is a good time to sand all the case parts to 220 grit or finer.

Rout the dadoes for the bottom

The chest bottom is ½" plywood trapped in dadoes in all four sides of the box. The front and back assemblies receive a through dado while the side assemblies receive stopped dadoes. The dadoes are ½"

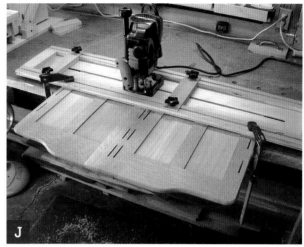

wide x ⅜" deep, placed ½" up from the bottom of the lower rails. Lay out the dado locations with a pencil and square. The stopped dadoes in the side frames stop ⅜" from the back and ⅞" from the front.

Use a router and jig to guide the cuts and support the router base (Photo J). The jig consists of a ¼" plywood bottom, two ¾" x 2" plywood guide fences, two end pieces and two ¾" plywood stops. The jig width will be determined by the width of your router base. I routed a T-slot in the guide fences for use with T-bolt hardware. The stops have a ¼" piece of plywood attached to the top of the stops to overlap the guide fences and

a hole is drilled to accommodate the T-bolt. Cut through the jig bottom with a ½" bit with sacrificial scrap placed underneath the cut.

To rout the stopped dadoes in the side assemblies, align the jig slot with the layout lines and clamp the workpiece and jig securely to your bench. Position the router in the jig with the bit just short of the dado stop line and set the jig stop for each stop location before routing the dadoes. Be sure to account for the ¼" jig base when setting the bit depth.

Use a chisel to square up the ends of the stopped dadoes. The operation for the front and back assemblies is the same, but without the use of the stops.

Glue up the case

With the bottom panel and all biscuits in place, perform a dry fit of the case parts and work out a clamping strategy. It's best to let gravity work in your favor. Assemble and clamp the case standing on its side with cawls placed underneath to allow clearance for the clamps (Photo K; page 179). If no adjustments are needed, glue up the case. The bottom sits in the dadoes dry. Once the clamps are in place, turn the case on its feet on a flat surface, check that its stance is level, and adjust violating parts if needed.

Make the lid

Flatten the lid glueup by scraping and sanding before cutting it to finished size. Measure the case opening width to confirm a match. I made my lid length ¼" less than the case opening, while the width overhangs the front panel assembly. Rip and crosscut the lid to final size using a panel sled for safety at the table saw. Rout a roundover profile on the front and side edges, leaving the back edge square.

The weight-rated lid support I used required a notch in the underside of the lid due to the location of the hinges in this project. You could mount a ½" block

between the support and the rear wall, but I thought that the notch looked better. I also recommend that you weigh your lid before ordering a support. The retailer provides a formula that lets you determine how much lift, and therefore which support, you'll need for a safe lowering by small hands.

Measure over 2½" right of center and lay out a notch with a pencil and square. The notch measures 1½" long x 1" wide and ½" deep at the back edge and tapers to 0" deep at the stop line. Carefully cut the notch sides with a hand saw. Remove most of the waste with a chisel, working with the grain. Smooth and refine the notch with a file and sandpaper wrapped around a block (Photo L; page 179).

Install the lid hardware & cleats

The lid rests on a set of cleats attached to the sides of the case interior. The cleats are mounted flush with the top edge of the front assembly stiles, and measure ½" wide x ½" thick x 13" long. Make a set of story sticks of equal length that will support and reference the cleats at the correct location. Laying the case on its side makes this operation much easier.

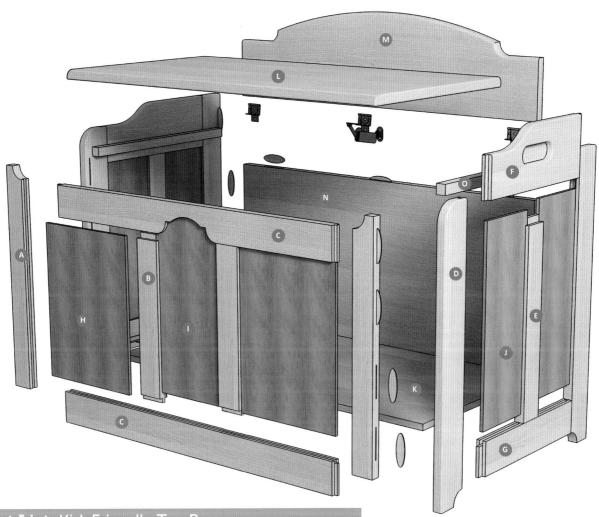

Cut List: Kid-Friendly Toy Box

A	Front stiles (2), oak	3/4"	x	1 3/4"	x	18"
B	Front center stiles (2), oak	3/4"	x	2"	x	13"
C	Front rails (2), oak	3/4"	x	2 1/2"	x	28"
D	Side frame stiles (4), oak	3/4"	x	2 1/2"	x	22"
E	Center side frame stiles (2), oak	3/4"	x	2"	x	15"
F	Upper side frame rails (2), oak	3/4"	x	4 1/2"	x	13"
G	Lower side frame rails (2), oak	3/4"	x	2 1/2"	x	13"
H	Front panels (2), plywood	3/8"	x	9 3/8"	x	12 7/8"
I	Front center panel, plywood	3/8"	x	6 7/8"	x	14 3/8"
J	Side panels (4), plywood	3/8"	x	5 7/8"	x	14 7/8"
K	Bottom, plywood	1/2"	x	15 5/8"	x	31 1/8"
L	Lid, oak	3/4"	x	16"	x	30 1/4"
M	Rear crest rail, oak	3/4"	x	7 3/4"	x	30 1/2"
N	Rear panel, plywood	3/4"	x	16"	x	30 1/2"
O	Lid cleats (2), oak	1/2"	x	1/2"	x	13"
	Story sticks (2)	1/2"	x	1/2"	x	16 1/2"
	Story stick	1/4"	x	1/4"	x	8"
	Finger pull template, MDF	3/4"	x	11"	x	16"
	Upper front rail template, MDF	3/4"	x	3"	x	33 1/2"
	Upper side rail template, MDF	3/4"	x	11"	x	16"
	Rear crest rail template, MDF	3/4"	x	7"	x	32 1/2"
	Dado jig base (for 7" router base)	1/4"	x	11"	x	48"
	Dado jig side rails (2)	3/4"	x	2"	x	48"
	Dado jig ends and stops (4)	3/4"	x	2"	x	7"
	Dado jig stop part B	1/4"	x	2"	x	11"

The cleats are attached with glue and two #6, 1" screws that will be concealed with plugs. Mark the screw locations 1" from each end, centered on the width of the cleat. At the drill press, drill a 3/8" hole 1/2" deep to accommodate a 3/8" plug. Position the cleat with the story sticks in place and carefully predrill for the screws. Use a drill depth stop or tape on the bit as a depth reference. Apply glue and drive the screws. Plug the holes by cutting plugs from scrap, cutting them off with a flush-cutting saw and sanding them smooth.

Install the center hinge first. Turn the lid upside-down and position the hinge on center, predrill using a Vix bit and attach with screws. To position the right and left hinges, I used an 8" story stick (Photo M).

Position the lid on top of the cleats and against the back wall, with the hinges still attached to the lid. I used ⅛" shims on each end of the lid to center it and ensure an even gap at both ends. Mark the position of the center hinge. Clamp a straight piece of stock to the back wall, resting on top of the hinge barrels, as a reference for mounting the hinges to the case. Remove the lid, and the hinges from the lid. Position the center hinge on the back wall of the case on center and butted up against the reference stick you clamped on (Photo N; page 180). Use the 8" story stick to reference the right and left hinges; predrill and attach with screws. Remove the clamps and reference stick.

Next, the lid can be attached to the case using the predrilled holes as your guide. Test the fit and operation of the lid. Now, install the weight-rated lid support. Align it with the notch and mark and predrill the screw-hole locations (following the manufacturer's directions).

Remove the hardware, prep for and apply the finish. Reinstall the hardware when the finish has cured.

An Oil-and-Varnish Finish

This finishing method was passed along to me by a superb box maker. It starts with a seal coat of blonde de-waxed shellac mixed fresh. When this coat has cured, the surfaces are buffed vigorously, re-exposing the surface fibers but sealing the pores. After the shellac has been buffed out, a mixture of oil and polyurethane is applied for a glowing hand-rubbed finish that accents the wood's natural beauty. The shellac sealer coat helps to even out the oil absorption, eliminating blotching and adding luster and a silky-smooth feel to the finish. Shellac can also be very effective for repairing small cracks or gaps. Before starting the first coat, sand the crack or gap with 220-grit paper and a sanding block, working sawdust into the gap. Without removing the dust, apply shellac to the area. Once dry, sand it level and repeat if necessary.

Applying the shellac

First, check your project for any imperfections, glue remnants or pencil lines, and sand to 220 grit or finer, then remove the dust. The seal coat of shellac is mixed at a 1-lb cut. A 1-lb cut means that 1lb of shellac flakes is mixed with 1 gallon of denatured alcohol. See the mixing ratio chart for mixing smaller quantities. Shellac has a short shelf life. It's best mixed fresh just a few days before it's needed. Mix and store it in a non-metal, airtight container. Swirl or agitate the mixture frequently for the first few hours to prevent the flakes from clumping. Before application, the shellac mixture must be strained. Use a piece of cheesecloth doubled over and strain it into a clean container. Submerge the staining pad and then wring it out a bit. The pad shouldn't create drips or runs while applying. Wipe on a single thin coat on every surface, inside and out, top to bottom. Shellac dries quite fast, but let it cure overnight before buffing it out. Use 0000 steel wool and buff all surfaces vigorously. Remove all dust and wool fibers by vacuuming and wiping with a clean soft cloth. The surfaces should be silky-smooth at this point.

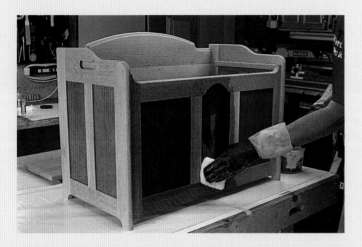

Applying the oil and varnish

The oil-and-varnish mixture consists of boiled linseed oil, pure tung oil and oil-based glossy polyurethane. (Note: the tung oil must be 100% pure; products labeled "tung oil finish" will not work.) Mix it up fresh just before applying. Use a measuring cup and mix at a ratio of 50% polyurethane, 25% boiled linseed oil and 25% pure tung oil. Or experiment with your own blend. I often use a ratio of equal amounts of each with excellent results. With the mixture ready, submerge your staining pad and soak it thoroughly, then wring out the majority of the oil and just wipe it on all the surfaces. Let the oil mixture stand for about 10 minutes, then wipe it off thoroughly. When you're done wiping the oil off, switch to a fresh, clean rag and go over everything again. The oil must be thoroughly wiped off or it will harden, leaving a shiny spot that will have to be buffed again with steel wool. Continue checking the finish for oil seepage, especially in areas the oil will hide and wick out, such as around the frames and panels or other joinery areas. Shine a bright light at an angle across the finish to spot areas that need additional wiping. The key to this finish is really wiping all the oil off well.

Let the finish dry for 24 hours, and then inspect it for shiny spots of hardened oil. Buff out any such spots before applying the next coat. No buffing of the other surfaces is necessary; just repeat the oil application steps. Two or three coats should be sufficient.

After the finish has cured for two or three weeks, or when the oil smell is gone, apply a coat of wax to protect the finish. To care for the finish, dust occasionally with lemon oil and re-wax as needed.

Shellac Conversion Table

Alcohol		Cut (in oz):	
	1#	2#	3#
1 gallon (128 oz)	16	32	48
2 quarts (64 oz)	8	16	24
1 quart (32 oz)	4	8	12
1 pint (16 oz)	2	4	6
1 cup (8 oz)	1	2	3
½ cup (4 oz)	.5	1	1.5
¼ cup (2 oz)	.25	.5	.75

For each fluid ounce, add the corresponding weight in shellac flakes.

Materials:

Pure tung oil
Blonde shellac flakes
Boiled linseed oil
Oil-based polyurethane (glossy)
Denatured alcohol
Mixing and storage containers
Cheesecloth or paint strainer
Painter's rags
Staining pads
0000 steel wool
Liquid measuring cup
Diet scale

SAFETY ALERT

Oil-soaked rags are a major fire hazard. If your rags and the staining pad are left in a pile or wadded up, they can and will self-combust. They should be carefully spread out to dry after use. I hang mine on the edge of my metal waste can or spread them out on a concrete surface outside.

PENCIL-POST BOOKSHELF

Sharpen basic turning skills as you turn 2×4s into No. 2s

BY JOE HURST-WAJSZCZUK, DESIGN BY ANDY RAE

For those who think that pencil post furniture is too "period," here's a literal reinterpretation that fits perfectly in a child's playroom or bedroom.

Knowing how quickly kids outgrow furniture, designer Andy Rae created this bookshelf to be fun, easy to build, and inexpensive. You'll find the bulk of the materials at your home center: the posts are laminated 2×4s; the erasers are turned from a 4×4 cedar fence post; and the ferrules are 2½" thick-walled PVC conduit. (I used Baltic birch for the shelves, but you can save money by substituting hardwood plywood.) The connector nuts and cross dowels not only lock the shelves to the posts but also make it easy to disassemble the pieces and transport them.

Depending on your clamp collection, assembling the pencil posts may take a few glue-up sessions, but after that, the shelving unit can be finished in a weekend. Despite its simplicity, there are a few interesting twists and turns. You'll learn how to lay out a hexagon; practice turning cones, cylinders, and tenons; and discover a few tricks for negotiating long columns with a short-bed lathe.

Bright colors add a nice dose of whimsy to the pencil posts, but painting the posts yellow or black—or leaving them bare—provide options that may work better with your home's decor.

Make the legs

1 Select six 96"-long 2×4s to make the posts (A): one for each leg, one to test your setups, and an extra in case you make a mistake. Avoid loose knots and waney edges. The best 2×4s are sometimes sold as *select* or *prime* stock.

2 Cut each 2×4 into two equal lengths. Then arrange them side by side for the best-looking grain. Mark the ends of each piece to ensure that each half stays properly paired with its mate.

3 Using a jointer, flatten the inside faces and edges of each matching pair. Next,

Figure 1: Pencil-Post Bookcase Exploded View

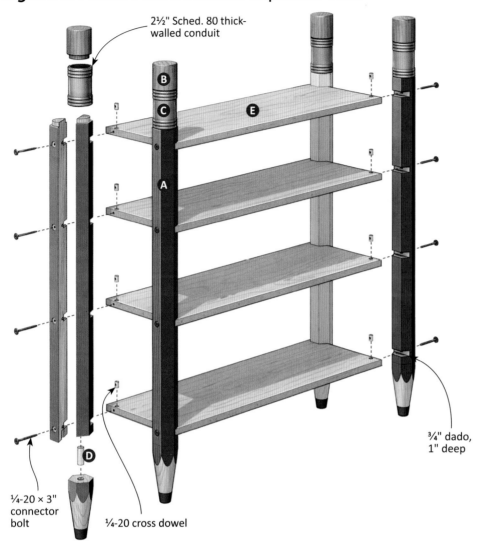

2½" Sched. 80 thick-walled conduit

¾" dado, 1" deep

¼-20 × 3" connector bolt

¼-20 cross dowel

apply glue to the inside face of one half, attach a small clamp across the edges to help align the halves, and then apply clamping pressure across the faces (Photo A). To ensure a seamless joint, space the clamps 6-8" apart. Glue up all six pairs, and let the assembled post blanks dry.

4 Referring to Figure 2 on page 189, Step 1, rip the post blanks to 3" wide. (You may need to rip a little material from the jointed edge to remove the remaining rounded corners.) Next, refer to Step 2 and lay out a hexagon on the end of your test piece, and mill all the blanks to the proper thickness.

5 Rip the first face, as shown in Step 3. Now flip the blank end for end, and rip the adjacent edge. (When you flip the stock for your second cut, the layout lines will be facing you.)

6 Rotate the blank 180° so that the cut edge rests against the fence, and rip the remaining two edges (Photo B; page 188). Double-check your cuts against your layout lines; if no adjustments are needed, cut the remaining legs. Finally, crosscut the posts (A) to length. Save your scrap. You'll use the rippings to prevent tear-out when dadoing the posts and a hexagonal offcut to make the dowelling jig.

QUICK TIP

To keep your wood handscrew clamps from sticking to your posts, protect their faces with packing tape.

Leg Detail

Use a threaded rod to trowel glue evenly across the face of the post, ensuring a good, clean glue-up.

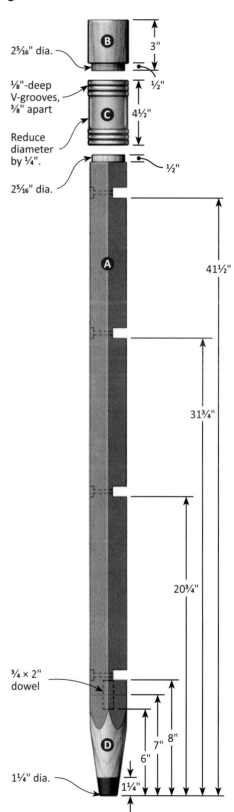

2⁵⁄₁₆" dia.

3"

⅛"-deep V-grooves, ⅜" apart

½"

4½"

Reduce diameter by ¼".

2⁵⁄₁₆" dia.

½"

41½"

31¾"

20¾"

¾ × 2" dowel

7" 8"

6"

1¼" dia.

1¼"

7 Finish the pencil posts (A). To add color but reveal some grain, I used BioShield Stain and Finish, a nontoxic, one-part stain and finish. An acrylic paint would create a more classic No. 2 pencil look, or you could finish the shafts with a clear finish. Whatever you choose, it's important that you finish the posts now in order to achieve the scalloped end when you "sharpen" the tip.

8 Chuck a ½" straight bit into your table-mounted router, and set the fence for a ½"-wide rabbet. Next, wrap the top end of a post (A) with painter's tape to protect the finish, and slide it into a 12"-long piece of 3" PVC. Guiding the pipe against a block of wood (or miter fence), feed the post into the bit, and then slowly turn the post/pipe clockwise, as shown in Photo C (page 188). Gradually raise the bit until the tenon fits inside the 2½" thick-walled conduit. Repeat with the remaining posts.

9 Build the dado sled shown in Figure 3 (page 190). Next, set up your dado cutter to the width of your shelf materia; to cut a 1"-deep dado. Tape a strip of wood (left over from ripping the hexagonal post) to the back face of the pencil to control tear-out, and cut the dadoes, as shown in Figure 1 Leg Detail and Photo D (page 188).

10 At the drill press, drill counterbores and through holes for the connector bolts through the posts (A), where shown in Figure 1 Leg Detail.

Turn the pencil parts

1 From 4×4 cedar stock, create three turning blanks for the erasers (B), each approximately 3 × 3 × 8". Next, cut four 4½"-long pieces of 2½"-diameter thick-walled conduit for the ferrules (C).

2 Using a tablesaw, chamfer about ½" from the corners of the eraser blanks to facilitate turning, and then mount the blank between your headstock and tail centers. Set the lathe to slow speed (around 1,500 rpm), and use a carbide cutter or roughing gouge to rough out a cylinder. Next, reposition the rest closer to the blank, and adjust the speed to around 1,800 rpm. Using a light touch, turn the cylinder to match the outside diameter of the conduit (approximately 2⅞").

3 Using a parting tool or square-edged carbide cutter, turn a 1⅛"-long tenon in the center of the cylinder, as shown in Photo E (page 190). (To obtain a snug-fitting tenon, use calipers rather than relying on dimensions.) Measuring up from the tenon's shoulders, cut the erasers (B) to size using a saw or parting tool, and then cut through the tenon to separate the pair. Repeat the procedure with the remaining two blanks. Cut the final blank in half but do not trim the ends; you'll use these pieces as jam chucks to turn the ferrules (C).

4 Using the jam chucks made in Step 3, mount the conduit. Leaving the speed at 1,800 rpm, lightly run a round carbide cutter against the conduit to smooth and true the cylinder. Now, locate the ferrule V-grooves, where shown in Figure 1 Leg Detail, and cut the grooves as shown in Photo F (page 189). Next, turn the center section. Complete the remaining ferrules (C), and then put the erasers (B) and ferrules aside for now. (Note: This is a good time to spray-finish the ferrules.)

As you rip and flip the hexagonal post, make sure that the glue line stays in contact with the rip fence.

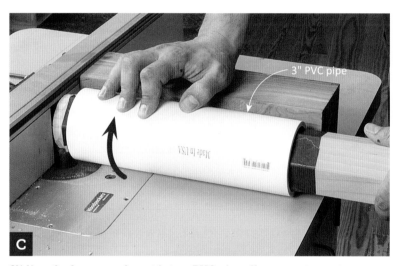

Sliding the hexagonal post into a PVC pipe allows you to rout a round tenon. Painter's tape protects the finish and packs the post in the pipe.

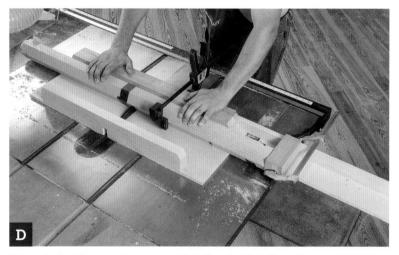

Use a sled with stops to ensure that the shelf dadoes line up. Cut the corresponding dadoes in each leg before readjusting the stop.

Figure 2: Turning a 2×4 into a No. 2 in 3 Steps

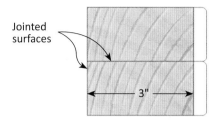

Jointed surfaces

3"

Step 1: Joint one face and edge, and glue up the leg blank. After the glue cures, rip the leg blank to 3" wide.

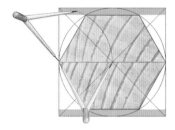

Step 2: Find the centerpoint, and draw a circle. Without adjusting the compass, "walk" it around the circle to find the hexagon's corners. Mill the excess material from the top and bottom faces.

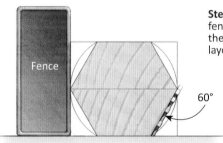

Fence

60°

Step 3: Adjust the fence, and rip along the outside of the layout lines.

5 With a mitersaw or tablesaw and crosscut sled, equipped with your best crosscut blade, trim 7" from the bottom end of each post (A). Mount one of the pieces into your lathe with the intended tip against the tailstock. Now, adjust the speed to 1,500 rpm. Staying 1" away from the headstock end, lightly rough out a cylinder. Stop the lathe to inspect the scalloped edge.

6 Using a parting tool or square edged carbide cutter, establish the tip's final dimension, as shown in Figure 1 Leg Detail. Now, working downhill from right to left, "sharpen the pencil." Finally, establish a "lead tip" line about 1¼" in from the tailstock end, as shown in Photo G (page 190). Repeat with the remaining pencil tips.

7 Using a post offcut, make a doweling jig, as shown in Figure 4 (page 191). Now, using the jig, drill ¾ × 1" holes in each pencil post end (Photo H; page 190). Reassemble the tips to the posts using glue and ¾"-diameter × 2"-long dowels (D).

8 Touch up the pencils' finish where needed. Finally, dip the pencil tips into Plasti-dip to create a nonslip tip, as shown in Photo I (page 190).

E

Using calipers to check your progress, turn the eraser blank and tenon to match the conduit's outside and inside diameters.

Groove positioning guide

Jam chucks

F

Use the corner of the square-edged carbide cutter to create the V-grooves, then use the flat edge to reduce the diameter between the coves.

Figure 3: Dado Sled

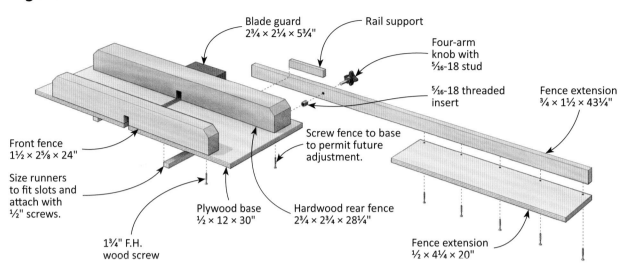

Blade guard
2¾ × 2¼ × 5¾"

Rail support

Four-arm knob with ⁵⁄₁₆-18 stud

⁵⁄₁₆-18 threaded insert

Fence extension ¾ × 1½ × 43¼"

Front fence
1½ × 2⅝ × 24"

Size runners to fit slots and attach with ½" screws.

Screw fence to base to permit future adjustment.

Plywood base
½ × 12 × 30"

Hardwood rear fence
2¾ × 2¾ × 28¼"

1¾" F.H. wood screw

Fence extension
½ × 4¼ × 20"

G

Lay out the lead line with a pencil. Note the wavy edge at the top of the sharpened tip.

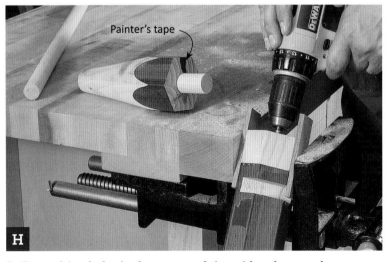

Painter's tape

H

Drill matching holes in the posts and tips with a shop-made doweling jig. Use painter's tape to keep track of matching faces.

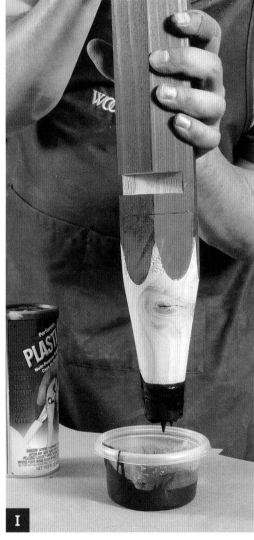

I

Dipping the pencil tips into rubberized paint creates non-slip, non-marring footpads.

Pencil Post Bookshelf Cut List

	Part	Thickness	Width	Length	Qty.	Mat'l
A*	Posts	2⅝" (approx.)	3"	44	4	P
B	Ferrules		2⅞" dia.	4½"	3	Schedule 40 PVC
C*	Erasers		2⅞" dia.	3"	4	C
D	Dowel pins		¾" dia.	2"	4	B
E	Shelves	¾"	12"	36"	4	BP

Materials: P=Pine, C=Cedar, B=Birch, BP=Baltic Birch Plywood.
*Indicates that parts are initially cut oversized. See instructions.

Figure 4: Doweling Jig

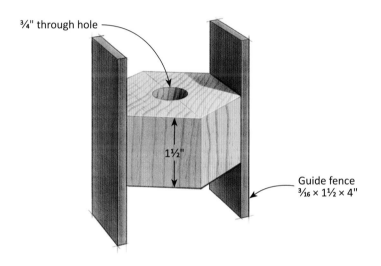

¾" through hole

1½"

Guide fence
³⁄₁₆ × 1½ × 4"

Figure 5: Leg-to-Shelf Detail

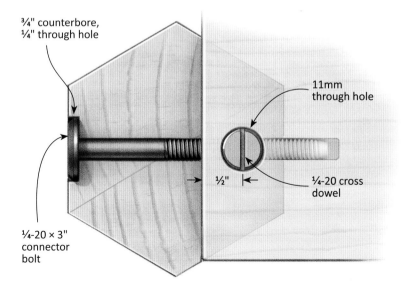

¾" counterbore,
¼" through hole

11mm
through hole

½"

¼-20 cross
dowel

¼-20 × 3"
connector
bolt

Make the shelves and attach the legs

1 From ¾" Baltic birch plywood, cut four shelves (E) to the sizes in the Cut List.

2 Sand the faces, knock off any sharp edges, and then finish the shelves with 2-3 coats of water-based polyurethane.

3 With a helper, fit the shelves (E) into the posts (A). Using the pre-drilled holes as guides, drill ¼ × 3¼"-deep holes into the ends of the shelves.

4 Remove the shelves, and drill 11mm holes through the face of each shelf for the cross dowels, where shown in Figure 5.

5 Insert the cross dowels into the shelves, and then attach the posts to the shelves with connector bolts.

6 Attach the erasers (C) to the ferrules (B) and the ferrules to the posts (A). (To join the wood to the PVC, I used Nexabond, but epoxy would also work). Consider leaving one ferrule unglued since kids appreciate a secret hiding spot for small treasures.

CONTRIBUTORS

Playtime Easel
Written, Designed, & Built by: Andy Rae
Photos: Larry Hamel-Lambert & Andy Rae
Illustrations: John Hartman

Kid-Pleasing Rocking Pony
Written by: Robert J. Settich
Designed & Built by: Chuck Hedlund with Ken Brady
Photos: Jim Osborn & Doug Rowan

Marble Race
Written, Designed, & Built by: Scott Emch
Photos: Jim Osborn
Illustrations: James Provost

Magic Coin Bank
Written, Designed, & Built by: Ken Burton
Photos: Jim Osborn
Illustrations: Frank Rohrbach III

Rainbow Thrower
Written, Designed, & Built by:
  William McDowell

Backyard Wagon
Written by: Jim Harrold
Designed & Built by: Tim Birkeland & Bob Poling
Photos: Chad McClung

Double-Duty Doll House
Written, Designed & Built by:
  Tom Whalley & Marlen Kemmet
Photos: Jonathan Whalley & Carson Downing
Illustrations: Christopher Mills

Toy Trucks from 2 x 4s
Written, Designed, & Built by: Don Russell
Photos: Larry Hamel-Lambert

Doll High Chair
Written, Designed, & Built by: Chuck Hedlund
Photos: Larry Hamel-Lambert
Illustrations: Mario Ferro

Trio of Toy Trucks
Written, Designed, & Built by: Ken Brady
Photos: Ken Brady
Illustrations: Shane Wiersma

Toy Truck
Written, Designed, & Built by: Chuck Hedlund
Photos: Jim Osborn & Larry Hamel-Lambert
Illustrations: Mario Ferro

Front-End Loader
Written, Designed, & Built by: Chuck Hedlund
Photos: Morehead Marketing
Illustrations: Mario Ferro

Road Grader and Bulldozer
Written by: Tom Whalley & Marlen Kemmet
Designed & Built by: Tom Whalley
Photos: Larry Hamel-Lambert & Caleb Rizzuti
Illustrations: Mario Ferro

Tugboat
Written, Designed, & Built by: Ric Hanisch
Photos: Ric Hanisch & Paul Anthony
Illustrations: John Hartman

Chomping Shark, Waddling Walrus, and Beaver
Written, Designed, & Built by: David Wakefield
Photos: Morehead Marketing
Illustrations: Mario Ferro

Treasure Chest
Written, Designed, & Built by: Andy Rae
Photos: Larry Hamel-Lambert & Andy Rae
Illustrations: Christopher Mills

Kid-Friendly Toy Box
Written, Designed, & Built by: Dewayne Baker

Pencil-Post Bookshelf
Written and Built by: Joe Hurst-Wajszczuk
Designed by: Andy Rae
Photos: Larry Hamel-Lambert
Illustrations: John Hartman

INDEX

Note: Page numbers in *italics* indicate projects.

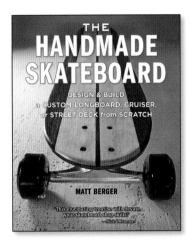
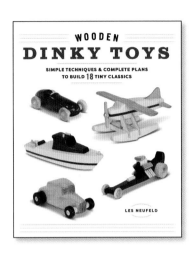
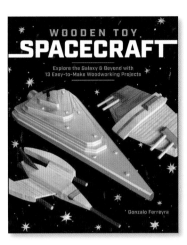
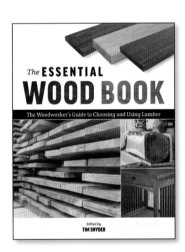

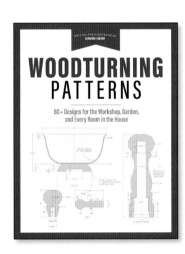

Cutting Boards
$22.95 | 168 Pages

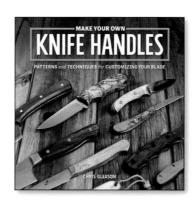

Make Your Own Knife Handles
$24.95 | 168 Pages

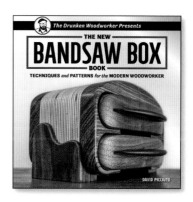

**The New Bandsaw
Box Book**
$19.95 | 120 Pages

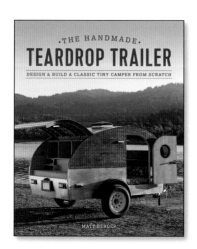

**The Handmade
Teardrop Trailer**
$27.00 | 224 Pages

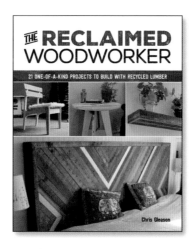

The Reclaimed Woodworker
$24.95 | 160 Pages

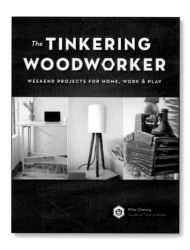

The Tinkering Woodworker
$24.95 | 152 Pages

CEDAR LANE PRESS

Look for these titles wherever books are sold or visit www.cedarlanepress.com.

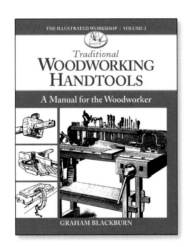
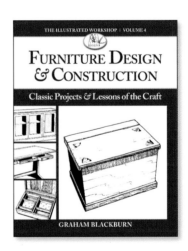